Scope and methods
of political science

AN INTRODUCTION TO THE
METHODOLOGY OF POLITICAL INQUIRY

Scope and methods of political science

AN INTRODUCTION TO THE METHODOLOGY OF POLITICAL INQUIRY

Alan C. Isaak

Associate Professor of Political Science
Western Michigan University

1969

THE
DORSEY
PRESS Homewood, Illinois
Irwin-Dorsey Limited, Georgetown, Ontario

First Printing, July, 1969

Second printing, February 1970

Library of Congress Catalog Card No. 70-90240

Printed in the United States of America

224302

To
my Mother and Father
and to Betty

Preface

This book has several objectives. Its first is to provide a description of what political scientists today are doing—what their main concerns are and what they are attempting to accomplish. Thus we will to some extent be characterizing the discipline called "political science." A second objective is to provide a methodological foundation for reading, understanding, and criticizing the literature of political science. This should also serve as a preparation for advanced work in the study of politics, including both graduate study and the doing of empirical research. Thus, it is our intention to serve several groups: first and primarily, the upper-level undergraduate student in political science who wishes to gain a systematic understanding of the foundations of his discipline; but in addition, the more advanced student of politics who is studying political phenomena in greater depth and therefore requires an understanding of the principles around which such study should be organized.

A good way to describe the general content of a book is to indicate what it is not about. This one is not an introduction to political science in the sense of providing a description of the fields of political science (comparative politics, international relations, and so on). Instead, it attempts to get at those elements which all political scientists should be interested in. A discussion of these elements is methodological, and thus this is primarily a book on the methodology of political science.

Let us at this early stage make clear the distinction between *methodology* and *research techniques*. We are primarily interested in the former, which refers to the basic principles and assumptions of political inquiry. Research techniques on the other hand are specific devices for gathering and analyzing data about political phenomena; examples are survey research, content analysis, and statistical techniques. It must be pointed out, though, that a discussion of methodology—or, as it is also called, the logic of political inquiry—must at times mention such techniques, since what we have here are two levels of scientific activity.

While this book deals with a complex subject-matter, it nevertheless is to a large extent based on several fundamental principles which are often stated as distinctions. That is, much of the detailed analysis revolves around a small number of distinctions—facts versus values, discovery versus justification, to name several—and if one has these clearly in mind, then the analysis should be much easier to assimilate. Therefore much time will be spent on basics.

Let us conclude these introductory remarks by briefly describing the three sections of the book. Each attempts to answer several basic questions.

I.   What is the nature and scope of political science?
II. What is the nature of political science as a science? What are the main elements of the logic of political inquiry?
III. How do political scientists attempt to discover and organize political knowledge? What are the main approaches to the study of politics?

Much of the analysis of this book is based upon work done by philosophers of science. This is especially true of Part Two. Our main objective has been to make this significant body of work relevant for students of politics. The book also owes much to the writings of a number of political scientists. They are mentioned in the footnotes. In addition, I would like to thank Professor Milton Hobbs for stimulating my interest in the philosophy of political science and for providing a framework for methodological analysis. Of course, I must add that any errors in fact and interpretation are entirely my own responsibility.

Finally, a special thanks to my wife Betty for her invaluable editorial assistance, encouragement, and patience which saw me through; to Eric who kept me going as only a two-year-old can; and to Greta, who postponed her arrival until her father's book was completed.

Kalamazoo, Michigan   Alan C. Isaak
June, 1969

Table of Contents

INDEX

Part One

THE SCOPE OF POLITICAL SCIENCE

1 The scope of political science: Political philosophy and political science

Probably the first question that a present-day student of politics ought to ask is, What is political science? Or putting it in more answerable form (that is, the way this book puts it), What is the *scope* of political science? This in turn is reducible to, What kinds of activities interest those who call themselves "political scientists"? There are a number of ways to go about answering this question. *Part One* examines several of these. This chapter takes an historical and comparative approach. That is, an answer, which at this point can only be stated in fairly general terms, is arrived at by describing the main concerns of traditional political thought and comparing them with modern political science. This also provides a foundation for the more analytic approach taken in Chapter 2, in which political science is characterized by analyzing its component parts "politics" and "science."

TRADITIONAL POLITICAL PHILOSOPHY

By traditional political thought, philosophy, or theory we usually mean the significant political analyses carried out by past political thinkers such as Plato, Aristotle, Locke, and Rousseau. But there is a more fruitful way of characterizing traditional political philosophy which allows one to speak of contemporary political philosophers. This method involves sorting out the main activities of political philosophers and indicating which of these receives the greatest emphasis. There are four types of activity; we have labeled them scientific, normative, instrumental, and analytic.

Describing a political system, an aspect of it, or a general political phenomenon, and *explaining* or accounting for such facts are *scientific* activities. We will say much more about "science" and what it means to be scientific in later chapters. It is enough at this early stage if "scientific" is roughly equated with talking about and explaining on the basis of the world of observation and experience: to use a word which we will come back to time and again, the *empirical* world. Traditional political philosophers have always been engaged in such scientific activities. For instance, Aristotle spent much time describing and comparing various kinds of constitutions, and in another section of the *Politics* he attempts an explanation of political change and revolution.[1]

However, several qualifications must be added. The political philosopher has rarely been a very good scientist, especially when it comes to explaining political phenomena. This is probably attributable to several factors. Two that may be cited are: his lack of sophisticated scientific methodology; and the fact that scientific activities have never been his primary concern. This latter point is also our second qualification. We can admit, then, that while political philosophers have described and explained they have usually deemphasized these activities.

The primary activities of political philosophers have probably been *normative*. These are activities which involve moral, ethical, or value judgments. While scientific activities deal with what *is,* value judgments express what a political philosopher believes *ought* to be. As we will see in a moment, the distinction between *is* and *ought* is fundamental to an understanding of present-day political science. There are several varieties of normative activity. First, many political philosophers spend much time *prescribing* the "best" state or political system. Perhaps the first and most famous attempt is Plato's discussion of the ideally just state in which the absolute knowledge of the philosopher-kings is proposed as the standard for political and social decision making.[2] Political

---

[1]Ernest Barker (ed., trans.), *The Politics of Aristotle* (New York: Oxford University Press, 1958), Books IV and V.

[2]Francis M. Cornford (ed., trans.), *The Republic of Plato* (New York: Oxford University Press, 1945), Part III.

philosophers also engage in the normative activity of *recommend-* *ing* the proper or true goals of politics. Thus Rousseau emphasizes the restoration of a sense of community and the fulfilling of man's moral and emotional needs as the legitimate ends of the political system[3] and Jeremy Bentham argues that happiness should be the basis of all political actions.[4]

Applied or *instrumental* value judgments are often confused with normative statements. There is however a fundamental difference in that instrumental judgments recommend the best way of achieving a given end, but do not attempt to justify the end itself. This is the significance of an alternate label, *means-ends* analysis. An instrumental judgment is therefore a scientific-empirical activity, for it is really an explanation of why certain conditions or actions lead to the desired end. But the confusion we just referred to is understandable when it is realized that political philosophers often combine normative and instrumental judgments. That is, an ultimate end or value is recommended and then the best means for achieving this end is described. Hobbes not only suggests that peace (the absence of civil discord) ought to be the end of the political system, but then goes on to discuss the means to this end, namely, the absolute political sovereign, the Leviathan.[5] The first kind of analysis is, strictly speaking, normative; the second, scientific.

The last kind of activity we have labeled *analytic.* This category includes both the analysis of political words and concepts and the examination of certain aspects of political arguments, for instance their logical consistency. Plato, using the dialectical method, analyzes and criticizes a number of definitions of *justice* in his attempt to arrive at its "real" meaning.[6] Other political thinkers since Plato have engaged in such analytic activities—the doing of any kind of philosophy is impossible without analysis of this sort. However, not until recent years has it become a distinctive kind of political philosophy.[7] But more about that in a moment.

---

[3]Jean Jacques Rousseau, *The Social Contract.*

[4]Jeremy Bentham, *Introduction to the Principles of Morals and Legislation.*

[5]Thomas Hobbes, *The Leviathan.*

[6]Cornford, *op. cit.,* Parts I and II.

[7]See, for instance, T. D. Weldon, *The Vocabulary of Politics* (London: Penguin Books, Ltd., 1953).

Some significant conclusions about traditional political philosophy can be stated at this point. First, in engaging in all four types of activity the traditional political thinker was in effect a complete political scientist, even though he was a poor scientist. The second conclusion, a qualification of the first, is that the emphasis in most "political philosophies" is on the "ought" questions, the normative ones. This leads to a present-day distinction between political *philosophy* and political *science,* a distinction which will be clarified in the next section. The emphasis of traditional political philosophy on normative questions has been explained in several ways. Alfred Cobban has presented one of the most reasonable arguments by pointing out that all of the great political philosophers considered their writings as part of the political process. In Cobban's words, "They all wrote with a practical purpose in mind. Their object was to influence actual political behavior. They wrote to condemn or support existing institutions, to justify a political system or persuade their fellow citizens to change it...."[8] These activities are basically normative.

CONTEMPORARY POLITICAL SCIENCE

Political scientists, using the term at *this point* to include all those persons found in academic departments of political science, engage in the same kinds of activities as traditional political philosophers. Thus they describe and explain political phenomena and attempt to construct empirical theories so as to explain them more completely. They also recommend both ends and the means to achieve the ends. Finally they analyze the definitions of political concepts and the logical relationships between propositions about politics. However—and this is the significant fact toward which our analysis has been moving—it is becoming increasingly evident that there exists a distinction between normative and analytic activities on the one hand and scientific activities on the other, with the former constituting political philosophy and the latter political science. Thus those who do the former can be called political philosophers, those who do the latter, political scientists. It seems fair to conclude, then, that

[8]Alfred Cobban, "The Decline of Political Theory," *Political Science Quarterly,* Vol. LXVIII, No. 3 (1953), p. 330.

there has been a division of labor of sorts within the discipline of political science, and therefore "political science" has both a narrow and a broad connotation. It should be made clear, however, that while we can make the distinction between political science and political philosophy and use it meaningfully in our analysis, as a matter of fact many of those within the discipline of political science (broad connotation) will be both political scientists and political philosophers, either simultaneously or alternately.

The nature of political philosophy can and should be made more explicit. What we have really said is that there are two kinds of political philosophy, the distinction between them following the more basic one between two conceptions of philosophy. The first claims that the philosopher seeks true knowledge, of reality, goodness, or beauty; and thus successful philosophical reasoning produces knowledge different in kind but on a par with the results of scientific research. It is from this orientation that Plato proceeds in quest of the nature of absolute truth and the goodness of society. The other conception of philosophy rejects the notion that philosophical analysis produces any ultimate knowledge of reality or goodness. Instead, philosophy can only analyze language in order to straighten out "linguistic muddles" or clear away "philosophical rubbish." Thus the results of the analytic or linguistic philosopher's work are not ultimate truths but logical clarifications of philosophical discourse. It can be seen why one opponent of this interpretation has labeled it the "underlaborour" theory.[9]

This chapter's discussion can be placed in a broader context by pointing out that throughout the book our attention will be focused upon those activities which can be placed within the boundaries of political science in the narrower sense. In short, normative questions lie outside the scope of the book except in so far as they relate to the scientific nature of the study of politics (for instance, Do values influence empirical research?). It will also become evident that we will be functioning as analytic philosophers when we examine the nature and logical foundations of political science.

---

[9]Peter Winch, *The Idea of a Social Science* (New York: Humanities Press, 1958). The term is originally John Locke's.

FACTS AND VALUES

The distinction between political science and political philosophy rests upon a more basic distinction between *facts* and *values,*
or in terms we have already used, between the *is* and the *ought.*
Let us now develop this distinction in a little more detail. Our
analysis follows that of the 18th-century philosopher David Hume,
who to a large extent provided the foundations for modern
philosophy and science and who incidentally said a great many
perceptive things about politics.

Empirical or *is* statements are about and based upon evidence
referring to the world of experience. They are therefore verifiable;
that is, it can be determined if an empirical statement is true or
false. A true empirical proposition states a *fact.* "Truth" then has
something to do with jibing with the world of observation.
However, it should be made very clear that empirical statements
are never *necessarily* true. They simply state facts or relationships
which we have observed or discovered through various methods
such as experimentation or statistical control procedures. This
then is why we call empirical statements *contingent.*

Normative propositions state value judgments. They are neither
true nor false because no amount of empirical evidence can prove
or disprove a value judgment. As Hume pointed out, an *is* never
implies an *ought.* This then is a statement of the fact-value
distinction. Rather than being factual, a normative proposition is a
statement of individual preference and perhaps in addition an
attempt to change the values of others. The influence of this
position on scientific thinking has been labeled "scientific value
relativism," that is the realization that science is neutral in regard
to normative values—it views them as relative to individuals and
cultures not as absolutes.

Many philosophers and political thinkers have held the view
that the truth or falsity of normative statements can be demonstrated. Since this is contrary to the position we have just stated, it
is incumbent upon us to discuss some of these ideas and indicate
where they fail.

Some thinkers have argued that the "good" (or the good state)
is discoverable through a *rational* process. The "good" is therefore
objective in the sense that it is independent of human desires or

needs. It might exist, as it did for Plato, in a "World of Forms" or it may be defined within a system of natural law. In any case the assumption is that given the proper mental equipment, the nature of the good state can be *discovered.*

Another variant of this basic philosophical position is *intuitionism.* It postulates a moral faculty or sense which "tells" man what is ethically or politically good. Intuition seems to differ from reason in that the former is not itself describable or explainable, while the process of rational analysis is itself subject to analysis. When we reason we follow a series of methodological steps (which vary from rationalist to rationalist), but when we know the good state through intuition we simply know or intuit it.

This distinction should not be exaggerated, for in the end the claim of each variant can be reduced to the following: there is an objective good which is knowable by reasonable men; or, when a man is rational the good will become obvious to him.

The trouble with this philosophical position is that two "rational" men may disagree over what the good is, and there is no way to resolve the disagreement. No outside criteria exist against which normative-rational claims can be measured. It does no good for one man to settle the argument with an appeal to reason—"I am rational, you are not"—because the second man can use the same strategy. The result is a return to the original unresolvable position. We are not questioning the importance of reason. Rather we are rejecting the position which argues that rational analysis can lead to true or ultimate value judgments, for what is reasonable to one may be unreasonable to another.

Another method which some philosophers have used in their attempt to give normative propositions objective status is the equating of "desired" and "good." This position, developed most fully by the 19th-century Utilitarians, confuses an "is" question with an "ought" question. The fact that a majority of a population want or desire something is surely of great interest to the decision maker concerned with a stable political system. But the fact does not make the desired policy good in any ultimate sense. A restatement of our original position summarizes the reply to utilitarianism. A normative judgment, whether made by an individual or a large population, is an expression of subjective values, wants, needs, desires. Its truth is in no way demonstrated by the proportion of those making it.

There is a philosophical tradition which views *existence* and *survival* as legitimate criteria for goodness. Such widely divergent thinkers as Thomas Hobbes, Friedrich Nietzsche, and Herbert Spencer have in effect argued that what exists, survives, or triumphs is what ought to exist, survive, or triumph. Thus in politics the system which lasts the longest is clearly the best.

It doesn't require extensive training in philosophy to see that "existence" and "survival" are actually values which have come in through the back door, so to speak. If one believes that they should be the ultimate values or objectives of a society, then he will naturally evaluate favorably those political systems which have achieved or at least try to achieve them. But this does not demonstrate their truth. How does one, arguing from this position, refute the contrary position which values freedom above existence? If to be free implies the breakdown of the political system, then breakdown it must be. Clearly, there is no solution, for what we have here is a conflict between ultimate values.

Aristotle developed the idea, usually called teleology, that everything, including men and political systems, has an end sown in it from the time of its origin. Thus the acorn's end is to become an oak tree and man's end is to become, let us say, a good citizen. The significance of teleological thinking lies in the claim that every man and social institution has an objective end which is knowable and that this end can provide the basis for normative judgments. If a political system's end is to become a democracy then it is morally right that it become a democracy; or those actions which tend to lead to democracy are morally commendable.

There are several criticisms which can be made of this position. First, how do we determine a person's or system's proper end? We know that acorns become oak trees, but would we want to conclude that they ought to? The teleological argument is really based on an empirical observation logically the same as, "education leads to higher salaries." But what about the ends of men? Can we say that every man has an end toward which he is moving? How do we discover them? Ability or skill might be equated with "end." But is a mediocre baseball pitcher who has great musical ability immoral in pursuing a baseball career? In the final analysis the teleological grounding of value judgments is guilty of the common is-ought confusion. Even if ends are discoverable, and this possibility is not one which we have uncritically accepted, one need not agree that they are what ought to be realized. An opponent might agree that most conflicts become wars, yet still bemoan the fact as being morally unjustified.

Returning to our analysis of propositions, the third kind is labeled *analytic* or *logical*. Unlike empirical statements, which can be contingently true, valid logical statements are necessarily true, that is for all time and for all possible worlds. But they have this quality because they are true within a specific logical system—they are true by definition, so to speak. Thus, for instance, the propositions of symbolic logic, the truths of arithmetic, or the theorems of geometry are necessarily true. But necessary truth comes at a price; an analytic statement says nothing new about the world: "2 + 2 = 4" does not give us the same kind of information as "businessmen tend to be Republican." Still this is a clarification and not a criticism of analytic statements, for the powerful apparatuses of logic and mathematics are of immeasurable value to the political philosopher and political scientist.

The basic distinction that we have been discussing should be obvious by now. It is between *empirical* political science and *normative* and *analytic* political philosophy. It must be realized, of course, that both political scientists and political philosophers employ analytical propositions.

2 Politics and science

We have now described the general nature of contemporary political science by contrasting its interests with those of political philosophy. But the result, while basic to the arguments presented in this book, is nevertheless a skeleton in need of flesh. Some of the latter will be provided in the present chapter, where a second, more analytical approach is taken to answer the question, What is the scope of political science?

We have already described the nature of analytic propositions and analytic political philosophy, so the use of the word "analytic" here should not generate any problems of comprehension. We will *analyze* "political science"; that is, examine and explicate its component parts, "political" and "science." Another way of looking at this activity is to say that we are interested in two aspects of the discipline or field of political science; its content or *what* is studied, and its structure or *how* the content is studied. The first is politics or "the political," the second "science." In examining the meanings assigned to these concepts by political scientists we will in effect be describing the scope or boundaries of political science. "Science" itself refers to the *methods* of political science, the general topic of Parts Two and Three. But the methodology which a political scientist adopts, the basic assumptions he makes, will to some extent influence the image he has of his discipline. Therefore, "scope" and "method" cannot be completely divorced. Methodology can and should be studied in its own right (as most of this book does); but in addition it ought to be considered as an important influence on the scope of political science, for it indicates to some extent what it can and cannot do.

POLITICS

Most of us use the word "politics" without providing an explicit definition, yet we all seem to know what others are talking about. When a political issue is being discussed the discussants seldom begin by working out an acceptable definition of "political." This probably indicates that there is a basic commonsense understanding of the term. However, at this point some people, especially those interested in studying politics in a more rigorous fashion, point out that in order to really gain knowledge of politics one has to formulate a more explicit definition; that is, one can't simply rely on common sense.

In a later section we will examine in detail the differences between scientific and commonsensical knowledge and see how the former, while to a large extent based on the latter, nevertheless goes beyond it in its ability to describe and explain the world. One might argue that perhaps the most important factor leading to the development of knowledge in a field of study is agreement among its members about the content of that field.[1] In other words, you can't expect knowledge in a particular area to develop and accumulate unless those working in the area share a conception of what it is they are studying. In the context of our present discussion this means a fairly clear-cut definition of politics.

The next task, then, is to examine several definitions or types of definition of politics which have been given by political scientists. However, in doing so we should keep in mind an alternative position which claims that it is a waste of time to attempt an explicit definition of politics. It is more sensible to simply plunge in and study whatever the student of politics finds interesting and significant. In effect, the definition of politics, or scope of political science, is contextually determined. The argument is then that whatever political scientists say is politics, is politics, and one restricts the growth of political science if he prematurely

---

[1]See David B. Truman, "Disillusion and Regeneration: The Quest for a Discipline," *American Political Science Review,* Vol. LIX, No. 4 (December, 1965), pp. 865-73.

advocates a definition. Thus, the outer limits of political science can be determined only by listing all the topics which interest political scientists.

This seems to be an important tradition within political science. In their analysis of the historical development of American political science, Albert Somit and Joseph Tannenhaus point out that the discipline has never had a clear conception of its content. This has often bewildered observers. For instance, the English historian Morse Stephens, after teaching in the United States for two years, reported in 1896 that "he had not been able to find anyone who could tell him precisely what political science was."[2]

Despite this strong tradition of definitional disinterestedness, many definitions of politics have been given by political philosophers and political scientists. As a matter of fact, their diversity is no doubt another reason for the bewilderment experienced by observers of political science. While there has been a wide range of definitions, most of them can be classified as being one of two types. Some identify "politics" with "government," "legal government," or the "state," while others revolve around the notions "power," "authority," and/or "conflict." After examining the advantages and disadvantages of each, we will consider a contemporary attempt to formulate a more useful definition which many believe overcomes some of these disadvantages.

Government

To the average citizen, the man on the street, "politics" and "government" are synonymous. It seems natural to identify politics with what goes on in Congress, the state legislature, or the mayor's office. Many political scientists take the same position, but articulate it in a more sophisticated manner. The political scientist Alfred de Grazia says that "politics" or the "political" "includes the events that happen around the decision-making centers of government."[3] Charles Hyneman is more specific in claiming that most political scientists have assumed that *legal* government is the subject matter of their discipline. "The central

---

[2]Quoted in Albert Somit and Joseph Tannenhaus, *The Development of American Political Science: From Burgess to Behavioralism* (Boston: Allyn & Bacon, Inc., 1967), p. 24.

[3]Alfred de Grazia, *Political Behavior* (New York: Free Press, 1965), p. 24.

point of attention in American political science...is that part of the affairs of the state which centers in government, and that kind or part of government which speaks through law."[4] There are, then, in effect, two versions of this definition, a weaker and a stronger. The former speaks only about "government"; the latter adds the concept "legal." As we will see in a moment, they come down to the same thing. Thus to most political scientists, "legal government" is internally redundant.

If a political scientist identifies "politics" with "government" or "legal government," it is incumbent upon him to let us know what he means by "government." Here we, as students of politics interested in the meaning of this widely used term, are faced with a problem in part the result of its wide usage. Because of the number of definitions it is difficult to decide what is being referred to. However, if one is mainly interested, as we are, in discovering a basic or core meaning of "government," it becomes clear that the problem is more apparent than real. For after sorting through the definitions, one realizes that as it is used by most political scientists, "government" means something like "the legally based institutions of a society which make legally binding decisions." If this is an accurate statement, then clearly Hyneman's definition is simply more specific than de Grazia's. "Legal government" is redundant because "legality" defines government; it is the characteristic which distinguishes government from other institutions in society. But whether "government" or "legal government," it is clear that the political scientist who adopts this type of definition is focusing his attention on formal *institutions* of a certain kind.

We conclude, then, that the definition which equates politics with government has a commonsensical *basis.* However, many political scientists would probably warn us to be wary of its commonsensical *appeal,* for they see in it serious limitations. Perhaps the most significant is its limited applicability. In emphasizing government, such critics argue, the political scientist must overlook much that should, and as a matter of fact often does, interest him. In other words, this definition is unrealistically restrictive. Take, for instance, a political scientist interested in

---

[4]Charles Hyneman, *The Study of Politics* (Urbana: University of Illinois Press, 1956), p. 26.

studying the politics of an African nation. He no doubt spends much of his time examining tribal societies in which no governmental institutions exist. Yet he discovers that the tribal chief and elders are making basic decisions for the community. Because the decisions are not made by identifiable legal institutions such as a congress or parliament, in other words by a government or the state, are they to be classified as nonpolitical and therefore beyond the scope of the political scientist?

A large number of political scientists would answer that it is a sign of narrow-mindedness, a dangerous trait for a researcher, to use a type of political institution as the basis for a definition of politics. Perhaps the heart of the difficulty, as perceived by these critics, is a failure to look behind governmental institutions for that element which makes them all political. The emphasis should be placed, not on institutions, but, in David Easton's words, on "a kind of activity that may express itself through a variety of institutions."[5]

Power, authority, and conflict

Political scientists who make such criticisms of the "governmental" definition of politics and develop them beyond the negative stage usually end up on a positive note, formulating an alternative definition which equates politics with "power," "authority," or "conflict." Any of these could be the activity mentioned by Easton. Let us quote William Bluhm, a political scientist who provides a rather elaborate definition of this sort: "Reduced to its universal elements, then, politics is a social process characterized by activity involving rivalry and cooperation in the exercise of power, and culminating in the making of decisions for a group."[6] The appeal of the definition flows out of its apparent flexibility or wide scope. Politics is found wherever power relationships or conflict situations exist, which means that the political scientist can legitimately (i.e., as political scientist) study the politics of a labor union, corporation, or African tribe, as well as what goes on in a legislature or administrative agency.

---

[5]David Easton, *The Political System* (New York: Alfred A. Knopf, 1960), p. 113.

[6]William Bluhm, *Theories of the Political System* (Englewood Cliffs, N.J.: Prentice-Hall, Inc., 1965), p. 5.

The emphasis, then, is placed upon a type of activity or behavior rather than a particular kind of institution. Implicit in this definition is a refusal to prematurely answer the question, In what kinds of institutions is politics the most likely to occur? Or the more basic one, Does politics have to be institutionalized in the first place?

Underlying our comparative analysis of definitions is the by now obvious fact that a definition of politics based on government is simply a version of one based on power in general. The political scientist who adopts the first type assumes that only one kind of power is political and therefore relevant to his discipline, namely, power exercised within and by governmental institutions. Thus in the end all definitions of politics are based upon notions of power and/or conflict. This realization does not, however, make our categorization of definitions less significant. The purpose of the present chapter has not been to formulate the *real* definition of politics (as we will see later on, there is no such thing as a real definition), but rather to discover how political scientists use the term. And as a matter of fact, those who limit politics to governmental power do concentrate on the "governmental" rather than the "power." Thus, as the concepts are used in political science, there is a practical difference between a definition based on government and one based on politics. As Chapter 3 will demonstrate, this difference can influence the research orientations of political scientists. Just as we assumed that it was the responsibility of those using the first definition to define "government," it seems reasonable to expect that when the second is employed the meaning of "power" will be specified.

Once again the familiar problem of a diverse and ambiguous collection of definitions, seemingly defying analysis, faces us. Yet, once again, lying at the bottom of this agglomeration is a commonsense core which at least enables us to gain a rough notion of what power means to those adopting this definition of politics. Running through all concepts of conflict and power is the idea of people or groups competing for scarce values, with some of them influencing the behavior of others and/or the outcomes of decisions. In the third part of this book the concept of power will be examined in much greater detail and it will become obvious then that we have just provided an oversimplified, but nevertheless accurate, definition.

Despite the appeal (a growing appeal, by the way) of this more liberal definition of politics it has not gone without criticism. To some political scientists, especially those who feel the need for a discipline with clear-cut boundaries, it seems that the equating of politics and power destroys the possibility of specifying such boundaries. If the political scientist can legitimately study all forms of power and conflict, in the UAW, General Motors, or the local Kiwanis Club, then what is distinctive about political science? The sociologist does the same thing. Does this mean that there are no significant differences between sociology and political science? One answer is "yes"; another, "there is no reason to answer the question."

We will consider the nature and implications of these responses in a moment. But first, let us return to a consideration of the reply which claims that the content of political science is distinctive and therefore the discipline does have boundaries which are more restrictive than those provided by "any power or conflict situation." As we have seen, one set of boundaries is equivalent to the institutions of legal government. However, some political scientists have attempted to formulate an alternative definition of politics, an in-between position which is neither as restrictive as the "government" type nor as broad as the "power" variety.

The authoritative allocation of values

Perhaps the most widely known and used alternative of this sort has been provided by David Easton. His identification of the political system with "the authoritative allocation of values for a society"[7] has provided many political scientists with a useful guideline for delimiting the content of political science. We have already quoted Easton's plea for an emphasis on political *activity* rather than *institutions*. The "authoritative allocation of values" is, Easton argues, the kind of activity we should be interested in. The first assumption is that in every society values are desired, that is people have different interests or objectives and these must be allocated, distributed by someone or something. In a sense, then, this is a power and conflict situation. But saying that every

---

[7]Easton, *op. cit.*, pp. 129ff.

society allocates values authoritatively does not prejudge the question, How is this done? In the United States we would expect legal governmental institutions to make such decisions, while in an African tribe the activity would probably take place much more informally, without the need for elaborate institutions. Thus every society has a political system, defined as that which authoritatively allocates values; but this system takes different forms.

The first conclusion we can draw is that the political scientist adopting Easton's definition is not limited to the study of legal government. This is significant for two reasons. First, it means that the American political scientist is able to study other political systems or cultures objectively, without preconceived notions about political structures and behavior. Secondly, when studying his own political system, the political scientist is not limited to the formal institutions of government, such as Congress, but in addition can include interest groups, political parties, and other less obvious influences on authoritative decisions.

On the other hand, Easton's definition is not of the "anything goes" variety. He is not saying that the political system includes (is coextensive with) all power or decision-making situations. Only those decisions which are authoritative for the society are relevant to the political scientist. According to Easton, "A policy is authoritative when the people to whom it is intended to apply or who are affected by it consider that they must or ought to obey it." [8] In other words, it is considered binding. However, not every authoritative decision is made within the political system. What, for instance, of those which members of a Kiwanis Club accept as binding? How do they differ from acts of Congress? The answer is, of course, found in the qualifier "for society." From the class of all authoritative decision, the political scientist following Easton's definition selects only those which apply to *all* members of society (although only a few might be affected).

The argument for an Eastonian-type definition of politics is based, then, on the desirability of a compromise position which is neither too restrictive nor overly broad. Such a definition, it is claimed, is more useful for political scientists. However, this kind of definition does not go without criticism; in fact, to many

---

[8]Ibid., p. 132.

political scientists, its advantages are only apparent. Instead of one word ("politics"), several ("authoritative," "allocation," "values," and "society") have to be defined. Therefore anything which may be gained from an explicit definition of politics is canceled out because of the addition of several complex concepts. For instance, what does it mean to make a decision "for society," and how does this differ from one which is not made for society? To many political scientists, any elaborate attempt to answer this question is̄ a waste of time.

Why define politics?

In the early stages of this discussion mention was made of an alternative approach. It questions the usefulness of any attempt to define politics, on the grounds that since there is no final solution to a problem of definition (as we will see in Chapter 5), and since there are so many existing definitions of politics, the political scientist's time could be better spent in other activities. Although rarely articulated (by its very nature) this position has long been a significant one in American political science. For instance, in 1904 a leading political scientist wrote that, "Such an attempt [to define politics] is not only dangerous but even if successfully made, it is not in my opinion sufficiently fruitful of practical results to justify the expenditure of thought and time necessary to secure the desired end." [9] Our point is that many, if not most, contemporary political scientists agree with this statement. Thus, rather than concern themselves with semantical questions, they "plunge in" and either do their research without worrying about the scope or boundaries of their discipline or allow the results of their work to set the boundaries.

Let us reiterate that the primary objective of this discussion has not been to arrive at "the" or even "a" definition of politics. If the only conclusion drawn is that there is no such definition, then the discussion has been partially successful. But in addition, it is hoped that in becoming familiar with several of the more popular interpretations of "politics" or "political science," the student will

---

[9]Frank J. Goodnow, "The Work of the American Political Science Association," *Proceedings*, Vol. I (1904), p. 35; quoted in Somit and Tannenhaus, *op.cit.*, p. 65.

be able to make more sense out of the literature of his discipline.

Perhaps we can be more specific. Making it clear once again that no best definition of politics is being advocated, there nevertheless seems to be a recognizable commonsensical core meaning of the political scientist's subject matter. It is simply that politics has something to do with power. In effect, then, we are reducing all the definitions of politics to a single common element. This is acceptable—perhaps a better word is prudent—because it is the basis upon which most political scientists operate anyway. We have already seen that there are legitimate objections to any proposed definition of politics: someone is always dissatisfied. In addition, as the next chapter will demonstrate, many political scientists reject as unrealistic and overly restrictive the notion of boundaries between the social sciences. If the political scientist and sociologist often seem to be studying the same thing, it is because of the nature of the world. Perhaps it would be wise to work out an efficient division of labor, but there is nothing about the overlap which is sinister. No discipline is being "imperialistic." From this attitude can be derived the familiar conclusion that it is wrong to prematurely *define* the scope of political science. Political scientists commonsensically understand the label which has been assigned them. Unification of the discipline must come as a natural development from within, that is through the discovery of facts which have relevance for all those who call themselves political scientists, rather than from the imposition of an elaborate definition which arbitrarily classifies some things as political and others as nonpolitical.

SCIENCE

What does the "science" in "political science" mean? A survey of the discipline's literature uncovers several answers. However, a close examination indicates that these are different in degree rather than in kind. Each interpretation is really a simplified version of a set of scientific principles which ultimately provides the basis for all "scientific study." This is the model of science which will be the most closely analyzed here, for it is also the foundation upon which a science of politics must rest.

The most primitive and least fruitful interpretation uses science in an "honorific" sense. Just as a nation in the contemporary world is judged good if it is democratic, a political scientist's status rises if he is scientific. Therefore nations call themselves democratic and political scientists call their work "scientific" with a public relations payoff in mind. "Science" becomes a label to be used but not defined. If this were all that science involved, then there would be no point in going on. However, there is much more to say. We will survey in ascending order of sophistication several acceptable interpretations of the "science" in political science.

The first of these simply equates it with *serious study*. Almost by definition, then, all those who study politics professionally become scientists, for at the very heart of their profession lies a commitment to study political phenomena more seriously than, for instance, the man on the street or the journalist. While this is one step forward, it doesn't tell us what we really want to know: namely, What distinguishes scientific from unscientific study?

A familiar reply is that to be scientific is to be systematic or *rigorous*. Even when these adjectives are left undefined, as they often are, one at least senses what science is all about. Some rough operational guideline is provided to tell us in any given instance where the scientific ends and the unscientific begins. However, this kind of guideline is not going to take us far unless it is given more substance through explicit definitions of "rigorous" and "systematic." As we just noted, this is rarely done. When it is, the result is usually an explication of "scientific," for as they are commonly used "rigorous" and "systematic" are synonyms of our key word. "Science" has not been defined, it has simply been given a new name. Thus, while we know a little more now, we are still treading water rather than making headway. A political scientist who believes his discipline is scientific because it studies political phenomena systematically is right. But he hasn't said enough. What does it mean to be systematic or scientific? What are the distinguishing characteristics of a systematic or scientific discipline?

The answer which most have given or assumed is that a scientific discipline is empirical. An empirical proposition, let us recall, is one which refers to and is based upon the world of experience and observation. Since the political scientist, as a scientist, is interested in one aspect of the world around him, he must make sure his descriptions of politics are empirical. Thus, according to this interpretation of science, the political scientist lives up to his appellation if he deals only with the *facts. Naive empiricism* is the appropriate label by which it is known. We are all probably familiar with its consequences—the piling of fact upon fact; exhaustive descriptions of a single governmental institution; or detailed narratives of a particular political decision. In effect, the facts speak for themselves and usually there is only a limited attempt to organize and/or explain them. The naivete of this position should not be exaggerated, however, for it seems clear, no matter how sophisticated one's conception of science, that science begins with empiricism. There is no denying that one must look at the world if he is to explain the world.

Let us pause for a moment and summarize this section's main points. One significant interpretation equates "scientific" with "systematic" or "rigorous." Another recognizes the empirical basis of science. Now these two positions are not mutually exclusive. In fact, the political scientist who adopts one probably assumes the other, so that the composite picture of science which emerges is that of a kind of ordered study which stays close to the facts (observation). Charles Hyneman has described political science in these terms: "...the political scientist is pursuing scientific method if he makes a conscientious, careful, systematic effort to find out what actually exists and goes on...."[10] We might characterize this orientation which links systematic and empirical as a more liberal version of the set of scientific principles which have already been identified as fundamental to any science. A description of these principles provides the most sophisticated notion of science.

However, some political scientists accepting the more liberal interpretation would probably argue that they are principles of only the more highly developed physical sciences such as physics and chemistry, and are therefore not realistically applicable to political science or, for that matter, any social science. Therefore, the political scientist can be empirical and systematic only at a

---

[10]Hyneman, *op. cit.,* p. 78.

very general level. This point of view raises a host of issues which will be handled at appropriate times throughout the book. In the present context, only one reply is necessary. If all notions of science are derived from this set of basic principles, then there is no opposition between it and the liberal interpretation of science. Only a fool could fail to see the more highly developed nature of the natural sciences relative to the social sciences. However, this superiority is not derived from the acceptance of a different set of scientific principles. It has been achieved because of a clearer understanding of and more effective building upon these principles. The implications are that every science, natural or social, is based upon a common set of assumptions and this set is a more complete version of what has here been called the liberal interpretation of the "science" in "political science."

The assumptions of science

Let us, then, run through these assumptions and principles, realizing that a more thorough discussion will have to wait until Part Two. At this point we are mainly interested in a reasonably accurate *sketch* of an existing or potential science of politics based on the conception of science held by most practitioners and philosophers of science (this includes a growing number of political scientists). But first a preliminary point. There are two ways to approach science. On the one hand, it can be viewed as "a body of knowledge"; on the other, as "a method of obtaining it." According to the first approach, science or that which is scientific includes the laws, facts, what-have-you of physics, biology, economics, etc. According to the second, science is a particular set of principles which tells us now to obtain these facts. We will take the second approach, for what interests us are the *methodological* foundations of political science.

Remember that science is being viewed as the second aspect of political science—*how* political scientists go about studying political phenomena. Thus a discipline can be judged scientific if it makes certain assumptions and follows certain principles, even though the knowledge it has produced is not very impressive. It should be clear that there is no opposition between the two approaches. The adjective "scientific" can be applied both to the principles ("scientific" method) and the facts obtained ("scient-ific" knowledge). We emphasize the first here because it is logically prior—scientific *knowledge* is obtained only by following scientific *method.*

A further distinction can be made between two ways of looking at scientific method. One is exemplified in the work of the political theorist Arnold Brecht. He lists 11 "scientific actions" or "steps of scientific procedure," beginning with observation, which together make up scientific method.[11] The other approach is to sort out the basic assumptions and principles, rather than operations or procedures, which scientists make and follow. This then becomes a more fundamental analysis. But let us make it clear that these are simply two ways of looking at the same thing.

"Nothing in the universe just happens" is a simple way of stating the scientist's basic assumption. It is usually labeled "determinism" or the "principle of universal causation."[12] Most of us believe that there are reasons for everyday events or situations. This is the commonsensical basis of the scientist's assumption of determinism or causality. In effect he says, if we want knowledge of the world we have to assume that the world is coherent, that there are certain recurring relationships which can be expressed in such propositions as "If *A* occurs, *B* occurs." This is a causal relationship and it is what the scientist is searching for. If scientific knowledge is knowledge of such relationships, then the principle of determinism, or something like it, is a necessary starting point. However, it must be emphasized that the principle is not itself a scientific law which has or can be substantiated but instead is an assumption which directs the scientist's work. As one philosopher has said, "It expresses a resolve, 'Let us find uniformities in the world.' "[13] This is why he calls it a "leading principle." It can be said then, that a science of politics begins with the assumption that no political phenomenon just happens. This enables the political scientist to carry out his main task, namely, to account for the phenomena which interest him—to show *why* they happen or exist.

11Arnold Brecht, *Political Theory: The Foundations of Twentieth-Century Political Thought* (Princeton, N. J.: Princeton University Press, 1959), pp. 28-29.

12For a clear discussion of the principle see John Hospers, *An Introduction to Philosophical Analysis* (Englewood Cliffs, N.J.: Prentice-Hall, Inc., 1953), Chapter 4.

13*Ibid.,* p. 261.

The second characteristic of science is one we have already discussed. If the world is what we are interested in, then it is the world we must go to and examine. Describing and explaining politics implies speaking about and basing our explanations on what has been observed (directly or indirectly) about politics. This means that every scientific statement is in one way or another based upon an observation. The proposition, "There are 30 desks in this classroom," can be verified by counting the desks. Of course, matters are much more complicated in the sciences, but the principle is the same. In studying voting behavior, for instance, we have to do much more than count a few desks. But observing voters' attitudes (responses to questions) and measuring social status (income and occupation), to name only some of the factors which might interest us, are empirical for the same reason that counting desks is.

It is often said that to be scientific is to be *objective* as opposed to *subjective*. The scientist is one who keeps separate his professional and personal judgments. In the latter he is subjective, which means that values or normative considerations often influence his decisions. But when he is being scientific such influences must be excluded; the scientist "tells it as it is." Perhaps it can now be seen that *objective* is in many ways a synonym of *empirical*. To base your judgments on observation is to be empirical, and if your judgments are empirical in this sense you are being objective. Another way of saying all this is to call science "value-free." Recalling the discussion of the first chapter, science deals with "is," not "ought" questions; with empirical, not normative questions. Thus we see the relationship between "scientific" and "objective."

Many students of scientific method, however, prefer an alternate term to "objective" when they characterize science. "Intersubjective" seems more descriptive of how scientists actually operate, for it is not so demanding as "objective"; it doesn't conjure up the images of ultimate reality which "objective" seems to. For as Arnold Brecht has pointed out, to be intersubjective, knowledge has to be transmissible. He means by this, "A type of knowledge that can be transmitted from any person who has such knowledge to any other person who does not have it but who can grasp the meaning of the symbols (words, signs) used in communication and perform the operations, if any, described in these communications."[14] Thus, if one scientist performs an experiment, a second scientist can repeat the experiment and compare the two sets of findings. If the procedures are correct, then we would expect the results to be similar; although because of changing conditions and new factors, they might differ. This is scientifically acceptable. What is important is that one scientist can understand and evaluate the methods of others and can carry out similar observations so as to test the validity of scientific facts. This then is the significance of intersubjectivity. The requirement is simply that all proposed scientific facts be open to inspection and the procedures used to arrive at these facts be clearly enough described so as to be repeatable. Thus scientific knowledge is "transmissible." When we contrast a scientific proposition such as, "Most businessmen vote Republican," with the metaphysical one, "Spirits motivate businessmen," the significance of the former's intersubjective nature is made evident.

There is more to science than observation. We all look at the world and draw conclusions, yet this does not make us scientists. While science begins with common sense (everyone who looks sees the same chairs or analyzes the same attitude questionnaires), scientific knowledge is not the same as commonsensical knowledge. It is at this point that the systematic nature of science becomes relevant. For the scientist takes his observations and attempts to classify and analyze them. His first objective is to formulate useful *empirical concepts* that organize the phenomena which interest him. Then, starting with the assumption of determinism, he attempts to find relationships between these concepts. If successful, he discovers a scientific *law* or *generalization.* Further systemization of empirical knowledge is achieved by the construction of *theories,* which are collections of logically related generalizations. Finally, the scientist uses his laws and theories to *explain* events and situations which have occurred or exist and to *predict* future happenings. It can thus be said that the scientist's attempts to systematize are all leading up to this ultimate objective, to explain and predict—to show *why* things were, are, or will be. A glance at this book's Table of Contents will

---

[14]Brecht, *op. cit.,* p. 114.

indicate that Part Two has just been outlined. We have, in very general terms, mentioned the basic elements of science, and therefore of a science of politics—concepts, laws, theories, and explanation and prediction. The way in which these elements are developed and used gives science its particular character. In organizing, in looking for relationships, in trying to explain and predict, the scientist moves beyond the commonsensical kind of knowledge that most of us accept as sound.

This, then, is an outline of science as it is viewed by scientists and philosophers. It is the set of principles which more and more political scientists are accepting as the basis of their own work. Our analysis, of course, assumes that the "science" in "political science" is based upon these principles. The other, more liberal, interpretations of science are acceptable, for it should now be obvious that they are simply less complete versions.

However, it would not be fair to leave readers with the impression that all political scientists accept this interpretation of political *science*. Some reject the notion that politics can ever be studied *scientifically*. Thus, while they probably accept the previously discussed model of science (or one of its derivatives), they deny that political science can ever meet its requirements. Instead, the political scientist must rely on nonscientific methods to study politics. But no reliable knowledge of the sort found in physics will ever be produced in political science. The end result is usually a political science more closely related to literature and philosophy than the social sciences. In Chapter 4 we will consider some of the specific arguments these political scientists present in their attempt to prove that political science can never be scientific. We will attempt to refute these arguments and thus indirectly demonstrate the possibility of a science of politics.

Finally a characteristic which science does not have should be mentioned. We have already implied it several times. While science deals with the world of observation, it does not develop *necessary* truth. As was pointed out in Chapter 1, only analytic propositions can be necessarily true. Empirical propositions are by their very nature contingent. This is why we said that many scientists shy away from the concept, "Truth"; it seems to imply necessity.

To be empirical, and therefore scientific, a proposition has to be disprovable. If there is no way to show that it is false, if no amount of observational evidence can put its claim to question, then it cannot be called scientific. Thus, if a scientific proposition is always open to disconfirmation, it obviously cannot be necessarily true.

3 *Orientations in political science*

In Chapter 1, the broad interests of political scientists were described.Chapter 2 analyzed the meanings of "political" and "science." Now, in Chapter 3, the scope of political science will be viewed in a different light. We will deal with orientations, schools of thought in modern political science. There is a rough chronological order about them which allows us to talk about the historical development of American political science, an important topic in its own right. But more important to us is the fact that they are all still in evidence today.

This discussion will, hopefully, serve two purposes. First, it will put into clearer perspective the conclusions of Chapters 1 and 2. It is interesting, for instance, to note the tendency of particular interpretations of "politics" and "science" to cluster together to form particular schools of thought. These schools, then, represent definitions of *political science.* This was hinted at in the last chapter and will become more obvious as we move along. In providing such perspective, a foundation for the rest of the book is laid. But this second purpose, foundation-laying, is accomplished more directly by examining the most contemporary orientation in political science, *behavioralism,* for it is the orientation of this book (although it is not accepted uncritically).

A general and well-known distinction today is drawn between the *traditional* and the *behavioral* approaches to the study of politics. Before we go any further, one point of clarification should be made. While we can with some justification distinguish one school from another for the purposes of analysis, in the real world the boundary lines are usually blurred. Few professional political scientists would allow themselves to be classified as out-and-out traditionalists or behavioralists. The reason, in addition to the natural academic aversion to self-pigeonholing, is the legitimate realization that "pure" political scientists are rare. Most individuals' orientations are a mixture of schools, old and new. This chapter, then, is not a handbook for classifying professors of political science (although this is at times an enjoyable pastime). It is, instead, a characterization of the discipline of political science—an attempt to sort out and describe the major methodological tendencies in the discipline so as to gain a better understanding of the scope of political science.

TRADITIONAL POLITICAL SCIENCE

The so-called traditional approach includes several methods of analyzing politics which became popular among many American political scientists in the 19th and early 20th centuries and which continue to be conspicuous. It cannot be emphasized too strongly that traditionalism is a collection of approaches lumped together today mainly because of a common enemy, behavioralism. Perhaps the three most important ones are the historical, legalistic, and institutional approaches.

From its beginnings, in the 19th century, American political science was looked upon by many of its practitioners as primarily an historical discipline. Little difference was recognized between history and political science; the latter was considered a branch or division of the former. Thus political science was really political history, and included such fields as the history of political parties, of foreign relations, and of great political ideas.

While the historical approach had its heyday in the last century, it is still much in evidence today. One hears arguments, for instance, to the effect that historians and political scientists use the same methods. For instance, in 1938 the American political scientist Edward M. Sait wrote that, "The historical approach is indispensable. It affords the only means of appreciating the true nature of institutions and the peculiar way in which they have been fashioned."[1] And in how many colleges does a Department of History *and* Political Science still exist? A variation on the historical approach is used by those political scientists who might be labeled historians of the present. They give detailed descriptions of contemporary political events, done in the narrative style of the historian. The results are often called case studies. The well-done case study's realistic portrayal of politics is no doubt useful. However, Nelson Polsby, Robert Dentler, and Paul Smith have noted its shortcomings. "As more and more case studies are written, readers are overwhelmed by details. Case writers ... often resist the codification of their findings in any but the most primitive ways, however."[2] Thus, while he gives us much information about a particular political event, the historian of the present refuses to generalize, to compare and find the common elements in his and other narratives.

It seems and has probably always seemed natural to link the study of politics to law or the legal system. This provides the basis for the *legalistic* approach in American political science, an approach which views political science as primarily the study of constitutions and legal codes. In the last chapter we saw the importance of "legality" in many definitions of politics. At this point the relationship between the definition and approach becomes clear. If politics, the subject matter of political science, is distinctive because of its legalistic nature then it is only reasonable that the political scientist should concentrate on the specifically legal aspects of the political system. Some political scientists view the legalistic approach as an improvement over the historical approach because it makes a distinction between the realms of history and political science—the political scientist is now able to tell the historian what the two do *not* have in common. It should also be pointed out that in adopting a legalistic approach the political scientist is not limited to the study of the legal system per se. Rather, the legal and constitutional aspects of any political institution can be examined. One of the most respected works of this kind is Edward S. Corwin's thorough analysis of the

---

[1]Edward M. Sait, *Political Institutions: A Preface* (New York: Appleton-Century, 1938), p. 529.

[2]Nelson Polsby, Robert Dentler, and Paul Smith, *Politics and Social Life* (Boston: Houghton Mifflin Co., 1963), p. 4.

Presidency as a *constitutional office.*[3] Thus, the primary data employed are court decisions which interpret the powers of and limitations on the President. However, other political scientists consider the legalistic approach as simply one kind of historical study. The political scientist who assumes the former is going to study the *history* of constitutions or court decisions. The political scientist then can take a legalistic and an historical approach simultaneously.

A number of factors can be cited to explain this inclination toward legalism in American political science. We will mention only two which seem especially important. In the 19th century most American political scientists received their graduate training in European, usually German, universities. (Columbia University began the first successful graduate program of political science in the United States in 1880.)[4] The political science professors were members of *law* faculties, which tells us something about their approach to the study of politics. In fact modern German political science and political philosophy has always had an obvious legalistic strain. Thus the returning American political scientists with their new doctorates tended to think along the same lines as their European teachers. And, more significantly for contemporary political science, this has remained a tradition in the discipline.

Perhaps an even more important and deeper seated reason has to do with the American political system itself and the picture most Americans seem to have of it. We have been taught that ours is a government "of laws, not of men." While most intelligent citizens realize that it takes men to make, implement, and enforce laws, the doctrine or folkway of the rule of law has always influenced popular political ideology in America. And so it no doubt influences the study of politics. What methodological guideline follows more logically from such a political system (or image of a political system) then, "Study the legal system, not the structure of political institutions or the behavior of politicians"?

Reaction to the historical and legalistic approaches probably stimulated the third traditional school of thought, the *institu-*

[3]Edward S. Corwin, *The President: Office and Powers* (New York: New York University Press, 1957).

[4]Albert Somit and Joseph Tannenhaus, *The Development of American Political Science: From Burgess to Behavioralism* (Boston: Allyn & Bacon, Inc., 1967), Chapter 1.

tional. As political scientists realized that there was more to politics than legal codes and constitutions, a shift in emphasis took place. There was talk about studying political *realities,* that is, what politics actually is, not just its history or legal manifestations. The most obvious *reality* of politics is the political institution; legislatures, executives, and courts then receive the primary attention of the institutionalist. What we have called naive empiricism manifests itself, for his work is mainly descriptive— detailed descriptions of political institutions, and not explanations of the political system, are the goal of the institutionalist. So, for instance, the powers, roles, and functions of the President might be listed and described. One need not look far to discover examples of institutional political science, for many if not most textbooks are institutionally oriented.

BEHAVIORALISM

The traditional approach gains most of its meaning *as a single orientation* when it is contrasted with the behavioral approach.[5] For the latter seems to have begun after World War II as a sort of protest movement by some political scientists against traditional political science. The general claims of the new behavioralist were that, first, the political science which had gone before did not measure up as a producer of reliable political knowledge; many political scientists working in important wartime decision-making positions made this discovery when they had to draw upon existing knowledge of domestic and international politics. But, second, and on a positive note, more reliable knowledge of politics could be achieved through different approaches and methods. This turn in direction was not spontaneous, however. Beginning in the 1930's there had been an influx of European social scientists to the United States, and they were often skilled in the use of new research methods. They no doubt had some influence on their American colleagues. At least the European exposed the American

---

[5]This section is based upon the following discussions of behavioralism: Robert A. Dahl, "The Behavioral Approach," *American Political Science Review,* Vol. LV, 1961, pp. 763-72; David Easton, *A Framework for Political Analysis* (Englewood Cliffs, N.J.: Prentice-Hall, Inc. (1965), Chapter 1, and "The Current Meaning of 'Behavioralism,'" in James C. Charlesworth (ed.), *Contemporary Political Analysis* (New York: Free Press, 1967), pp. 11-31; Somit and Tannenhaus, *op. cit.,* Chapter 12.

to new ways of analyzing social and political phenomena. Despite the significant contributions of European political scientists, we must not overlook the solid foundation for the behavioral or new movement in political science which had been laid by several political scientists "way back" in the 1920's. Perhaps the most deserving of credit is Charles Merriam, who, at the University of Chicago, anticipated many post-World War II developments in political science, and educated and stimulated some of the best known contemporary behavioralists.[6] So there is reason to say that many of the ideas articulated by the behavioralists were not original with them.

Before proceeding any further perhaps we ought to say a few words about the label "behavioralism." Most importantly, its relationship to "psychological *behaviorism*" should be made clear, for the two are often mistakenly identified. Behaviorism refers to a type of psychology which uses as data only overt stimuli and responses, mainly actions or behavior.[7] Thus, only observable physical phenomena such as pieces of cheese, electric shocks, and *behavior* like the running of rats can be referred to by the behaviorist. Concepts such as attitudes, opinions, and personality traits which are mental in nature and not observable actions (à la leg-kicks or eye-blinks) are rejected as meaningless. To the behavioralist this approach seems much too restrictive. He does make extensive use of attitudes and similar concepts, attributing them to people on the basis of observed behavior. Attitudes do not therefore take on some mysterious existential quality, for they are still tied to experience, they are still linked to empirical referents. For instance, if a person scores high on a particular attitude scale we say he is a pacifist (he has a pacific attitude). To the behavioralist this simply means that any individual who gives a particular set of responses to a particular set of questions has by definition a particular attitude. The behavioralist, then, shares the behaviorist's desire to keep his work empirical (and the latter has no doubt influenced the former in this regard). However, he interprets this characteristic

---

[6]See especially Charles E. Merriam, *New Aspects of Politics* (Chicago: University of Chicago Press, 1924).

[7]For a short presentation of behaviorism see the relevant articles in T. W. Wann, *Behaviorism and Phenomenology* (Chicago: University of Chicago Press, 1964).

of science more liberally, so as to allow for the use of attitudes and other dispositional concepts.

If one moves beyond a consideration of the general mood of behavioralism, he is faced with several interpretations of this new orientation; that is, several arguments about how political science can improve upon traditionalism. One interpretation emphasizes subject matter or content. According to this view behavioralism is characterized by its concentration on the *behavior* of political actors, and is therefore to a large extent a rejection of the institutional approach. Let us recall David Easton's plea, asking political scientists to study activity, not institutions. It can now be seen that this is a statement of the first interpretation of behavioralism. The behavioralist argues that, although an important aspect of politics, the institution as a thing in itself is not the real stuff of politics. It is the activity within and the behavior around the political institution which should be the main concern of the political scientist. The major part of the behavioralist's energy is not, for instance, spent in describing the *structure* of the Senate or the *legal duties* of senators but rather in describing and explaining senators' *behavior* and therefore explaining how the Senate as an institution operates—*why* it passes a tax bill but not a civil rights bill. The behavioralist does not completely reject the traditional approaches. He still uses historical data when necessary; he still studies the legal aspects of political systems; he still realizes the importance of institutions. But he always comes back to behavior. History consists of human behavior; people make, follow, and break laws; and finally and most importantly, institutions are nothing more than combinations of behavior patterns.

In the broadest sense both individuals and groups (in this discussion "group" includes all organizations from the local city commission to the United Automobile Workers to the United States) behave—they act and react, they are stimulated and respond. However, there are two points of view about the respective significance of each level of behavior, and this disagreement is of some importance for behavioralism and political science. First there are those, and it seems that most behavioralists are of this opinion, who argue that groups are nothing more than their individual members. This position is, not surprisingly, labeled "individualism."[8] To say that an interest group is opposed to a particular legislative proposal means that a majority of its members is opposed. The behavior of the Supreme Court is really the individual behaviors of a small group of men. There are no properties of groups which are not reducible to individual properties. Thus, while the individualist does not deny that groups exist, he does deny that they have any independent status, that they are more than the sum of their parts.

Other political scientists argue that there are *emergent* group properties which are not reducible. Thus groups are more than the sum of their parts. This position, usually labeled "holism," represents an important tradition in historical and sociological thinking, and has no doubt influenced many political scientists. A holistic political scientist might argue, for instance, that an interest group has certain characteristics, such as "cohesion," which none of its members has and which cannot be reduced to, or defined in terms of, individualistic characteristics. To this the individualist would reply: of course no individual is cohesive in the way that a group is. But the group's cohesiveness can, in principle, be defined or explained by referring to characteristics of and relationships between its members. "A group is cohesive when a majority of its members belong to no other interest groups" might be a definition of cohesion, for instance.

Most behavioralists, it would seem, take the individualistic position. They stress the significance of individual behavior as the basic building block of political science. This, then, is a turning point in political science. The institutionalist studies structures, powers, and responsibilities; the behavioralist, attitudes, personalities, and physical activity (voting, lobbying). Behavioralism and individualism seem to go hand in hand. If one sees as the characteristic feature of behavioralism its emphasis on behavior, then the kind of behavior which seems the most reasonable to emphasize is that of the individual. We will assume, then, that there is a fairly strong correlation between behavioralism and individualism. But note that this does not preclude the behavioralist from studying groups or nation-states. Groups and nation-

---

[8]For a thorough analysis of the individualism-holism controversy see May Brodbeck, "Methodological Individualism: Definition and Reduction," *Philosophy of Science,* Vol. XXV, 1958.

states exist, this no one can commonsensically deny. It is accounting for the group which leads to the controversy, and the political scientist's own resolution of the controversy will have much to say about how he studies politics.

There is another interpretation of behavioralism which, while closely related to the first, is nevertheless important enough in its own right to deserve separate consideration. According to it, behavioralism is equated with the scientific study of politics. This suggests several more specific elements. First is a more or less explicit advocacy of scientific method, which can range from the weak or liberal notion of science (anything systematic and empirical) to the full set of scientific assumptions and principles. In any case, what the behavioralist appears to be doing is making a distinction between scientific-behavioral and unscientific-traditional political science. To many, this may seem unfair. But it is only unfair if it is inaccurate. Furthermore, remember that we are only trying to describe the linguistic uses of "behavioral," not its supposed "real meaning." According to this usage, behavioralism becomes the label applied to the scientific movement in political science. Its objectives are the development of empirical generalizations and systematic theory, and the use of these in the explanation of political phenomena.

There are variations on this interpretation. For instance, to some, many of them nonbehavioralists, behavioralism means counting heads (or votes), using numbers, quantifying. Often used for purposes of derogation (quantification dehumanizes political science; we can quantify only the more trivial features of politics), this proposed essential characteristic is really one important technique of science. Quantification of data is a significant goal of every science, and no science will develop beyond a fairly primitive level unless it does employ quantitative techniques of various sorts. But as we have seen, there are other characteristics of science which are more basic. To the outsider behavioralism may be defined in terms of quantification, and this is all right as far as it goes; but the behavioralist himself realizes the more fundamental foundations of his approach.

Finally, there is an assumption about the relationship between political science and the other social sciences which seems to go along with a behavioral state of mind. It expresses the hope that some day the walls which separate the social sciences will crumble. The time spent by political scientists defending their discipline against the onslaughts of outsiders (sociologists are perhaps the most visible) could be more fruitfully spent in doing research, for the battle is a bogus one. While indicating a pragmatic division of labor, the boundaries do not reflect a logically necessary division.

There is a methodological basis for this position, which is usually labeled "the unity of the social sciences." It states simply that all social scientists are studying the same thing, the behavior of individuals (or groups of individuals). Political scientists study what is defined as *political* behavior, economists what is defined as *economic* behavior. It is on this basis that the disciplinary boundaries are drawn. But the data, the basic observations of any social science, are of the same *type*. Thus the social sciences are, according to the behavioralist, unified because of their common interest in behavior. They are also unified on methodological grounds – all sciences, natural and social, make the same basic assumptions and follow the same principles. This was the gist of Chapter 2.

For the political scientist this unity of data and method has important consequences. Practically speaking, it means that he can legitimately move from sociological to economic to psychological data in his attempt to describe and explain political phenomena. To the antibehavioralist this lack of disciplinary patriotism is an indication of the dangers of behavioralism. Most serious is a lost appreciation among political scientists for what is truly political. As the boundaries between the social sciences become more and more blurred, the distinctiveness of political science will become less and less evident. The title of a recent book, critical of behavioralism tells it all: *Apolitical Politics.*[9] "Archaic" or even "reactionary" would probably be the behavioralists' characterization of this criticism.

Let us now try to bring some order to our discussion of behavioralism. A general conclusion which immediately comes to mind is the lack of a single interpretation of behavioralism. The ambiguity is more apparent than real, however, for the two basic interpretations of behavioralism are complementary. If one inter-

---

[9]Charles McCoy and John Playford (eds.), *Apolitical Politics* (New York: Thomas Y. Crowell Co., 1967).

prets behavioralism as the "scientific study of politics," then chances are the basic unit of analysis which he uses will be individual behavior. More specifically, to advocate the use of scientific method in political science is to assume the existence of, or the possibility of developing, an intersubjective observation language of politics. Recall that intersubjectivity is a basic characteristic of science. If one scientist performs an experiment or proposes a generalization, his findings must be open to the probing of other scientists. This is possible only if there is a basic language referring to observational units which enables all scientists to observe the same events. In political science, behavior seems to be the proper framework for such a language.

So what appear as two interpretations of behavioralism are in fact two aspects of the approach. The political scientist who advocates the scientific approach to politics (and is therefore a behavioralist in the second sense) will invariably formulate his scientific propositions in a language of behavior. Thus the behavioral approach comes full circle.

Part Two

THE SCIENTIFIC
STUDY OF POLITICS

4 *Is political science a science?*

In Chapter 2 a short description of science was given. The chapters of Part Two will develop in detail the main points made there. Each of the primary building blocks of science—concept, law, theory, explanation, and prediction—will be analyzed with the special needs of the political scientist in mind. Before beginning this task however, there is another which must be attended to. The discussion in Chapter 2 assumed that scientific method is applicable to the study of politics. It was noted, however, in conclusion, that some political scientists question this applicability. Let us, then, critically examine the assumption by analyzing several of the arguments made by those who are skeptical of or in opposition to it. An attempt will be made to point out the shortcomings of each argument, and thus to provide a sound foundation for the detailed analysis of the science of politics upcoming in Chapters 5 through 8.

ARGUMENTS AGAINST THE POSSIBILITY OF A SCIENCE OF POLITICS

Science or scientific method is characterized by a number of assumptions and principles. They have already been discussed, but let us run through them again. The reason for this strategy will become obvious in a moment. First, scientists assume some form of determinism or "law of universal causation." Once again, this means that the political scientist who accepts scientific method plunges into his work assuming that nothing in politics just happens. The second major characteristic of science is its empirical basis. This implies a number of features, including an observational foundation, intersubjectivity, and the value-free nature of science. The objectives of science are summarized in the third character-istic, which we might call its systematic nature. They are to formulate and verify empirical generalization, develop systematic theory, and finally explain and predict. Now the arguments against the possibility of a science of politics invariably attempt to demonstrate that political science does not and/or cannot have one or more of these characteristics. This strategy correctly assumes that if political science must have these characteristics to be legitimately labeled "scientific," then such a demonstration, if successful, would illustrate the quicksand upon which the scien-tific study of politics rests. At that point the behaviorally or scientifically oriented political scientist would be well advised to put the brakes on, admit the futility of his activities, and return to the more traditional ways of doing things.

The complexity of political phenomena

One argument against the possibility of a science of politics claims that no regularities can be discovered because political phenomena are too complex. Because of a variety of usages, the meaning of "complex" is not clear. However, the basic point seems to be that in politics there are too many variables, and possible relationships between them, to find any order. In contradistinction, physicists and chemists are able to discover relationships and construct theories because the phenomena which interest them are less complex. This, then, directly attacks the third characteristic of science. If political phenomena are so complex that they cannot be organized into generalizations, that is, if relationships are not discoverable, then there can be no science of politics—there can be no scientific explanations and predictions of political phenomena. Let us turn to the writings of the well-known contemporary political scientist Hans Morgenthau for a statement of this position. After noting the complexity of social phenomena and the difficulty involved in isolating causal factors, he concludes: "The social sciences can, at best, do what is their regular task, that is, present a series of hypothetical possibilities, each of which may occur under certain conditions— and which of them will actually occur is anybody's guess."[1]

A reply to this argument should first point out that the degree of complexity of political phenomena is an empirical, not a logical, question. That is, it is debatable whether the social sciences are more complex than the natural sciences, and the debate can only be resolved by systematically examining each science. But it is not even necessary for our purposes to resolve the controversy, since there are no logical grounds for this criticism of scientific political science. From the fact that it is difficult to sort out political factors and measure relationships (research oriented political scientists need not be reminded of this), one cannot logically conclude that generalizations are *impossible.* And note that the critic is not denying that relationships exist, only that the political scientist can discover them.

This is the logical—methodological answer. But in addition, several empirical points can be offered to strengthen our case. The philosopher of science Adolf Grunbaum has wondered what someone living before Galileo and holding to the complexity thesis would have thought about the possibility of a science of motion. This observation is perhaps especially relevant in today's rapidly changing world, in which the word "impossible" is used with greater and greater discretion. The point is, of course, that it is foolish to state on empirical grounds (even assuming that the evidence is sound) that something is logically impossible. In Grunbaum's words, "This argument rests its case on what is not known, and therefore, like all such arguments, it has no case."[2] Furthermore, we can refer the skeptic to the relationships which have been discovered in the fields of psychology, sociology, economics, and yes, even political science; the discovery of a single law logically refutes the impossibility argument, and on a positive note, the social sciences are more highly developed than many of their critics care to admit or seem to realize.

---

[1] Hans J. Morgenthau, *Scientific Man Versus Power Politics* (Chicago: University of Chicago Press, 1946), p. 130.

[2] Adolf Grunbaum, "Causality and the Science of Human Behavior," in Herbert Feigl and May Brodbeck, *Readings in the Philosophy of Science* (New York: Appleton-Century-Crofts, 1953), p. 770.

This argument then boils down to the mistaken translation of a practical problem into a logically insurmountable barrier. As we already implied, every political scientist knows how difficult it is to find order in the world of politics—but this does not prevent him from attempting to discover generalizations. Sometimes he even succeeds. Contrary to the image of science held by many laymen, scientists, whether natural or social, realize that no complete description or explanation of any empirical phenomenon is possible. Something is always left out. Thus, to chastise political science for something which is true even of physics is perhaps unfair. If the political scientist is sobered by the practical wisdom implied by the complexity argument, if his rose-colored glasses are shattered, then it has been useful—utopian optimism is out of place in science. But if his reaction is to give up the scientific enterprise, then political science has been dealt a destructive blow.

Human indeterminancy

So much for the complexity thesis. Another argument against the possibility of a science of politics is based upon the so-called "indeterminancy" of human behavior. Russell Kirk, one of the most vigorous opponents of the scientific study of politics, has put it this way: "Human beings are the least controllable, verifiable, law-obeying and predictable of subjects."[3] On the one hand, this is in part a version of the complexity argument—one of the reasons for the complexity of political phenomena is the unpredictable behavior of political actors. The reply, then, is the same given in the last section. But on the other hand there is an additional feature which makes the argument a new and probably more uncompromising one. This feature boils down to a belief in freedom of the will. Because humans are free to choose their course of action at any given point in the political process, their actions cannot be classified, and so generalizations describing their behavior cannot be formulated. This argument is more uncompromising than the previous one, because the claim is not that it is

---

[3]Russell Kirk, "Is Social Science Scientific?" in Nelson W. Polsby, Robert A. Dentler, and Paul A. Smith (eds.), *Politics and Social Life* (Boston: Houghton Mifflin Co., 1963), p. 63.

extremely difficult to isolate causal factors but that there are no causal factors in the first place.

As many philosophers have shown, this is a bogus argument. The ability to formulate laws of human behavior and freedom of the will are not incompatible. Those who opt for freedom of the will are usually saying that people are able to act without external restraints. "But would they also claim that what they do is not determined even by the sort of people they are, considered as whole, individuals possessing a certain disposition, a certain character, certain motives, and so on?"[4] In other words a free choice need not be uncaused. It is rather determined to a great extent by the makeup of the person choosing. And this makeup (attitudes, personality traits, etc.) is subject to description, that is, inclusion in general laws which relate the individuals' characteristics to other factors. John Hospers neatly summarizes this whole reply when he points out that, "Freedom...is the opposite of compulsion, not of causality."[5]

Some critics would now reject the defense just presented with a statement of inderterminism—"not every fact has a cause." Unfortunately for social scientists, most of the uncaused ones are found in the social, economic, and political realms. This position, then, strikes directly at the first assumption of our model of science. Now, let us recall that determinism should not be considered an empirical statement about the universe; there is no point in trying to disprove it, for the failure to discover determining conditions does not prove that there are none. This, of course, is why it is not empirical—it fails to meet the testability and verifiability criteria. Instead, the thesis of determinism should be "construed as a regulative principle that formulates in a comprehensive way one of the major objectives of positive science, namely, the discovery of the determinants for the occurrence of events."[6] In other words, without some sort of assumption that events have causes, the whole attempt to describe and explain the

---

[4]Quentin Gibson, *The Logic of Social Enquiry* (London: Routledge & Kegan Paul, 1960), p. 22.

[5]John Hospers, *An Introduction to Philosophical Analysis* (Englewood Cliffs, N.J.: Prentice-Hall, Inc., 1954), p. 271.

[6]Ernest Nagel, *The Structure of Science* (New York: Harcourt, Brace & World, 1961), p. 605.

world of politics might as well be given up. This suggestion is no doubt appealing to some. But why end science at this point? And I say *end* because progress has been made in the social sciences, including political science. For one engaged in the enterprise of understanding political phenomena, the assumption of determinism seems unavoidable. Why, when starting out to gain knowledge should one want to limit himself before he begins? Perhaps political science will never produce the kind of knowledge which characterizes physics and chemistry, but it is worth the try, and something is better than nothing. We can't tell what we can't do until we try to do it.

The influence of values

Another argument against the possibility of a science of politics questions its presumed value-free nature. Here is the main difference between the natural and social sciences; practitioners of the former do not have to deal with values—protons and molecules are neither good nor bad—but the latter do. This is especially true of political science, for several reasons. First, political science is a policy science in the true sense of the word. Politics is mainly concerned with goals and the means to achieve them—policies. Politics involves policies and policies involve values.

A second reason is the importance of value concepts—attitudes, opinions, and ideologies—to political science. No political scientist denies that values hold a significant place in his discipline. The first claim of the antiscientist is, however, that because political scientists study values, they must be influenced by them. It would seem that no lengthy argument is required to demonstrate the weakness of this claim. There is a *logical* difference between *having* one's own values and studying attitudes and opinions. The latter can be treated in the same manner as any other political phenomena. They are just as susceptible to scientific treatment. And to admit this the political scientist does not have to deny that he himself has values—this is patently foolish.

Looking now at the other value aspect of political science, to say that we are interested in policies is not to claim that we are formulating *basic* values or goals for a society. This the political scientist may do, but not, legitimately, as a political scientist.

While playing his professional role he can only give instrumental value judgments, answers to *means,* not ends, questions. This, of course, is what a policy science is all about. Given the objective of preventing urban riots, the political scientist's task is to demonstrate how the goal can be achieved. This then becomes an empirical question—the normative aspect (urban riots should be prevented) is no longer the concern (as an ultimate value) of the political scientist (although it may deeply concern the man).

However, the antiscientist might accept this analysis and then point out that because the political scientist is also a value-holding man, he cannot prevent his own values from influencing his professional research. Thus every study, every approach in political science is value-influenced. This is the heart of the matter. To quote Russell Kirk once again, "Although the complete behaviorist may deny the existence of 'value-judgments' and normative understandings, nevertheless he does not escape, in his researches, the influence of his own value-judgments...."[7]

What we are faced with here is a half-truth. That values influence research is undeniably true; but this influence is not inevitable. Furthermore, there are ways to tell when values are distorting supposedly objective work. After all, when someone like Kirk argues that values do exert an influence he must believe that there is a way to uncover this influence. Otherwise, how else could he make the claim? Every social scientist knows how difficult it is to prevent his values from intruding. But he does not have to throw up his hands; scientific method enables us to sort out what is *fact* and what is *value.* If the principle of intersubjectivity is followed by observant and critical scientists, then few biased propositions in political science will long exist.

A common rebuttal is that even if one admits the possibility of purging the content of political research of its value-biasedness, the fact remains that the political scientist must make other kinds of value judgments which inevitably affect his objectivity. First of all, when he decides to use scientific method he is making a value judgment—he could just as well choose not to use it. There are several replies to this confusing position. One will be discussed in a moment because it is significant in its own right. We need say here

---

[7]Kirk, *op. cit.,* p. 63.

only that one does not select a way of studying politics the way he does a new automobile—either one is as good as another or it is all a matter of personal taste and cost. Scientific method is, as we have seen, a label applied to a set of assumptions and principles which those studying the world have formulated, developed, and accepted as the best foundation for their work. Scientists do not arbitrarily impose science upon a society. Thus while a political scientist might "choose" the scientific approach it is really not the same kind of choice as, "Democracy is the best form of government."

A second kind of value judgment which takes place before the research is done has to do with the selection of research topics. No one denies that the political scientist chooses to study the causes of urban riots, for instance, because the problem interests him or because he thinks that the black ghetto is dysfunctional or evil. But the results of his work *need* not be biased by his values. Once he plunges into his research, the original value choice is methodologically irrelevant. His claim that ghetto living conditions lead to urban riots can be tested intersubjectively. Until it is, it should be considered an hypothesis—a guess, educated or otherwise, about a relationship between two factors. It is difficult, then, to understand why the selection of a research topic *has to* bias the results of research. Of course, the political scientist might, because of his value commitment, ignore certain kinds of factors so that his conclusions agree with his values. But here, once again, we see the significance of scientific method; this kind of biased research will simply not survive the criticism of his colleagues. This argument really ties in with the one we just considered which emphasizes political science's interest in policy questions. Whether beginning with a society's, government's, or individual political scientist's attempt to solve a particular social or political problem, there is no doubt that much political science research begins with a normative commitment. This refers both to the President who wants to decrease the incidence of urban disturbances because they threaten the existing political system,[8] and the individual political

---

[8]Two recent studies resulting from such motivations are *The Report of the National Advisory Commission on Civil Disorders* (New York: E. P. Dutton & Co., 1968); and *The Walker Report to the National Commission on the Causes and Prevention of Violence* (New York: New American Library, 1968).

scientist who studies racism because he believes it is morally wrong. We can conclude from this sampling of arguments that on the one hand, there are no valid arguments demonstrating the impossibility of a science of politics. On the other hand, many of them are useful if they make manifest to the political scientist some of the difficulties of his discipline. For instance, while the complexity of political phenomena is no *logical* barrier, it does create serious problems. The same can be said of values and free will. Let it be made clear, then, that in criticizing arguments against the possibility of a science of politics we are not taking a complacent attitude toward the many problems facing political science. There is no full-blown science of politics just around the corner. As we have already said, utopian optimism is out of place in any science. The crucial point is simply that a science of politics is possible, and any attempt to end the pursuit of political knowledge at this point is premature and unreasonable.

ALTERNATIVE ROUTES TO POLITICAL KNOWLEDGE

All political scientists who reject the viability of *scientific* political knowledge do not reject the possibility of all knowledge of politics. Some claim that scientific method provides one route to knowledge, but there are other routes, such as metaphysics, theology, and intuition. The scientist is then usually characterized as a sort of scholarly bigot, applying the seal of approval only to facts ground out of his own rigid set of rules, which he labels "scientific method." This, however, is an unfair criticism and it fails to see what science is all about.

The scientist does not deny that theological, metaphysical, or intuitive knowledge exists. He only claims that none of these is knowledge *about the world.* There is no way to verify a theological or intuitive explanation of an empirical event. Thus the scientist does not have to be arrogant about the knowledge he produces or might produce. All he has to say is, "If man can ever *know the world,* it must be through the application of scientific method." He might then go on to argue that "science" is not a conspiracy to impose a particular approach or methodology on the study of politics (or anything else). Scientific method develops as scientists do scientific work. It is, then, the basic set of principles which have been formulated and refined in order to describe and explain the world of observation and experience. The logic or foundation of this activity is the concern of philosophers of science (including us). But neither the scientist nor the philosopher of science arbitrarily creates this foundation. Given the objectives of accurately describing and soundly explaining the world (of politics for instance), certain principles seem to follow—they are necessary to do the job. It is interesting to note that even he who advocates a nonempirical approach such as theology to analyze the world, usually somewhere along the way begins making observations about the world and using them as evidence. At this point, whether he realizes it or not, he is using the same methods as the scientist. The point is, then, that science is not imposed upon society by scientists. Rather, it is simply a more sophisticated version of the methods we all use to cope with the world in our day-to-day lives.

But why bother with the difficult and often frustrating enterprise of science if it is really nothing more than common sense with trappings? Is the scientist perpetrating a fraud, going through the motions and accepting credit which he doesn't deserve? Another kind of attack on a science of politics questions the superiority of scientific over commonsensical knowledge and claims, in effect, that pursuing scientific method is a waste of time. How many of us have heard someone comment after reading a report of political research, "We knew this already"? The philosopher of science Ernest Nagel has given us a number of answers to this significant charge.[9] We will here only summarize and reinterpret them so as to make them directly relevant to students of politics. In effect, we will examine several reasons why scientific knowledge is superior to commonsensical knowledge and why, therefore, an attempt to create a science of politics is a worthwhile undertaking.

An initial shortcoming of common sense is its tendency to accept presumed facts without question, as a matter of faith. Propositions such as, "All politicians are corrupt," become part of the folk wisdom of American politics and are either never

---

[9]Nagel, *op. cit.,* Chapter 1. Also see Karl W. Deutsch, "The Limits of Common Sense," in Polsby, Dentler, and Smith, *op. cit.,* pp. 51-58.

explained or explained improperly. If we accept a "fact" simply because it is "obvious," "reasonable," or "self-evident," we may never be aware of the underlying conditions which account for it. The same can be said of the superficial explanations which often pass as scientific. For instance, several commonsensical propositions which are accepted by many as sound historical explanations claim that economic depressions are caused by Republican administrations and a Democratic administration will always be followed by war. First, of course, their truth can be questioned. But assuming that there is a correlation between political parties and economics or war, accepting such a commonsensical "fact" as an explanation of an historical or societal trend *might be* incorrect. The point is, commonsensically we will never know—scientifically we might find out. Perhaps the correlation is spurious, to speak statistically. It might be purely coincidental that the election of a Democratic President usually precedes a war; or the relationships may be deeper and more complex. Scientific method, with its stress on empiricism, intersubjectivity, and systematic generalizations, can probably be employed to sort out some of the more basic factors which common sense does not perceive. Once again it must be emphasized that scientific method is not a philosopher's stone, capable of providing ready answers to every question. Nor is common sense being rejected out of hand. In our day-to-day lives, there is usually no other basis for decisions. We are, instead, taking a more modest position which claims that the application of scientific method to problems of political analysis uncovers many of the mistakes and inconsistencies of commonsense knowledge and therefore leads to a more reliable brand of knowledge than its more primitive ancestor.

These shortcomings of commonsensical knowledge lead to several practical problems for those attempting to use it for purposes of explanation and prediction. First, although commonsensical knowledge may be true up to a point, because it isn't explained its limits are seldom realized. A user of scientific method, on the other hand, knows approximately how far he can go in applying the knowledge he discovers because in sorting out explanatory factors he has become aware of its limits. Suppose we explain the relatively low rate of voting turnout in the United States on the basis of a widespread apathy, which in turn is interpreted as an expression of basic satisfaction with the political system. This makes sense, so we accept it as commonsensically true. But suppose that as a matter of fact it is applicable only to certain segments of the population, the white middle class for instance. Other segments, Negroes, the poor, and the isolated, don't vote because they feel alienated from society. Their behavior has nothing to do with satisfaction; on the contrary, much dissatisfaction goes along with alienation. Now the point is, the scientific study of voting behavior would be more likely to discover these facts than common sense. Therefore, the scientist would be less likely to overapply his explanation. He would know the basic difference between middle-class and lowerclass non-voting, a difference which the advocate of common sense would be more likely to miss. The relevance of this analysis for practical policy making is clear.

Another serious problem which commonsense knowledge must face is its deficiency in accounting for political change. If explanatory factors are unknown, then if conditions change, especially the less obvious ones (which usually means the more important ones), a realization of inadequacy possibly leading to disillusionment might be the result for an advocate of common-sense knowledge. But if a sound scientific explanation has been given, and if therefore we are aware of the implications of changing conditions, we will have a much better chance of anticipating or even predicting the change. For instance, taking another oversimplified hypothetical case, let us assume that it is a commonsensical truth that urban disturbances come about primarily because of an increasing disrespect for law and order. However, if the primary conditions for such disturbances are urban living conditions (the ghetto, unemployment, etc.), then if such conditions become worse, the commonsense explanation will not be able to explain and predict the increase in riots and demonstrations and thus to point out what steps ought to be taken to prevent them. Once again, common sense in most cases is not so much wrong as incomplete and superficial.

But isn't common sense sometimes correct? is a common reply. Correct, perhaps; substantiated, no. This is the gist of the last few pages. Knowledge is not knowledge until it has been substantiated, using the procedures which have been labeled "scientific method."

While we might say, "I knew that all the time," we didn't know it—we sensed it, we intuited, we believed it.

On the other hand, common sense is useful as a source of hypotheses—relationships to be tested. No productive scientist can ignore the world of his own psychic experiences; it might not be a totally reliable world, but because he is a man, it is his starting point. It is often said that a poet experiences and sees the same things as the average man except that he sees them differently. The same could be said of the scientist. The great scientist is great not because he knows more about scientific method; all competent ones have that knowledge.[10] He is great because of imagination, insight, and the ability to draw implications from what he observes. But every imaginative insight must be subjected to the test of intersubjectivity. It is at this point that scientific method becomes relevant. This is what distinguishes the insights of the scientist from those of the poet.

In conclusion, let us make several points. First, while science begins with commonsense *observation,* scientific knowledge is not equivalent to commonsensical knowledge. Second, while the accumulated wisdom of common sense is sometimes duplicated by scientific procedures, it does not follow that science is a waste of time. Nothing is obvious until it has been empirically and systematically substantiated. This is not, of course, to deny that at times political science devotes its resources to the more easily studied at the expense of the perhaps more significant and harder-to-get-at phenomena. But, finally, let us note that political science discovers things which are unknown by, even in violation of, common sense.

---

[10]One of the objectives of this book is to provide a description of scientific method for students of politics.

5 Scientific concept formation in political science

Assuming that the study of politics can to some extent follow the basic principles of scientific method and that this is desirable (the last chapter, of course, attempted to demonstrate the validity of both assumptions), the question before us becomes, How do we go about constructing a science of politics? Chapter 5 begins a detailed discussion of the building blocks of scientific political inquiry. They will be analyzed as stages in the scientific process, beginning with the formation of *concepts,* then the formulation of *generalizations* (relationships between concepts), the construction of *theories* (interrelated sets of generalizations), and finally the primary objective of science, the use of laws and theories to *explain* and *predict* political phenomena.

We will adopt a simple, step-by-step approach. This is not, of course, to say that the nature and logic of scientific political inquiry is an easy subject; only that the discussion of science can be organized around a compact set of notions. There are others which are significant, and many of these will be discussed as they become relevant, for they are in every case directly related to one of the basic notions—i.e., the relationship between generalizations and causality. Uppermost in our mind, though, is the clearness, coherence, and overall usefulness of the next four chapters. If a few topics which some consider important are left out, we hope the justification contained in the last sentence is acceptable. This, after all, is not a complete survey of the philosophy of science—such an attempt would be a perfect example of social scientific overkill—but an analysis of scientific method *for students of politics.* Some topics in the more general field can be deemphasized. The main objective here is to discuss the relevant points and to provide a foundation for further work and reading in *political science.*

Science begins by forming concepts to describe the world. While we have referred several times to the importance of explanation, it should be realized that whatever is explained must first be described—*what* questions are logically prior to *why* questions and the former are answered within a framework of concepts which characterize, classify, order, compare, and quantify worldly phenomena. It is, then, the "concept" that serves as science's empirical base. Although it is usually the elaborate and awe-inspiring scientific theory which attracts the attention and stimulates the interest of the layman, it is the unsung concept which supports the whole scientific enterprise. A science will never progress if it does not move beyond the concept-formation stage, yet no science can begin without such activity.

CONCEPTS AND LANGUAGE

Description requires language, a language which includes descriptive words. Let us then continue our discussion by placing the concept in the context of language. There are several kinds of words and a number of ways to classify them. Perhaps the simplest and most useful classifies all words as either *logical* or *descriptive.* [1] A logical or *structure* word, as it is sometimes called, such as "and," does not *refer* to anything. There is nothing "out there" in the world which serves as the empirical referent of "and." Rather, logical words act as connectives between descriptive words; thus the alternate label "structure"—the scientific language is structured, shaped, given its outline by its logical words. Examples, besides "and," are "all," "some," "none," and "or." We might also want to include the terms of mathematics, although they are derivable from the basic set of words we just mentioned. But the purpose is not to memorize a list of words labeled "logical"—any

---

[1] Gustav Bergmann, *Philosophy of Science* (Madison: University of Wisconsin Press, 1957), pp. 12-24.

competent logic text provides such a list—but to understand what a logical word is.

But more than this, we want to know something about descriptive words. Unlike logical words, they refer to or name something. "Chair," "hard," and "power" are descriptive words because they refer directly or indirectly to observables. This is why they are descriptive. To say that something is a chair is in a sense to describe it. A simple concept such as "chair" presents fewer problems than a more complex one such as "power"—a chair is an assemblage of a small number of directly observable parts, while power is only indirectly observable. Yet in both cases something about the world of observation comes to mind when they are mentioned. We see a chair, or we see power being exercised. But we don't see "and" or "all."

There is another kind of descriptive word which does not directly concern us. It does not refer to a class of observable things such as "chair" or "man," but instead to a particular example of something: "the brown chair in my office," or "George Washington." This kind of descriptive word is called, in the first case, a *definite description*; in the second, a *proper name*. In either case, something is being described, but the something is specific and identifiable. The picture which enters our mind when "man" is mentioned is not the same as the one which is produced by "George Washington" (unless, of course, the latter is our ideal of manhood).

There are two kinds of descriptive words, then, one referring to classes of things—all things having certain characteristics; the other to particular things—one man out of the class of all men. The first kind of descriptive word might be called a *universal;* the second, a *particular.* It should be clear by now that we are interested only in the first, the universal descriptive word or *concept.*

Concepts, or character words, are the stuff of science. While the set of logical words structures a science—and their importance cannot be exaggerated—concepts manifest its content. Furthermore, while logical words are given to the scientist, so to speak, concepts have to be formulated. He has to struggle with the task of developing a set of concepts which can describe the range of phenomena which interest him. This is why so much emphasis is placed upon concept formation. The political scientist ought to be especially aware of this. Nothing holds up the development of an underdeveloped (or should we say, newly developing) science so much as an outmoded, inapplicable, and ambiguous set of concepts.

THE INTRODUCTION OF CONCEPTS

It is one thing to demonstrate the importance of concepts. It is another to describe how they are introduced into a scientific language. And how they are introduced determines to a large extent their usefulness. There is a rather obvious answer to the question: concepts are defined, they are given meanings, and in this way enter our scientific language. This is generally true. However, for several reasons, it is not enough to say that concepts are defined. First, there are two interpretations of definition and only one is acceptable within the framework of scientific method. Second, given this scientifically acceptable notion of definition, there are still several ways to define concepts. Let us examine each of these points in greater detail.

The question, "But what does it *really* mean?" is a fairly common one in everyday conversation.[2] It assumes that every descriptive word has an *essential* meaning which will become evident if we only dig deeply enough. Everyday conversation, however, is not the only context in which we find evidence of this interpretation. There is a strong and articulate philosophical tradition which argues in favor of *real* definitions. As early as Plato's *Republic* we find attempts to *discover* the essential characteristics of a particular concept, in Plato's case, "justice." A concept's meaning is not assigned; rather its essential nature is discovered. When applied to science, this interpretation of definition creates a problem. Time is spent searching for the true essences of, rather than empirical relationships between, concepts.

The scientist does not have to face this problem when he adopts the other interpretation of definition, usually called the *nominal.* According to it, in defining power we say in effect that from now on, when phenomena *X, Y,* and *Z* occur, power exists—we are

---

2The discussion of this section is based primarily on Carl G. Hempel, *Fundamentals of Concept Formation in Empirical Science* (Chicago: University of Chicago Press, 1952).

naming that particular set of phenomena "power." The same analysis holds true in regard to the definition of the concept "chair." "Chair" is simply the word or linguistic expression we assign to a physical object with certain specified characteristics. It should be emphasized that there is a difference between the concept "chair" and the label or name "chair" we assign to it. A nominal definition, then, is neither true nor false. You may have your own definition of "power," and I cannot reject it on the grounds that "it is not what 'power' really means," because "power" has no real meaning. The set of characteristics which have been so labeled can be clearly described and, hopefully, related to other concepts, but political science will never discover its true essence. I might, however, be able to point out that my definition is sounder or more useful than yours for reasons which we will discuss later in this chapter. In other words, all concepts are not of equal scientific value, although none are more real than others. The point, then, is that in science we deal only with nominal definitions. Science has no place for *real* meanings and *essential* characteristics. Concepts are used to describe the world as we observe it, and so the very notion of essentiality is foreign to science. A nominal definition then takes the form: "power" (the name of the concept) = characteristics X, Y, and Z. In effect, real and nominal definitions start from different directions. The former begins with a word and tries to reveal its essential nature. In the case of a nominal definition, on the other hand, a configuration of empirical characteristics is observed and described, or postulated and assigned a label.

Having discussed the general nature of definition, let us now analyze the several methods available for defining concepts—that is, the several ways of introducing concepts into our scientific political language. To begin with, we are *directly acquainted* with some concepts. It is easy for us to define "chair" because its characteristics are directly observable. Putting it another way, the concept which we have labeled "chair" is directly tied to physical objects having a particular set of properties with which we are all familiar. It is probably fair to say that we are directly acquainted with many of the concepts used in everyday conversation. However, as we move beyond common usage and into scientific discourse, the concepts with which we are directly acquainted become less common.

Operational definition

As our science develops it becomes necessary to think about other methods of definition. If we want to be able to describe and explain the wide range of phenomena which are relevant to political science, then we cannot rely simply upon those concepts with which we are directly acquainted. Some political concepts, such as "Australian ballot" and "single-member district," are related directly to observables and so can be defined according to the first method. But what of the concepts which give politics so much of its scope and depth, concepts like "conservative," "group cohesion," and "power"? Do we ever observe them directly? The answer, of course, is no. We define "power" by means of observable phenomena or behavior, but the concept itself does not correspond to a directly observable entity. This, then, is a second kind of concept introduced by a second method of definition. Such concepts are said to be *operationally* or *dispositionally* defined.

There is a substantial body of philosophical literature on the nature and problems of operational and dispositional definitions, but there is no need for us to become deeply immersed in it. All we want to do is gain a basic understanding of what is involved in defining a concept operationally. The notion of operational definition was controversial at one time, and there are still scientists and philosophers who resent the slogan, "We must operationalize." But today, the controversy seems at an end. The operational definition is an accepted, in fact indispensable, piece of scientific hardware. This is due in part to the more realistic analyses of operational and dispositional concepts produced in recent years.[3] Instead of being a panacea for all problems of scientific concept formation, operationalism is now viewed as one basic method for introducing concepts into a scientific language. More generally, it refers to the attempt by all scientists to link

---

[3]See, for instance, the articles contained in Chapter Two of Phillip G. Frank, *The Validation of Scientific Theories* (New York: Collier Books, 1961).

their concepts to observational properties. To a large extent, then, operationalism is nothing more than a more flexible approach to empiricism. Everything still comes back to what is observable, but now we can indirectly *infer* concepts from directly observable properties. We are not directly acquainted with "power" or "conservatism," but it makes sense to say that someone has power or is conservative. Let us see what this means by giving several examples.

A classic case of operational definition from the natural sciences is the definition of solubility. The chemist might say that a substance such as salt is water soluble if, when placed in water, it dissolves. The structure of this kind of definition is straightforward enough. If we perform an operation (*O*) on something, and a particular result (*R*) takes place, we say it has a particular characteristic (*D*) which is our operational concept, in this case water solubility. Let us see if we can apply the same kind of reasoning to concepts in political science.

Take our familiar friend "power." Imagine a bargaining situation—negotiations between two diplomats. When, in such a situation, diplomat *A* can get diplomat *B* to do something *B* would not otherwise have done, *A* has power over *B*. We have just given an oversimplified but nevertheless valid operational or dispositional definition of "power." One thing must be made clear, however. In political science we cannot usually *perform* the operations which give the operational definition its label. The political scientist cannot manipulate people the way the chemist manipulates chemical elements. In this strict sense, the definition of "power" is not operational. However, the *structure* of the definition is the same, and that is what matters. If in a given situation—the placing of salt in water, or the negotiations of diplomats—a particular result occurs—the dissolving of the salt, or the acceptance against his will by one diplomat of the proposals of the other—then we attribute a particular characteristic to the entity: solubility to the salt, power to the second diplomat. The meaning of "operational" for the political scientist, then, is not the performing of operations so much as the more general requirement of observing reactions to given situations and defining concepts in terms of these reactions (or behaviors). It would no doubt be less confusing if this method of definition had another

name without the connotation of manipulation—perhaps "dispositional" is such a word. But as long as we know what "operational"
means *in political science* we can continue using the label. Or if
one still anticipates confusion, "dispositional" can be adopted.

Another kind of dispositional concept is exemplified by
attitudes or opinions. We might say that an individual is a pacifist
if he answers a set of questions in a certain way; if he answers
questions *X, Y,* and *Z* "yes," he has a pacific attitude. Some
political scientists argue that there is something in a person's mind
which the questions to some extent reflect or measure. Others
reject this kind of analysis, saying that the attitude is nothing
more than a set of answers to a set of questions. It makes no sense
to talk about entities which no one can see—to act as if our ques-
tionnaire is an imperfect reflection of the real attitude. There is a
more moderate way of stating the second position. Perhaps this is
also the most sensible position to take. It simply says that since we
can't see inside people's heads, the whole controversy is a waste of
time. We can use attitudes and other kinds of dispositional
concepts to summarize sets of observables; this holds true for
attitudes, opinions, ideologies, and personality traits. What really
interests us is behavior, and relationships between types of
behavior. We broaden the scope of political science immensely by
using such concepts, and their use does not force us to talk about
mysterious invisible entities.

Theoretical concepts

Concepts can be defined even more indirectly through their
placement in theories. This, then, provides us with a third method
of introducing concepts into our scientific political language.
While a full understanding of theoretical concepts must await the
analysis of theories which is upcoming in Chapter 8, we can say
enough now to make them understandable. In simplest terms, a
theoretical concept is defined within a theoretical system. Think
of a theory as a set of interrelated concepts, some of which are
defined directly or operationally, and some of which are not.
The latter are theoretical concepts. They gain their meaning
from the theory—remove them, take them out of context, and
they become meaningless. However, if the first two kinds of

concepts are removed from a theory which employs them, they retain their meaning.

A theoretical system which is familiar to everyone is Euclidean geometry; it is formal-mathematical rather than empirical-scientific (the distinction will be explicated in Chapter 8), yet because at this point we are interested only in the structure of theories and their relationship to theoretical concepts, geometry is a useful example. "Line," "point," and other Euclidean concepts gain their meaning from their placement within the system, from their relationships to other concepts. Remove a Euclidean "point" from its natural habitat and you have not only a lonely concept but a meaningless one.

Now, as we have just hinted, there is a vast difference between a scientific theory and a mathematical system, even though their structures are similar. The difference lies in the fact that the former is somehow linked to the world of observation—it describes the world; while mathematics, geometry for instance, has no link to the empirical. Such a system is merely a logically related set of symbols; X, 1, or A would do just as well as the Euclidean "point" because the structure, the logical relationships, are what count. Structure is also important in an empirical theory; this is, as we have said, what makes the theoretical concept distinctive. But in addition the empirical theory has empirical content—structure is not everything—and the content is achieved by making sure that some of its concepts are tied to the world; in other words, are directly or operationally defined. If in addition the theory is logically sound (put together correctly), those concepts not defined according to the first two methods will be theoretically defined. Thus they will not be without empirical meaning as are the concepts of Euclidean geometry, but neither will they have meaning outside their theory, a trait they share with "line" and "point."

An obvious and legitimate question which comes to mind at this point is, Why does science need theoretical concepts?[4] There are two points which have to be clarified in order to answer the question and demonstrate the significance of theoretical concepts.

---

[4]Carl G. Hempel attempts to answer this question in "The Theoretician's Dilemma," in Herbert Feigl, Michael Scriven, and Grover Maxwell (eds.), *Minnesota Studies in the Philosophy of Science* (Minneapolis: University of Minnesota Press, 1958), pp. 37-98.

First, the distinction between operational and theoretical concepts might not be entirely clear. What, for instance, is the logical difference between a concept in atomic theory, let us say "meson," and the concept "power" in political science? It would seem that power is no more visible to political scientists than mesons are to physicists—we are directly acquainted with neither. Yet there is a difference. "Power" is independently defined; there is a set of empirical circumstances which we call "power." Therefore it is misleading to say that power cannot be seen. The nature of an operational definition is that a concept is defined *in terms of* directly observable properties. "Meson" cannot be analyzed in the same manner. A theoretical concept is not defined independently but within a theory. This is the key point. Its meaning depends upon the other concepts in the theory and their interrelationship. That mesons are not visible is obvious. But neither are they invisible. A theoretical concept has no separate set of observables which defines it.

Granted that theoretical and operational concepts are logically distinct, that the former are not directly tied to observable properties. The question remains, Why does the scientist use them? This question cannot be completely answered at this point because it really asks for a justification of theory. All we can say now is that theories expand our ability to explain. A theory is wider in scope than any set of purely empirical generalizations (generalizations using directly acquaintable or operational concepts), and this widening of scope is due in large part to those theoretical concepts which act as connective links between the other two kinds of concepts.

We have now made some general points about the third method of introducing concepts; as students of the methodology of political science we need say no more about theoretical concepts, because, strictly speaking, there are none in political science at the present time. Theoretical concepts are found only in sound empirical theories, and there are no fully developed theories of politics. However, the last few pages were not written in vain; for, as we will see in Chapter 8 and Part Three, there are potential theories—political scientists are presently trying to formulate theories which might account for wider segments of political phenomena. Thus, even though for the time being we will be working primarily with directly acquaintable and operational concepts, there is, hopefully, a future for theoretical concepts in political science. We can make the point even more strongly: until political science begins constructing sound scientific theories, it will be considered an immature discipline.

EVALUATING CONCEPTS IN POLITICAL SCIENCE

Running through our discussion of concept formation has been an implied requirement of all sound concepts. Perhaps best labeled "empirical import," it is a straightforward requirement and, given the basic arguments of this book, not a surprising one.[5] "Empirical import" suggests that since concepts are the basic building blocks of empirical science, they must be linked to the world of observation. As the political scientist formulates his concepts, he must make sure that they have empirical import. Recall the three ways this is achieved. Some concepts are directly linked to corresponding observables and so we are directly acquainted with them. Could anyone doubt, for instance, that "Australian ballot" has empirical import? Another type has no observable characteristics to which it directly corresponds, yet is defined in terms of observables. Such an operational or dispositional concept as "power" also has empirical import, then. The third type of concept we analyzed is the theoretical. We hope that the last few paragraphs made clear that although it is neither directly linked to observables nor operationally defined, a theoretical concept nevertheless has empirical import. A scientific theory is, of course, empirical—some of its concepts are directly or operationally related to observables. Therefore, those which are not defined according to these methods also have empirical import because of their logical relationship to the other concepts. Thus there is a world of difference between the term "ghost" and the concept "meson," even though neither is directly tied to observables, and so far as we know neither ghosts nor mesons exist the way chairs do.

There is another characteristic which scientists would like their

---

[5]Hempel, *Fundamentals of Concept Formation in Empirical Science, op. cit.,* pp. 39-45.

concepts to have. Labeled *systematic import,* it has to do with the relationship between concepts.[6] Stated as a criterion of usefulness, it asks that they not be constructed in isolation. This is significant because a concept is of little use if it cannot be related to other concepts. Consider the following example—it is extremely absurd, but extremes and absurdities often make important points better than perfectly reasonable examples. Suppose a political scientist doing research on the personal characteristics of politicians constructs a concept labeled "shame," which is defined as a product of more than 150 resulting from the multiplication of the number of letters in the last name and shoe size. In other words, a politician who wears a size 13 shoe and has 12 letters in his last name has the characteristic "shame." Now clearly, the concept has empirical import; it is rather easy to discover a shoe size, count the letters of a name, and multiply the two. However, can "shame" be related to any other characteristics of politicians or the political system? At this point we would probably have to say no, unless there is some less than obvious relationship between politics, large feet, and long names. So we would conclude that for political science "shame" has no systematic import, and thus is not a useful concept even though it is an empirically sound one.

Notice that this is not the same kind of requirement as empirical import. The latter is a necessary characteristic of concepts. We might even say it is the characteristic which makes a concept a concept—it is its primary defining characteristic. Systematic import, on the other hand, is desirable but not necessary. In the more advanced sciences such as physics and chemistry, concepts will have both characteristics. In political science we *demand* that a concept have empirical import and *hope* that it has systematic import. To make the latter a necessity would be to prejudice the usefulness of concepts. We don't know, when we formulate a concept, even an absurd one like "shame," that it won't some day be useful, that there doesn't exist a relationship between it and other political concepts which simply awaits discovery. Or, turning things around, we can't determine the systematic import of an "obviously" sound concept such as "power" until we have discovered that it is, as a matter of fact,

---

[6]*Ibid.,* pp. 45-49.

related to other concepts. A case in point is the concept of "alienation." Developed and refined by Marxian theorists, it went out of favor and was rejected as a useful empirical concept (a concept with systematic import, that could be related to other concepts). Recently it has been rejuvenated, as social scientists speculate about and test possible relationships between it and other phenomena; i.e., alienation leads to urban disturbances.[7] The usefulness of a concept, then, is relative to the accumulated knowledge of the particular field in which it finds itself. However, as a practical matter, the political scientist usually begins his work with those concepts—power, influence, policy, participation, law—which do seem to have systematic import rather than concepts which have a less certain payoff. The political scientist's task is not an easy one. He must be aware of the immediate needs of political research, while at the same time anticipating its future development.

THE FUNCTION OF SCIENTIFIC CONCEPTS IN POLITICAL SCIENCE

Concepts are used to describe political phenomena—at least this much is clear from the foregoing analysis. When we identify a set of observable characteristics as "power," we have defined a concept and designated a class of observable phenomena. More can be said about the descriptive qualities of concepts than that they are used to identify political phenomena. In other words, there is more to description than identification. If we are serious about developing a science of politics, we would probably also like to use concepts to classify, compare, and measure. As a matter of fact, there are several kinds of concepts each with its own particular function, each with its own usefulness. More specifically, there are classificatory, comparative, and quantitative concepts.[8] Let us spend the next few pages describing the nature of each and determining its applicability to political phenomena.

---

[7]For a summary of findings on alienation, see Robert Lane, *Political Ideology* (New York: Free Press, 1962). Also see Murray B. Levin, *The Alienated Voter* (New York: Holt, Rinehart & Winston, 1960).

[8]Hempel, *Fundamentals of Concept Formation in Empirical Science, op. cit.,* Part III.

Classification

Some concepts provide the basis for classification—the placing of types of political actions, systems, or institutions into two or more classes or categories. As is true of science generally, classificatory concepts have a commonsensical basis. A substantial portion of our everyday thinking is spent classifying, arranging, sorting out the phenomena which confront us. This is a primary method for making sense out of the world. Similarly, it is the way the scientist begins his scientific analysis.

The scientist, of course, sharpens the classificatory apparatus of common usage. Instead of characterizing all nations as Communist or pro-American, as the "man in the street" is inclined to do, the political scientist might formulate a concept of "democracy" and then classify all political systems as either democratic or non-democratic. This is an example of *dichotomous* classification, the simplest variety. It involves defining a concept, "democratic," according to the scientific procedures already outlined; linking it to observables, such as "number of political parties and their rate of turnover" or "ratio between total adult population and eligible voters"; and then treating it as a characteristic of political systems, placing all systems which have the characteristic in one slot or category, and all those which don't in another. A dichotomy is thus created: there are only two categories according to this classificatory concept. If the concept has been soundly defined and is applicable to the population being considered, then the classification will be exhaustive (all members of the population will be classified) and exclusive (no member will be placed in both categories).

Science also employs multiple classificatory concepts, that is, concepts which enable us to place the members of a population into more than two categories. Once again, the same procedure is used in non-scientific activities, as for instance when we list the positions of a football team. Quarterback, halfback, fullback, end, tackle, guard, and center are the classes of a multiple classification. In political science the ancient but useful monarchy-oligarchy-democracy classification can be cited as a fairly straightforward example of a multiple classification scheme. Whether we are classifying football players or political systems, the principles of exhaustiveness and exclusiveness still apply. If, after classifying the members of the Cleveland Browns according to the above scheme, we still have a player, let us say the punting specialist, left over, we can conclude that our scheme is incomplete. The same criticism might apply if we come across a nation which does not fit our three-fold classification.

Comparison

Classification is important. Every science begins by sorting out the phenomena which seem relevant to it. As we have already said, this is the first method of making the world coherent and comprehensible. However, how far can a science go with concepts which only classify? The answer, it would appear, is, not far. We would probably like to know more than which political systems are democratic and which are not; perhaps, for instance, which in the first category are the most democratic. A logical step of progression from classificatory concepts, then, is to comparative or ordering concepts.

A comparative concept is, in the last analysis, a more complex and useful type of classificatory concept. The members of a population are sorted out and placed in categories; but in addition, because the categories represent more or less of a particular property, the members are ranked according to how much of the property they each have. For instance, returning to a previous example, we might want to compare those nations which are very democratic, those which are moderately so, and those which are much less democratic. This would be done by categorizing the empirical referents of democracy. Those political systems which fall in the upper one third of a list of ratios of total eligible voters to total population would be classified as very democratic, for instance. So we could say that a nation placed in the first category is *more* democratic than one placed in the second or third categories.

Usually, however, a comparative concept will allow a more refined analysis than this, for the categories will probably be more than three in number. In fact, a sophisticated comparative concept (such as "hardness," in geology, or "power," in political science) will allow us to compare every member of our population (whether a collection of rocks or a group of politicians) with every other member; thus, practically speaking, the number of categories is theoretically infinite, practically limited only by the number of members of the population. The result of this analysis, then, is a rank order of items, of *every* item — of more or less democratic nations, or more or less powerful senators, or of harder or softer rocks. In a recent study of the social conditions of democracy, Deane Neubauer has developed such a comparative concept which provides the basis for an "Index of Democratic Performance."[9] The empirical indicators used are (*a*) percent of the adult population eligible to vote; (*b*) equality of representation; (*c*) information equality, and (*d*) competition.

In every case, the advantage of the comparative over the classificatory concept is based upon the additional knowledge produced by the finer distinctions of the concept and the fact that the question is not either-or, but more or less. To know how 10 senators rank on a power index is to know more than that 6 have power and 4 don't, or that all 10 have power. Let us pursue the second possibility further. Suppose that according to our original dichotomous classification, all senators are placed either in the powerful or nonpowerful category. What does this tell us? A great deal depends, of course, on the concept of power which is used as the basis of classification. A choice might have to be made, for instance, between calling all senators who have 50 percent of their bills passed powerful, or those who have only 25 percent passed. The comparative concept does not present us with this problem of definition, for it is not, as we just said, a matter of either-or, of having power or of not having power. Rather, we are interested in how a number of senators are ranked in regard to the concept "power—how they measure up against one another. Thus, the claim that "Senator Smith is powerful" makes sense only if we expand it to read, "more powerful *than most other senators,*" which means the following: in a rank order of all senators on the concept "power," Smith comes out near the top of the list.

The advantages of comparative or ordering concepts over classificatory concepts should be manifest by now. The more

---

[9]Deane Neubauer, "Some Conditions of Democracy," *American Political Science Review,* Vol. LXI, No. 4, 1967, pp. 1002-9.

refined and explicit descriptions make possible the development of more sophisticated generalizations about, and theories of, politics. In using classificatory concepts we might discover, for instance, that *democratic* political systems tend to be unstable. Analyzing the same phenomena with comparative concepts could produce the following generalization: the more democratic a nation is, the more unstable it is. We may hope that political science will develop a greater number of comparative concepts. At this point we can say *optimistically* that such concepts are being formulated and applied by political scientists—examples are conservative-liberal attitude scales, and indices of political power; but *realistically* that the kinds of concepts most evident in a science roughly reflect the maturity of the science. The fact is, at this point political science is relatively immature (on a rank order of all natural and social sciences).

Quantification

Take a population which has been ordered by a comparative concept; then give the concept certain mathematical characteristics so as to allow one to say, not just "Senator Smith is more powerful than Senator Jones," but "Smith is twice as powerful as Jones." A *quantitative* concept has been formulated. Our rank order of senatorial power tells us nothing about *how much more* powerful one senator is than another. This, of course, gets to the very nature of the comparative concept and is its basic limitation. More significant to the political scientist interested in more reliable knowledge of politics is the development of concepts which allow us not only to rank items on a particular characteristic, but also to say something about how much of the characteristic each has. And if "how much" is the question, we have to perform certain mathematical operations which are impossible when classificatory or comparative concepts are being used. Thus the label "quantitative."[10]

---

[10]We will not say much about the mathematical foundations of quantitative concepts. For discussions of mathematics and political science see Hayward R. Alker, Jr., *Mathematics and Politics* (New York: Macmillan Co., 1965); and the more general but advanced John G. Kemeny, L. J. Snell, and G. L. Thompson, *Introduction to Finite Mathematics* (Englewood Cliffs, N.J.: Prentice-Hall, Inc., 1956).

There are really two levels of quantitative concepts. The first, and less rigorous, is usually introduced into our scientific language in the form of an *interval* scale.[11]   For the purposes of this discussion, we can think of a scale as a device for ordering items. An interval scale has the additional feature of equal intervals between its categories. A good example of an interval scale with which we are all familiar is the thermometer. Thus, temperature is a quantitative concept measurable on an interval scale. The distance between, let us say, 30° and 40° degrees Fahrenheit is equal to the distance between 40° and 50° and so on. But notice that it is not the case that 60° is twice as warm as 30°. The significant fact about an interval scale, then, is that we can quantitatively compare (carry out certain kinds of mathematical operations on) the intervals between items on the scale, but not the items themselves. This is attributable, speaking as nontechnically as possible, to the interval scale's lack of an absolute zero, or point of origin.

Take temperature again. The zero point on the thermometer does not represent the absence of temperature. A leisurely walk outside on a -15° winter day will convince anyone of this. As long as there are temperatures below zero, we cannot say that 30° is twice as cold as 60°. Thus we can say that 0° F. is an arbitrary cutoff point, manifesting convenience and not truth. The concept "temperature" can be viewed, then, as a property having an indeterminable beginning and end. We can measure heat or cold by means of our everyday thermometer, which marks off equal amounts of the property and in effect limits itself to the normal ranges of temperature. There is no difference in kind, then, between above- and below-zero temperatures, despite the almost mystical characteristics often attributed to the zero point.

There are some quantitative concepts in the social sciences which allow for the construction of interval scales. For instance, a refined concept of intelligence defined as the score made on a test might be so characterized. While it makes sense to say that an IQ of 100 is exactly halfway between 90 and 110, it doesn't to say that a man with an IQ of 200 is twice as smart as one with an IQ

---

[11]The following discussion of scales is based on S. S. Stevens, "On the Theory of Scales of Measurement," *Science,* Vol. CIII, 1946, pp. 677-80.

of 100. As far as political science goes, quantitative interval concepts are few and far between. Some political attitude scales might be so classified, and there are no doubt others; but, by and large, the knowledge of politics which has been accumulated is based upon classificatory and comparative concepts. This is not to say, of course, that the development of quantitative concepts will not become more common. On the contrary, the future of political science no doubt depends to a large extent upon the extent to which political scientists can develop quantitative concepts.

If it is true that quantitative interval concepts are rare in political science, then we would expect the second variety of quantitative concept to be even more rare. For it forms the basis of the most highly developed quantitative scale, usually called the *ratio* scale. Like the interval type, it begins with a rank order, adds equal intervals, but then grounds the intervals with an absolute zero point. While this allows many technical refinements, the only one which need concern us here is the newfound ability to say, by means of a ratio scale, "*X* is twice as big as *Y*." In other words, no longer are our mathematical operations limited to the intervals between points on the scale. Now the points themselves can be measured and compared. The reason is the zero point, the fact that there is an end to the scale: there is a point at which an item no longer has the characteristic.

The ratio scale most familiar to most of us is the system of cardinal numbers—the scale that is employed when we count. Obviously, eight chairs are twice as many as four chairs, because we start from a nonarbitrary zero point; it is impossible to have fewer than zero chairs. Unfortunately, almost all interval scales are found in the natural sciences.

6 Generalizations in political science

A scientific generalization expresses a relationship between concepts. To identify those nations which have democratic political systems (according to a dichotomous classificatory concept) is significant. To discover that democratic nations tend to have a higher level of education and economic prosperity is probably more significant, for our knowledge is broadened; the world of politics makes more sense because we begin to see its patterns, that is, the relationships between apparently individual facts. It is at the point when concepts are connected and the connections tested and either confirmed or rejected that science begins to take off; in other words, when concepts begin to have systematic import.

We might say, then, that generalizations are important to political science first of all because they give us a more sophisticated and wideranging description of political phenomena. To know that a particular senator has more power than another senator is an interesting and often useful bit of information. But to be able to say that in any competitive situation, the competitors who are the most highly motivated will dominate (have power over) their less highly motivated opponents, is clearly more impressive, and in the long run probably more useful. This forms the basis of a difference between the journalist or historian of the present, interested in the facts, in detailed case studies, and the political scientist, whose goal is the development of systematic knowledge of politics. Systematic here, of course, means *generalized.*

The second reason for the importance of generalizations follows from the nature of scientific explanation and prediction. In the next chapter the argument will be made that the primary functions of science (for political science, perhaps "objectives" is a better word) are the explanation and prediction of empirical phenomena—the demonstration of *why* they are or will be. Furthermore, every sound explanation and prediction contains at least one generalization; without generalizations there could be no explanations or predictions. This scientific fact of life will be clarified in this chapter and fully analyzed in the next. At this point, let us keep in mind that the development of generalizations is essential if political science is to not only describe political phenomena, but also explain and predict them.

THE NATURE OF GENERALIZATIONS

Let us first make a distinction between two forms of generalization, *hypotheses* and *laws*. Both are generalizations because they share certain characteristics: they have the same form and must meet the same structural requirements. We cannot tell whether the sentence, "Democratic political systems tend to be stable," is a law or an hypothesis if we are unaware of its context. The major difference can be traced to the claim which each makes (or which is made about it). An hypothesis is, in effect, a guess about a relationship between concepts. After being tested against available evidence according to the principles of scientific method, it is accepted or rejected. If accepted, it is labeled a law. We might say, then, that a law is a true hypothesis; or for those who prefer a weaker notion than truth, a *well-confirmed* hypothesis.[1] The latter formulation might be more desirable, for it implies the nonnecessary or contingent nature of all scientific knowledge. The use of "truth," on the other hand, seems to many to imply that scientific laws do express eternal and immutable relationships. For the scientist, however, the difference between "true" and "well-confirmed" is largely semantical, for he realizes the conditional nature of scientific knowledge, whichever label is used.

Since hypotheses and laws have the same form and differ only

---

[1] See Arnold Brecht, *Political Theory* (Princeton, N.J.: Princeton University Press, 1959), pp.48-52, for a statement of this position.

in regard to whether or not they have been empirically confirmed, we can in a methodological analysis talk about "generalization" without concerning ourselves with the distinction between its two main varieties. Later, when the basic principles of hypothesis confirmation are being analyzed, this distinction will move closer towards the center of our attention.

Conditional

A scientific generalization states an empirical relationship (confirmed or merely hypothesized) between concepts in the form of a generalized *conditional*. This rather technically phrased sentence compactly describes the nature of generalizations. But in order to make sense of it, it must be, as the philosopher might say, "unpacked," which in this case means explicating "empirical," "generalized," and "conditional."

Let us take the last characteristic first. Assuming that *B* and *R* are concepts, let us say "businessman" and "Republican," respectively, and *X* stands for any person, the general schema or form of a generalization is: "For every *X*, *if X is B then X is R*." In other words, every person who has the characteristic of being a businessman also has the characteristic of being a Republican. Of course this could also read, "If *X* is *B*, then *X* is *R* 75 percent of the time." The distinction between statistical laws, which say that only a certain percentage of a population has a given characteristic, and universal laws, which, of course, argue that all of them do, will be analyzed later in this chapter. At this point we need not concern ourselves with it. An alternate statement of the generalization is, "All *B* are *R*," all businessmen are Republicans. The two statements are logically the same. The second is translatable into the conditional form of the first — to say that all businessmen are Republicans is simply shorthand for, "If a man is a businessman then he is a Republican."

Structurally, then, generalizations are marked by the conditional "If...then...," which expresses the basic relationship between their concepts.[2] If you find someone with characteristic *A* then you can also expect him to have characteristic *B*. The law *itself* does not

---

[2]See Ernest Nagel, *The Structure of Science* (New York: Harcourt, Brace & World, 1961), Chapter 4.

say you will ever find a person with *A*. It only tells you what to expect or what to be looking for if you do. Thus, "All unicorns have poor eyesight" is an acceptable generalization (based on what we know so far), even though no one has yet confronted "a horselike animal having a single horn growing from the center of its forehead." But if someone who takes this hypothesis seriously does cross paths with a unicorn, he will be confident of getting a close look. The *if* sorts out certain things (those with characteristic *A*), the *then* tells us to expect them to have another characteristic, *B*.

Empirical

All generalizations have, or are translatable into, conditional form. But not every conditional statement is a valid scientific generalization, for several other requirements must be satisfied. Given the nature of science, the one which probably comes most readily to mind is the need for scientific generalizations to be empirical—somehow grounded in observation and experience. But what does it mean to call a generalization empirical?

First of all, since generalizations are basically proposed or confirmed relationships between empirical concepts, we would expect the soundness of a generalization to be dependent to a large extent upon the soundness of its concepts. The expectation is justified. A generalization which contains concepts not meeting the criterion of empirical import cannot itself be empirical. The hypothesis, "All ghosts are liberal," would have to be classified as nonempirical because "ghost" has no empirical import. This initial fact is obvious. But in addition, a generalization must be grammatically correct if it is to be considered empirical. This means, in simple terms, the generalization as a whole must make sense. Thus the combining of any two good concepts with the proper logical words does not insure the empirical soundness of the resulting generalization. What this requirement comes down to is the need to make generalizations *testable*—susceptible to confirmation or disconfirmation. If it is logically impossible to disconfirm a generalization, then it cannot be labeled empirical. And a major reason for this impossibility is the failure to put concepts together meaningfully, so as to allow for testing.

An example should clarify this criteria of grammatical sound-ness. Consider the generalization, "All political power is blue," which is translatable into the standard "If... then..." form. Taken individually, each word or concept of the generalization is meaningful: the logical words "all" and "is" present no prob-lems, and "power" and "blue" have or can be given empirical import through one or another kind of scientific definition. Yet there is something strange about the generalization. When all of its component parts are assembled, the result is untestable because it makes no sense—incompatible concepts have been placed together. Given any reasonable definition of power, it is absurd (note, not just difficult) to imagine a situation in which it is blue. Thus we can conclude that because of its absurdity, the sentence, "All political power is blue," is nonempirical. But let us emphasize again the more important methodological reason, namely, that such absurd or meaningless sentences are not testable. And, since empirical generalizations must be testable or potentially confirm-able—this is the very nature of "empirical"—an absurd generaliza-tion is not empirical.

Thus we have returned to the basic foundation of empirical science, the basing of knowledge upon experience and observation. If there is no way that experience, observation (empirical-scientific method) can influence our acceptance or rejection of an hypoth-esis, then it cannot be counted as scientific, although, of course, it might be part of another kind of intellectual system such as religion or metaphysics. Finally, notice that we have not been using "true" or "confirmed" as the test of a generalization, but confirmability (or disconfirmability). Thus, disconfirmed general-izations are still empirical in the sense that they have met the criteria of (1) containing concepts with empirical import, and (2) being formulated so that they are testable, so that they *can* be disconfirmed. According to this analysis, then, *absurdity* and *falsity* are not synonymous.

So far our examples have been absurd. But as we have said before, absurdity is often a useful device in making a methodo-logical point (which is not the same as saying methodology is absurd). At this point, however, it must be pointed out that the empirically unsound generalization will not always be so absurd and thus easily rooted out. There are other, more subtle, ways to accomplish this scientifically undesirable end which every scientific discipline ought to be aware of, especially a developing one such as political science. A generalization so generated will usually appear as sound as any other and so will be adjudged acceptable. In fact, it will often have an important place in the literature of the discipline. Thus it is especially crucial to be able to recognize and criticize this kind of proposition.

Like all nonempirical generalizations, these ultimately fail because they are not testable—there is no way to confirm or disconfirm them. But unlike those already considered, this characteristic is not attributable to the juxtaposition of incompatible empirical concepts, but to the way the concepts are defined and interpreted within the generalization.

Let us consider an example. Studies of community power often produce such generalizations as, "All important decisions in city X are made by a single elite." Apparently this is a valid empirical generalization—the concepts have or can be given empirical import, and the sentence as a whole makes sense; it might even be accepted as a commonsensical truth (which in itself is not important but indicative of the generalization's sound grammar). Thus, it appears that it can be tested; it is possible to devise methods for confirming or disconfirming it. But now let's see what might happen when the generalization is employed by political scientists, especially when as an hypothesis it is being tested.

Suppose a researcher studying decision making in a city hypothesizes that, "All important decisions in community X are made by a power elite." Then, let us say, he begins examining a number of local issues—building a swimming pool, providing busses for parochial schools, passing an open-housing law—to see which persons within the community are the most influential in regard to each decision. His findings might indicate that on the first two issues the same small group of business and political leaders had the greatest influence, but not so with the third. Here a second group carried the day. Now if the political scientist concludes that the third issue is not important (because it was not made by the power elite) and thus not the basis for a refutation of his hypothesis, he has defined away its empirical nature. Let us consider what has happened. The concept "important decision" has been defined in terms of a particular group of men who are called "the power elite." The "power elite," on the other hand, is defined as "that group which makes the important decisions." Thus, if we come across a decision not made by the elite we can conclude that it is not important. The result, then, is an hypothesis which is true *by definition*. It cannot be refuted by evidence; decisions not made by the elite are summarily labeled unimportant. Therefore, since it is impossible to disconfirm, it cannot be considered empirical and so cannot be counted as a scientific generalization.[3]

This method of insuring the "truth" of generalizations, not uncommon in the literature of political science, is usually the result of methodological sloppiness rather than intentional trickery. Its roots go back to the problem of concept formation. As we have pointed out several times, a generalization expresses a relationship between concepts, and thus the soundness of the generalization depends to a large extent upon its concepts. This implies the point we want to make now. The concepts of the generalization must be *independently* defined—not defined in terms of one another. The hypothesized or confirmed relationship between them is *empirical*, a question of fact, not *analytical,* a question of definition. Returning to the example, "important decision" and "power elite" must each be defined so that they are logically independent—it is logically possible for one to exist without the other one. This is just a backhanded way of stating our basic criterion. If it is logically impossible for one to occur without the other, then the hypothesis is not testable, in the sense that no amount of evidence could disconfirm it, and so not empirical. To make the hypothesis testable, the concept "important decision" would have to be defined in terms of a set of empirical criteria (how many people the decision affects; how much political, social and economic change it causes, etc.). Then political scientists could study those who influenced the decisions to see if a single group did play the major role in most.

---

[3]For a discussion of this kind of methodological shortcoming in the study of community power, see Nelson Polsby, *Community Power and Political Theory* (New Haven, Conn.: Yale University Press, 1963), especially Chapter 4.

There is another requirement of generalizations to think about. It is designed to prevent sentences which refer to finite objects (President Truman, for instance) from being classified as generalizations. Consider the sentence, "President Truman always vetoed tax-increase legislation." That it is empirical no one can deny; there are ways to test the assertion. However, do we want to include it in the same category with, "All businessmen are conservative," or "Radical ideologies tend to become less radical as they become more successful"? An immediate response might be, "Yes, why not? They are all empirical, so why make a distinction?" Upon closer examination, it becomes clear that there is a meaningful distinction that can be made. It has to do with the scope of each sentence's concepts, and ultimately, the scope of the sentence itself.[4]

The second two sentences use such concepts as "businessman," "conservative," "radical," and "ideology." These are concepts which are operationally defined, or with which we are directly acquainted. But so is "President Truman." The difference is that in regard to the first set of concepts, we identify a particular assemblage of characteristics and say that any entity which has these characteristics (meets the definition of concept) is included within the scope of the generalization. The generalization then tells us something about those entities possessing the first set of characteristics; that they possess another. So, all things which have the characteristics of being a businessman will also be expected to have the characteristic of being conservative. But how many President Trumans are there? The answer, "Just one," provides the basis for our distinction between generalizations characterized by unlimited scope and particularistic factual assertions. A sentence which includes "President Truman" cannot be a generalization because its scope is limited to one man (and the importance of the man is methodologically irrelevant, of course). The power of a generalization stems from this very fact, the fact that it makes no reference to specific things or individuals. Let us recall from the

---

[4]For a general discussion of the criteria of scope in generalizations, see Nagel, *op. cit.,* Chapter 4.

last chapter the two kinds of empirical or descriptive words, particulars and universal concepts. This is the basis of the present distinction, and indicates that the requirement of unlimited scope is intimately related to the requirement of properly formed concepts. The fact is, "President Truman" is not a concept, but rather a particular—a proper name, to be specific. We can at this point draw a significant conclusion: a sentence which contains particulars (common names or definite descriptions) cannot be counted as a generalization. The label "generalization" means, then, that something is being said about a *class* of entities, not just a single identifiable one.

It ought to be recognized, though, that a generalization can be made more or less restrictive through the use of qualifiers. Thus, instead of "All politicians are extroverts," we might hypothesize that "All *local* politicians are extroverts." But this does not call for a limiting of the generalization's scope. It still applies to an entire class; methodologically, it makes no difference whether it is the class of politicians, local politicians, or local politicians with long names and big feet. In fact, it might be possible to define our concept so closely that only one person is included in the class it designates. For instance, how many politicians have been a senator, Vice President, and President? Suppose we hypothesized that politicians who have been all three tend to have strong egos. Is this a generalization? The answer is yes, even though its scope is *narrow*; but note, it is not *limited*, for it is open to any politician who meets the requirements. Compare this situation with the one in which "President Truman" was used. In that case the result was not an open class, because a particular word was used instead of a general concept.

While generalizations can have broad or narrow scope depending upon the size of the population which they cover, it seems practically desirable to discover as many of the broadly gauged kind as possible. Thus we have two criteria of scope to keep in mind. The first says, no sentence can be a generalization which is limited in scope by definition, that is by the definition of its constituent descriptive words. The second one is not a logical requirement like the first, but an empirical guideline of sorts. It tells us to develop generalizations which have wide scope, for the more the generalization includes, the greater its power. At the same time, one must be wary of achieving generality through vagueness or ambiguity. If generalizations and their constituent concepts are vague or ambiguous they can appear to have greater scope than they actually do. For instance, a definition of democracy might be so vague that a generalization containing it applies to every existing political system. Surely, on the face of it, we would have doubts about the usefulness of such a generalization. At the other extreme are those generalizations which are overqualified, in the sense that their applicability to the real world of politics is severely limited.

UNIVERSAL AND STATISTICAL GENERALIZATIONS

Earlier in the chapter reference was made to statistical generalizations. Let us pick up the discussion again, for the distinction between universal and statistical generalizations is crucial, especially for a discipline such as political science which has few, if any, of the former.[5]

A universal generalization, as we have seen, takes the form, "All *A* are *B*," or, "If *X* is an *A*, then *X* is *B*." The key word here is "all," for it tells us that something is being said about *every* member of a particular class—every man who is a politician is also an extrovert. One need not be a specialist in scientific method to realize that the universal generalization is the most powerful kind in the scientist's arsenal. But what if the scientist is not confident that every politician is an extrovert; or suppose his evidence is not so clear-cut as to allow him to make a claim of universality (really the same thing)? Must he forsake the hope of developing meaningful generalizations of politics? The answer is, of course, no, and the reason is the statistical generalization.

Statistical generalizations take several forms. Weaker versions are, "*Some A* are *B*," "*Most A* are *B*," or "*A tends* to be *B*." A stronger and more useful version might say, "75 percent of *A* are *B*," or, "The probability that *A* is *B* is 0.75." The superiority of the latter is obvious. "Seventy-five percent" tells us a great deal more about a population than "most." Yet they are not logically

[5]For an easily assimilated account of universal and statistical generalizations, see Carl G. Hempel, *Philosophy of Natural Science* (Englewood Cliffs, N.J.: Prentice-Hall, Inc., 1966), pp. 54-67.

dissimilar; both are statistical, because only a portion, hopefully a substantial one, of a population is being referred to.

The philosopher of social science Quentin Gibson makes another distinction between two kinds of statistical generalizations. The first, labeled by Gibson the "statement of chance," is equivalent to all the varieties we have been talking about, from "75 percent of *A* are *B*" to "Most *A* are *B*."[6] The second is the "tendency statement."[7] According to Gibson, such statements attempt to get around the probabilistic (nonuniversal) nature of statistical laws by using phrases like "other things being equal." So, when used in the generalization "other things being equal, all politicians are extroverts," the phrase is supposed to indicate to us that all politicians are not extroverts because of unknown factors; other things are not equal. The "other things being equal" phrase is a kind of disclaimer added to what appears to be a universal law in order to indicate that there are exceptions. In effect, one gives a statistical generalization the form of a universal generalization, by saying, "If no other factors were operating, then 'all *A* would be *B*,'" fully realizing that other factors are exerting an influence.

This tells us something else about the nature of statistical generalizations. Most social scientists assume that statistical knowledge is simply imperfect universal knowledge.[8] This implies that all imperfect statistical knowledge can eventually be made more perfect, for the basis of its inferior status is incomplete knowledge of influencing factors, not the inherent statistical nature of the universe. That is, the statistical notion "chance" is not a throwback to such ideas as Machiavelli's "Fortune": "I hold it to be true that Fortune is the arbiter of one half of our actions, but she still leaves us direct the other half or perhaps a little less."[9] The difference is that while "Fortune" and similar concepts from the pages of traditional philosophy and political science stand for or symbolize the segment of social life which is presumed to be fundamentally unpredictable and so unknowable, "chance" as used by most contemporary social scientists stands

[6]Quentin Gibson, *The Logic of Social Enquiry* (London: Routledge & Kegan Paul, 1960), Chapter 12.

[7]*Ibid.,* Chapter 13.

[8]For a contrary view, see Nagel, *op. cit.,* p. 23.

[9]Niccolo Machiavelli, *The Prince,* Chapter 25.

for all the factors influencing a particular phenomenon which are unknown (not unknowable). This interpretation is reinforced by observing the development of knowledge in particular areas of political behavior. Take, for instance, the study of voting behavior—why people vote, and why they vote for one candidate rather than another. An examination of the four leading voting studies published since 1944 indicates that the amount of unexplained behavior, and therefore the significance of chance, has been steadily eroded as new variables and relationships are worked into the explanations.[10] The most obvious tendency has been a movement away from gross sociological explanations toward more refined psychological accounts of voting behavior. The important point to keep in mind is that progress has been made in the explanation of voting behavior, and in consequence less variance is attributable to chance. Even the "chance" of the gambler is of this empirical kind. If we were able to scientifically analyze a roulette wheel and its ball in terms of weight, balance etc., it would be possible to predict its behavior (or predict to some extent). The influence of chance would be decreased because of the identification of more influencing factors. Thus, it is *logically* possible that some day every presently statistical generalization in political science will take a universal form because of the discovery and incorporation of these new factors.

Statistical and universal generalizations are cut from the same cloth and differ only in regard to the claims that they make. Certainly it is more impressive and significant to say, "All *A* are *B*," then, "The probability that *A* is *B* is 0.75"; but notice that in both cases a percentage or probability is being referred to, 100 percent and 75 percent respectively. It is necessary to emphasize this perhaps obvious point in order to make clear that a sound statistical generalization does not suffer from lack of scope. For as in the case of the universal generalization, an entire class is being referred to. It is simply that in the one case only 75 percent of its members have been found to have another characteristic, while in the other, all its members can be so characterized.

---

[10] The studies are, in order: Paul F. Lazarsfeld *et al., The People's Choice* (New York: Duell, Sloan & Pierce, 1944); Bernard Berelson *et al., Voting* (Chicago: University of Chicago Press, 1948); Angus Campbell *et al., The Voter Decides* (Evanston, Ill.: Row, Peterson, 1954); Angus Campbell *et al., The American Voter* (New York: John Wiley & Sons, Inc., 1960).

One general conclusion which seems justified at this point is that political science rests upon a solid empirical foundation even though it employs statistical generalizations almost exclusively. While it would be desirable to have a body of scientific knowledge in the form of universal generalizations, and the development of such knowledge is surely the objective of any science, the statistical nature of existing political science generalizations should not act as a damper upon further attempts at discovery; disillusionment is not a constructive reaction to a statistically oriented discipline.

HYPOTHESES AND LAWS

At the outset of this chapter we noted the distinction between hypotheses and laws, between those generalizations which have been formulated but not tested and those which have been tested and either confirmed or not rejected. But then the distinction was ignored because of our initial interest in the structural or logical characteristics of generalizations. At this point, let us return again to the content of generalizations and ask the question which has been dangling for some time now: namely, How do we go about confirming or rejecting hypotheses? In other words, What is the difference between a hypothesis and a law?

Since this is a book about the methodological foundations of political science, we will discuss only the logical basis of hypothesis testing and not particular techniques for collecting and organizing evidence. The basic process, usually called "induction," which involves going from a particular body of concrete evidence to a generalization, is really quite commonsensical.[11] We test a hypothesis by seeing if it fits the world of observation. Suppose we want to test the hypothesis, "Businessmen tend to be conservative." A sample of businessmen would be questioned (it would be practically impossible to study all businessmen) to determine their ideological orientations. On the basis of this sample—and the confidence we place in our conclusion depends

---

[11]For a straightforward discussion of the logic of inductive reasoning, see Wesley C. Salmon, *Logic* (Englewood Cliffs, N.J.: Prentice-Hall, Inc., 1963), Chapter 3. A more advanced analysis of the logic of the confirmation of hypotheses is Israel Scheffler, *The Anatomy of Inquiry* (New York: Alfred A. Knopf, 1963), Part III.

92   *Scope and methods of political science*

upon its size and randomness—we accept or reject the hypothesis.[12] If three out of four businessmen score high on a test of conservatism, our hypothesis would be confirmed. In effect, we would be making a claim about the class of all businessmen on the basis of what we have discovered about some of them. Wesley Salmon has given us a similar example from the natural sciences: "According to Kepler's first law, the orbit of Mars is an ellipse. The observational evidence for this law consists of a number of isolated observations of the position of Mars....Clearly, this law (conclusion) has far more content than the statements describing the observed positions of Mars (the premises)."[13]

That scientists use induction to construct laws is indisputable. Every generalization, whether it claims that most or all *A* are *B*, is based on a number of concrete observations. This is why the scientist is said to take an *inductive leap* from his evidence to his generalization. And note that while it is most obvious in the case of generalizing from a sample to the entire class (How can we be sure that the members we didn't sample have the characteristic in the same proportion?), it is logically no less a leap when, in a rarer situation, we have sampled all the members. Even though we have more confidence in the conclusion, can we be sure that all members of the class have been sampled, or that future members (not yet sampled) will have the same characteristic? The single question which lies at the root of these is, just because we have observed that something is the case, can we conclude that it is always and will continue to be the case?

This question implies another, namely, How do we demonstrate the validity of induction itself?[14] If we are going to use inductive reasoning to confirm or reject hypotheses, then, the argument goes, we had better be certain of the logical validity of induction. Returning to our example, how do we justify the movement from, "Three out of every four businessmen whom I have talked to are

---

[12]For a readable introduction to sampling, see Charles H. Backstrom and Gerald D. Hursh, *Survey Research* (Evanston, Ill.: Northwestern University Press, 1963), Chapter 2.

[13]Salmon, *op. cit.*, p. 15.

[14]For various approaches to the justification of induction see the articles reprinted in Part 6 of Edward H. Madden (ed.), *The Structure of Scientific Thoughts* (Boston: Houghton Mifflin Co., 1960); and Wesley C. Salmon, "Should We Attempt to Justify Induction?" *Philosophical Studies*, Vol. VIII, 1957, pp. 33-48.

conservative," to "0.75 of all businessmen are conservative?" In Edward Madden's words, "What reason justifies the belief that something will happen simply because it has happened?"[15]

The justification cannot be based upon deductive logic; the generalization is not a logical consequence of the evidence in the sense that it would be a contradiction to reject the truth of the former while accepting the latter. Nor can induction be justified inductively, that is on the basis of empirical evidence; it is the use of such evidence in confirming general hypotheses which is being questioned. In the same sense, one cannot prove the validity of the Bible by quoting the Bible. So what have we left? Was David Hume right when he pessimistically concluded that scientific generalizations, that is, observed relationships between events or variables, are simply accepted as matters of faith?

In response to this well-worked controversy many contemporary philosophers of science have adopted a pragmatic approach to the problem of induction. This approach does not justify induction in any final or absolute sense—we have just demonstrated that this is impossible. It only moderates Hume's pessimism by pointing out that if there is any way to know the world, it must be through induction. That is, the only method available for the testing of generalizations is observation. Thus if we want to explain and predict empirical phenomena, there is nothing else to do but take the inductive leap, move from concrete observations to universal or statistical generalizations. In the words of Hans Reichenbach, the philosopher who more than any other has developed the pragmatic justification of induction, "The justification of induction is very simple; it shows that induction is the best means to attain a certain aim. The aim is predicting the future...."[16]

Remember that we began this section with the observation that induction is quite commonsensical. The pragmatic justification of induction simply reaffirms this by pointing out that scientific knowledge, that is, knowledge about the world, can never go beyond our ability to observe. It would be satisfying to have a

---

[15]Madden, *op. cit.*, p. 287.

[16]Hans Reichenbach, *The Rise of Scientific Philosophy* (Berkeley: University of California Press, 1951), p. 246.

demonstration of the infallibility of our inductive methods of hypothesis testing (that is, moving from observation to generalization), but given the contingent nature of our existence we must do the best that we can without one. Although it cannot be demonstrated that this will lead to truth, it is reasonable to argue that if there is any way to test our assumptions about what is true or false, it must follow the inductive method.

GENERALIZATIONS AND CAUSALITY

One interpretation of, "If *A*, then *B*," is, "*A causes B*" – being a businessman causes one to become conservative. That there is a relationship between the notions of generalization and cause is obvious. However, the assumption underlying the above-mentioned interpretation, namely, that generalizations are reducible to causal relationships, is not the only one which can be made. As a matter of fact, we will argue that it is the other way around: "causual relationship" is reducible to "lawful relationship." This fact has led some students of scientific method to view the notion of cause as expendable, that is, unnecessary, in any description of the fundamental elements of science. This section has as its main objective the clarification of these views about causality.

Modern conceptions of causality have their origins in David Hume's analysis which replaces the necessary connection of events with a mere constant conjunction. As we have seen, empirical relationships are contingent and not necessarily true. Hume's position was that all we can conclude from our observations is that one event or situation always or usually follows another. In his commonsensical style, he wrote: "Having found, in many instances, that any two kinds of objects—flame and heat, snow and cold—have always been conjoined together; if flame or snow be presented anew to the senses, the mind is carried by custom to expect heat or cold...."[17] There is no way to demonstrate that the relationship is necessary, that the events or variables must be invariably linked. Thus we are justified in noting the constant (or nearly constant) conjunction of events (this, in effect, is what we

---

[17]David Hume, *The Treatise of Human Nature*, Book I, Part III, Section III.

do in every generalization); but it is going beyond the limits of our knowledge to view this conjunction as a *necessary* connection. The latter interpretation makes the relationship analytic—it is a logical contradiction to say *B* occurred but *A* didn't; assuming that the relationship is intended to be empirical, and recalling that analytical propositions are nonempirical, it follows that causal statements do not express necessary connections.

The relationship between "cause" and "generalization" can now be briefly explicated. If saying that "*A* causes *B*" is tantamount to "*B* always follows *A*," then they are both reducible to the generalization, "If *A*, then *B*."[18] In other words, we can express what is traditionally known as a causal relationship without using the term cause. Suppose a political scientist who wants to explain the outbreak of war hits upon, "If economic rivalry, then war," which is simply the generalized form of the observation that "economic rivalry between nations tends to be followed by military conflict." The notion "cause" adds nothing to the analysis just given, or so it would seem.

However, even while accepting this analysis which demonstrates the logical expendability of "cause," it is not inconsistent to admit that there is a practical reason for distinguishing between causal and noncausal generalizations, and thus for continuing to use the concept "cause." What of a generalization which describes a relationship between two variables at a given moment? This kind of *cross-sectional* generalization is clearly noncausal in that one variable or event is not known to come or take place before another. In Gustav Bergmann's words: "Such laws state functional connections obtaining among the values which several variables have at the same time."[19] If we discover, for instance, that two political attitudes are usually associated—a person who has one tends to have the other—we will probably not be able to say that one causes the other, because we don't know which one comes first. Thus, Herbert McClosky has examined the relationship between conservatism and person-

---

18Herbert Feigl, "Notes on Causality," in Herbert Feigl and May Brodbeck (eds.), *Readings in the Philosophy of Science* (New York: Appleton-Century- Crofts, 1953), p. 410.

19Gustav Bergmann, *Philosophy of Science* (Madison: University of Wisconsin Press, 1957), p. 102.

ality.[20]   He discovers that high scores on a conservatism scale and high scores on a number of clinical-personality variables (hostility, rigidity) hang together so that an individual with the former tends also to have the latter. While the relationship is clear, McClosky refrains from drawing the commonsensical conclusion that personality "causes" conservatism. "The association between conservatism and the traits outlined exists in the form of correlations which only tell us that the two go together. How they go together, and which is antecedent to which is a more difficult and more elusive problem."[21]   In other words, because no temporal sequence has been identified, the relationship must be considered *cross-sectional* and not *causal.*

There does seem to be a difference, then, between cross-sectional and causal generalizations, and the difference is one of sequence or time. Carl Hempel's terminology makes this point very well. He calls the former laws of coexistence (*A* and *B* occur together), and the latter, laws of succession (*A* is followed by *B*).[22]   Thus a causal generalization is distinctive because it refers to a temporal sequence. Our conclusion seems to be, then, that while "cause" is logically expendable there are still times when a political scientist might want to refer to "causal laws" in order to distinguish them from the cross-sectional variety; but let us reiterate, this is primarily a pragmatic distinction, for in either case, the generalization is an expression of a "constant conjunction."

The search for causal relationships in political science is most profitably viewed as the search for and refinement of lawful relationships. This last point should be emphasized, for a conclusion which might be drawn at this point is that if we reduce "cause" to "lawfulness," one observed relationship is as good as another. However, even without a concept of necessary connection to direct us toward final or ultimate causes, we can distinguish between sound empirical and spurious relationships. A

---

[20]Herbert McClosky, "Conservatism and Personality," *American Political Science Review,* Vol. LII, 1958, pp. 27-45.

[21]*Ibid.,* p. 44.

[22]Carl Hempel, "Deductive Nomological vs. Statistical Explanation," in Herbert Feigl and Grover Maxwell (eds.), *Minnesota Studies in the Philosophy of Science,* Volume III (Minneapolis: University of Minnesota Press, 1962), p. 108.

discussion of the methods available for such analysis would take us far afield into the realm of research techniques.[23] Suffice it to say that the political scientist can work with empirical relationships in the form of statistical correlations; he can compare, sort through, and accept, reject, or refine them, and in so doing roll back the frontiers of political knowledge—and all this within the framework of Hume's constant conjunction.

Let us conclude our discussion of generalizations and causality with a brief consideration of several types of causal situations, emphasizing those which are especially relevant to political scientists.[24] It is not inconsistent to argue, as we have just done, that "cause" is expendable while simultaneously discussing its several forms. Remember that we have adopted a pragmatic approach to causality which allows us to recognize the usefulness of the distinction between laws of succession and coexistence without adopting any notion of necessary connection or final cause.

Causal situations are usually analyzed in terms of sufficient and/or necessary conditions.[25] *A* is a sufficient condition for *B* when (1) if *A* occurs, *B* does; and (2) *B* might have other sufficient conditions. For example, based on historical observation we might conclude that economic rivalry between nations is usually followed by military conflict, but that, in addition, an arms race often precedes such conflict, even in the absence of economic rivalry. We have then two independent sufficient conditions for military conflict.

If we observe that military conflict never occurs without economic rivalry preceding it, no matter what other factors are present, we would conclude that economic rivalry is a necessary

---

[23]For a discussion of correlational techniques, see any good statistics books. Perhaps the best, but not necessarily the easiest, for social scientists is Hubert M. Blalock, *Social Statistics* (New York: McGraw-Hill Book Co., Inc., 1960).

[24]Some social scientists have attempted to develop notions of causality which are useful in the description and explanation of social and political phenomena. See especially Hubert M. Blalock, *Causal Inferences in Non-Experimental Research* (Chapel Hill: University of North Carolina, 1961); and Herbert A. Simon, *Models of Man* (New York: John Wiley & Sons, Inc., 1957).

[25]For a discussion of "necessary" and "sufficient" conditions, see Stefan Nowak, "Some Problems of Causal Interpretation of Statistical Relationships," *Philosophy of Science,* Vol. XXVII, 1960, pp. 23-28. Also see Blalock, *Causal Inferences in Non-Experimental Research, op. cit.,* pp. 31-35.

condition for military conflict. Thus *A* is a necessary condition for *B* when (1) if *B* occurs we know that *A* is present; but (2) *A* is not alone a sufficient condition for *B*. Let us make it clear that this notion of "necessary" can be handled within our constant conjunction framework, for it does not imply a necessary connection between *A* and *B*. It would be logically possible for *B* to occur without *A*'s preceding it. Observation has simply led us to conclude that, as a matter of fact, this never happens.

From what we have already said about political science, it would be reasonable to assume that the discovery of necessary conditions is a rarer occurrence than the discovery of sufficient conditions. It is even rarer to identify a condition (*A*) which is both necessary and sufficient; for if we do, we have in effect found the one and only "cause" of *B*. Remember that a necessary condition need not be sufficient—we know it always takes place before a particular event but other conditions may also be necessary. But when a condition, economic rivalry, always precedes an event, military conflict, and military conflict never occurs without economic rivalry, we have an example of a necessary and sufficient condition.

Perhaps the kind of causal situation which has the most relevance for the political scientist is one in which a combination of factors is sufficient for an event. In this case we can call any one of them a *partially sufficient* condition, to indicate that by itself it is not sufficient. Returning again to the causes of military conflict, suppose we discover that economic rivalry and an arms race are *in conjunction* sufficient conditions. We can't say that economic rivalry alone is sufficient; but it is significant when other factors are added. There is evidence to suggest that this is the situation which confronts the political scientist more often than not. With the recognition of the complexity of social phenomena and the acceptance of a research framework which assumes multiple causes, the single sufficient condition becomes an exotic idea, so exotic that most political scientists push it to the back of their research minds. The political scientist does his scientific work by sorting through a number of possible partially sufficient conditions, rejecting some, accepting others—in other words, by testing hypotheses.

7 Explanation and prediction in political inquiry

The philosopher of science Ernest Nagel has written that "...the distinctive aim of the scientific enterprise is to provide systematic and responsibly supported explanations."[1] If Nagel's view is representative of most students of scientific method we can conclude that those doing political research and those reading the results of such research ought to know something about the nature of scientific explanation. Furthermore, it is evident that political scientists are forever trying to answer, explicitly or implicitly, "why" questions: Why did the Supreme Court make the *Baker* v. *Carr* decision? *Why* does the United States have a two-party system? *Why* do workers tend to vote left? When a question begins with "why," an explanation is being asked for. In addition, such frequently used words as "consequently," "hence," "therefore," "because," "obviously," and "naturally" are good indicators that one is face-to-face with, or in the midst of, an explanation.

Of course, much of political science is descriptive, and, as we have seen, many political scientists devote their energies to discovering and describing political facts. However, while recognizing the importance of description to a science, especially an immature one, we must not assume that it is the end of science.

---

[1] Ernest Nagel, *The Structure of Science* (New York: Harcourt, Brace & World, 1961), p. 15.

99

Emphasizing this point for behavioralists (but really for all political scientists) is Heinz Eulau: "No piece of political behavior research is content to describe the universe of politics.... The goal is the explanation of why people behave politically as they do and why, as a result, political processes and systems function as they do."[2]

One more justification of the political scientist's concern with explanation should be mentioned. A characteristic of scientific explanation which will be examined later in this chapter is its logical identity with scientific prediction. That is, the logical structure of explanation and prediction is the same; the difference between them is pragmatic, i.e., based on the way they are used. Is the objective to account for a past event or a present state of affairs (explanation); or is it to describe a future event or state of affairs (prediction)? If this identity is valid, then prediction, and therefore explanation, ought to be a major concern of political scientists. For one of their primary activities is to provide advice on policy matters; and policy decisions are always based on an expected outcome. a prediction about the best means for implementing a given end. In fact, David Truman has written, "we cannot...escape the necessity to predict. Governmental officials and private citizens anticipate as best they can the consequences of political actions with which they are involved."[3] Consider the two examples of a farmer trying to decide which of two senatorial candidates will be more likely to support his interests, and the President developing a policy to slow down inflation. In both cases a prediction (whether realized or not) is necessary; in the first instance about the behavior of potential senators, in the second about the reaction of the economy to alternative policies.

There are, then, some fairly convincing methodological reasons for political scientists' taking an interest in the logic of explanation. But there is a more commonsensical way of making the point. One merely has to consider how everyone, both the scientist and the man in the street, attempts to cope with the world. It is by trying to account for his environment—by

---

[2]Heinz Eulau, *The Behavioral Persuasion in Politics* (New York: Random House, 1963), p. 24.

[3]David Truman, *The Governmental Process* (New York: Alfred A. Knopf, 1951), p. 504.

attempting to explain the things that happen to him. We have argued in Chapter 2 that scientific knowledge is superior to common sense. This is not contradicted by the present argument, for we are now claiming that since explanation and prediction are basic human activities, it is not unfair to request that those dealing with the empirical world at more sophisticated levels have a basic understanding of the nature of the explanatory process.

The nomological model of explanation

Philosophers of science admit that there are many uses of the word "explain." We can explain (describe) the structure of the Interstate Commerce Commission or explain (explicate) the meaning of "writ of certiorari." These are both acceptable dictionary uses of "explain." Yet neither calls for a *scientific* explanation, that is, the answer to a *why* question. The "why" can be answered only by showing that the event or entity to be explained either follows logically from premises or is highly probable based on the premises. One might say that a specific event(s) causes another event, *X*. But we can explain *X* only by stating the general law which indicates that the relationship is normal — to be expected under the circumstances.

Political scientists appear to employ many kinds of explanation to account for political phenomena. But these are all patterns of one model of scientific explanation; they are variations on a single theme, not distinct logical types. This single logical type of explanation is usually called the "nomological" or "covering-law model." Stated simply, it claims that explanation is achieved by subsuming what is to be explained under general laws.

Let us now examine the structure of nomological explanation in more detail. Our objective, in addition to describing the model, is a demonstration that it is a flexible and not unrealistic basis for explanation in political science. That is, in addition to the fact that the nomological model can include within its boundaries many of the patterns of explanation used by political scientists, it is also useful even though it must be considered an ideal, not yet fully realizable in political science.

In the first place, an explanation can be divided into that which explains and that which is explained. Using Hempel and Oppenheim's terminology, the former will be called the "explanans," the latter the "explanandum."[4] The explanans includes two kinds of statements: general laws, and sentences stating initial or antecedent conditions. Together, they imply the explanandum. More accurately, initial conditions are necessary only when the explanandum is an individual fact. For instance, the fact of the United States' two-party system might be explained by (1) the *generalization* that all political systems with single-member districts have two-party systems, and (2) the *initial condition* that the political system of the United States is one of single-member districts. However, suppose that we would like to explain the generalization itself. The point can be made if we translate the two arguments into simple deductive logic. If A = "single-member district system," B = "two-party system," C = "third parties are undercut," and $\supset$ = "If....then," the explanation of the singular fact would be:

$$(1) \quad \frac{A \supset B,\ \text{and of the law:} \quad (2) \quad A \supset C}{\begin{array}{c} A \\ \hline B \end{array}} \qquad \frac{\begin{array}{c} C \supset B \end{array}}{A \supset B}$$

Several things have come to light in addition to the types of statements required in an explanation. First, both singular facts and generalizations can be explained. Secondly, an explanation can be expressed in the language of deductive logic. A deductive argument is of the form, "If X, then Y." This is the nature of the logical connection between the explanans and the explanandum. *If the premises are true, the conclusion must be true.*[5] Here is where the necessity of the argument exists; note that within logic nothing is said about the truth, let alone necessity, of the premises. But if the argument is valid and the premises are true, then the explanadum must follow. As Abraham Kaplan puts it, "In the deductive model the necessity does not lie in the premises, but rather in the relation between the premises and the conclusion which they entail."[6] Let us add, however, that the generalizations

---

[4]Carl Hempel and Paul Oppenheim, "The Logic of Explanation," in Herbert Feigl and May Brodbeck (eds.), *Readings in the Philosophy of Sciences* (New York: Appleton-Century-Crofts, 1953), p. 321.

[5]For the nature of deductive logic, see any logic text. Two of the most highly respected are Irving M. Cope, *Symbolic Logic* (New York: Macmillan, 1954); and Patrick Suppes, *Introduction to Logic* (Princeton, N.J.: Van Nostrand Co., 1957).

[6]Abraham Kaplan, *The Conduct of Inquiry* (San Francisco: Chandler Publishing Co., 1964), p. 339.

of an explanation must have empirical content. They must be testable.

One more point should be made before we move on. While it is fair to say that the logical validity of an explanation is independent of its empirical truth or falsity, we would probably like to add something about the truth of the explanatory generalizations. Thus, for an explanation to be truly explanatory, its generalizations must be well confirmed by empirical evidence. This is an obvious requirement; but notice that, unlike the others, it is not about logical structure. So a nomological explanation accounts for a fact by showing that it is one instance of a general tendency. This is what a political scientist does if he explains a political phenomenon.

It might be thought that we have equated nomological explanation and deductive logic. Certainly, this is the proper starting point; to understand the nature of the logical connection between the explanans and the explanandum is to grasp the power of scientific explanation. However, we must at this point make a distinction between two kinds of nomological explanation, deductive and statistical-probabilistic. As the label implies, the former is an exercise in deductive logic. As already noted, in a valid deductive explanation the logical connection between the explanans and the explanandum is such that if the former is true the latter must be. A deductive explanation employs universal laws or generalizations stating that *all* A's are B's. This is why the explanation can be deductive. Now, as we saw in Chapter 6 a universal law is never necessarily true. An empirical generalization must be testable and potentially falsifiable. The difference between a universal law and a statistical law is the kind of claim we make about each, based on the evidence. Neither is necessarily true.

A statistical or probabilistic explanation is one in which statistical laws are employed. It should be of greater interest to political scientists because the generalizations which political science has generated have up until now been statistical. Unlike a deductive explanation, the inductive-statistical explanation of an individual event does not necessarily imply that event; the premises can be true and the conclusion false. The explanation, then, consists not of showing why the conclusion is true, but why it is probable. Thus the explanation of the voting behavior of a certain group or the behavior of Congress may be explained by statistical laws, their actions accounted for by showing that they were highly probable based on the evidence contained in the laws and initial conditions of the explanans. But let us repeat, a single event cannot be accounted for deductively by means of a statistical law. The law and initial conditions can be true and the event might not take place. Thus even if we have a well substantiated law to the effect that approximately 75 percent of all businessmen are strong Republican party-identifiers, we cannot *deductively* explain the Republican beliefs of a single Republican as we could if the law stated that all businessmen are Republican. Thus his party identification is explained because it is highly probable or rationally credible that he is a Republican[7] — But, of course, he need not be, given the evidence, and this is what makes it a probabilistic and not a deductive explanation.

All this about inductive logic applies to statistical explanations accounting for individual events. What about the explanation of statistical laws? We have seen that universal laws are explainable by deductive logic. It is the same with statistical laws. That is, a statistical-probabilistic law can be explained with other laws, universal and statistical; yet this will be a deductive argument—if the premises are true, the conclusion is. For instance, the statistical law that 12 percent of all registered voters in city X are cross-pressured and identify with the Democrats can be explained by two other laws: (1) 30 percent of registered voters are cross-pressured, (2) 40 percent of registered voters who are cross-pressured are Democratic. Let us repeat, this is a deductive explanation, since if it is a valid argument and the premises are true (the probabilities are true), then the conclusion must follow. From the standpoint of logic then, the explanation of universal laws and that of statistical laws exhibit no differences, since they are both "universal" statements. The distinction is that one states that in a certain universe all individuals exhibit a certain characteristic; while the other states that 60 percent have the

---

[7]The concept "rationally credible" is Carl Hempel's. See "Deductive Nomological vs. Statistical Explanations," in Herbert Feigl and Grover Maxwell (eds.), *Minnesota Studies in the Philosophy of Science*, Vol. III (Minneapolis: University of Minnesota Press, 1962), p. 149.

attribute. So the tricky facet of statistical explanation is the explanation of the single event.

Other notions of explanation

We must now consider an alternate notion of explanation and try to describe its shortcomings. Robert Brown speaks for many philosophers and social scientists when he gives the following definition: "All explanations are attempts to explain away impediments of some kind."[8] This implies an interpretation of scientific explanation that is psychological. That is, "to explain" means "to make understandable," to reduce the unfamiliar to the familiar. In the words of the well-known physicist P. W. Bridgman, "Explanation consists merely in analyzing our complicated systems into simpler systems in such a way that we recognize in the complicated system the interplay of elements already so familiar to us that we accept them as not needing explanation."[9] This notion of explanation is in opposition to the nomological interpretation advocated in this book, and, as will be demonstrated, it misses the point of what explanation is all about.

The power of scientific explanation lies in the logical connection between the evidence and the conclusion (fact to be explained), not in the degree of psychological familiarity the argument has. According to Carl Hempel, "the covering-law concept of explanation ... refers to the logic, not the psychology of explanation...."[10] Thus there is a clear distinction between *having* an explanation and *understanding* it. One can give a good explanation of a political phenomenon using unfamiliar concepts and newly discovered relationships. On the other hand, one might think he has explained a fact because his argument appeals to common sense, while in reality, no explanation has been provided; the required generalizations do not exist or those used do not properly imply the conclusion. Thus, their familiarity is neither a

---

[8]Robert Brown, *Explanation in Social Science* (Chicago: Aldine Publishing Co., 1963), p. 41.

[9]P. W. Bridgman, *The Nature of Physical Theory* (Princeton, N.J.: Princeton University Press, 1936), p. 63.

[10]Carl Hempel, "Reasons and Covering Laws in Historical Explanation," in Sidney Hook (ed.), *Philosophy and History* (New York: New York University Press, 1963), p. 147.

necessary nor a sufficient condition of valid explanations. The distinction can also be stated as one between a psychological and a cognitive meaning of explanation. In explaining an event to someone we study his reactions as clues to his understanding of the explanation. He comprehends and accepts the explanation to a greater or lesser degree. This has to do with *communicating* a fact and depends in part upon my ability to articulate and his power of intellect and is thus psychological; it has no *logical* relation to the cognitive soundness of the explanation. In short, the soundness of an explanation and its psychological familiarity or attractiveness are distinct properties.

We have based our argument upon the requirements of scientific explanation; psychological understanding is neither a necessary nor a sufficient condition. But there is a more pragmatic reason for rejecting this interpretation of explanation. It is the simple fact that an idea or argument will appear more or less familiar to different people and at different times. Thus, psychological familiarity cannot serve as an objective standard for assessing the soundness of an explanation. An explanation is objectively valid to one degree or another; its cognitive value can be uniformly evaluated by numerous analysts—each will reach the same conclusion. This is how a science operates. It does not base its knowledge on psychological familiarity. It must be admitted, however, that we would like our explanations to be understood. Even the soundest explanation is of limited use if only one man understands it. This is, however, another attribute of the explanation, independent of its soundness. And this is the gist of our argument.

A related model of explanation assumes that a fact has been explained when it can be fitted into a pattern[11] or system. [12] "According to the pattern model, then, something is explained when it is so related to a set of other elements that together they constitute a unified system. We understand something by identifying it as a specific part in an organized whole."[13] If this model proposes another mode of explanation which is nonnomological,

---

[11]Kaplan, *op. cit.*

[12]Eugene Meehan, *Explanation in Social Science: A System Paradigm* (Homewood, Ill.: Dorsey Press, 1968).

[13]Kaplan, *op. cit.*

then it should be pointed out that one does not account for something simply by showing that it fits into a pattern. This might describe some of its relationships, but it doesn't answer the "why" question. On the other hand, the pattern model might be interpreted in a nomological sense if the relationships of the pattern or system are taken as manifestations of generalizations. In this case, it cannot be considered a distinct model.

There is another intellectual position that comes to mind in a discussion of the nature of explanation and psychological understanding. It is the argument that the nomological model of explanation does not really explain at all. Using the generalization, "Workers tend to vote left," and the statement, "*X* group is made up mainly of workers," to explain the group's voting left, does not, according to this criticism, really show why the behavior occurred. Something else is required, so the argument goes. For instance, W. G. Runciman has written, "Given that being a Catholic is correlated with being a Democrat, the question why is not so much answered as asked."[14] At one level, this is a version of the claim that no explanation is final. All explanations are, to use Abraham Kaplan's terminology, "indeterminate." That is, "every explanation is in turn subject to being explained."[15] This is a reasonable claim, and one that the practicing political scientist would do well to keep in mind. However, it tends to cast doubt upon an argument such as Runciman's, for it makes clear that there are different levels of explanation. One of the tasks of any science is to search constantly for more refined laws to account for more variance (speaking statistically); in other words, to explain a wider range of phenomena more completely. But this does not mean that the initial rough generalization fails to provide an explanation of sorts.

Returning again to Runciman's example, one can explain a group's being Democratic (it is predominantly Catholic) using the law provided, and still seek to explain why Catholics tend to be Democrats. There is no contradiction here. The next step will simply be a more refined and inclusive law. Thus, if this argument

---

14W. G. Runciman, *Social Science and Political Theory* (Cambridge, Eng.: Cambridge University Press, 1963), p. 92.

15Kaplan, *op. cit.*, p. 354.

merely boils down to a noting of the infinite regress of explanations, it need not trouble us. However, it can be pushed further. "There is a widespread notion that the hierarchy of explanations must ultimately ascend to the final comprehensive theory which is itself as ineluctable as a brute matter of fact...." [16] What underlies this notion is a belief that the laws of nature represent the necessary order of the universe. That is, science's ultimate task is to show why things must be as they are. But as we have seen, this is not at all the objective of an empirical science. The laws of any science are contingent; they describe the relations of things as we observe them. Science cannot demonstrate their necessity.

EXPLANATION AND PREDICTION

One of the reasons we mentioned for a political scientist's taking an interest in explanation is the fact that all policy scientists have to predict. This justification is valid because of the logical identity between explanation and prediction. The identity is based upon the fact that both explanation and prediction require laws and initial conditions. Thus, if one has a valid explanation he should be able to employ it to predict, and vice versa. If, given the proper initial conditions, one could not have predicted the event that was explained, the explanation was not adequate in the first place. Thus the claim made by philosophers such as Michael Scriven that social scientists would make better use of their time if they tried to discover nonpredictive explanatory laws is difficult to understand.[17] If it is possible to explain adequately without having a potential prediction, then the door is left open for any pseudoexplanation of a given phenomenon. Hempel and Oppenheim have warned against ex post facto explanations, or explanations that *seem* to account for a fact after it has happened. Thus one can conjure up causal factors (motives are a favorite) and explain a politician's behavior. But no prediction could have been made, for this was not a sound explanation; the behavior was not really accounted for.

16*Ibid.*

17Michael Scriven, "Explanation and Prediction in Evolutionary Theory," *Science,* Vol. CXXX, 1959, p. 477.

As we shall see, an explanation may be incomplete and yet be accepted by political scientists. This has led some to argue that while one can explain, using such partial explanations prediction is impossible. Abraham Kaplan then raises the question, "What shall we say, because they do not allow for prediction, that they are not really explanations at all?"[18] In the strictest sense they are *not* explanations, and so naturally they do not predict. In this period of a developing science of politics, we must often content ourselves with partial explanations, or even less. But this practical concession does not allow us to weaken the model of explanation to the point that it no longer explains. It is not a game we are playing, a game of providing the most reasonable-appearing explanation; an explanation either does or does not account for a fact and, as we have argued, its psychological appeal has nothing to do with its soundness.

Kaplan also implies that statistical laws can often explain better than they predict. However, once again, the explanation only appears sounder because the event has already happened. If the laws of voting behavior assert that it is 80 percent probable that country *X* will vote for candidate *A*, we can predict as well as explain the county's behavior with 80 percent certainty. The fact that it does behave in the *predicted* manner does not make the explanation sounder than a prediction.

There is another argument often used by those who claim explanation is possible without prediction. A well-worked example has to do with the explanation of earthquakes. We can explain them after they have taken place (using the proper laws and citing relevant conditions), but it is usually impossible to predict a quake. Rather, the last clause should read "technically difficult," because we are often unable to know about the initial conditions. Shifting the example to politics, we might have rather sophisticated laws accounting for revolutions and civil wars, but the initial social, political, and economic conditions existing right now in a small Latin American republic that would allow us to apply the laws may never come to our attention until after the revolution has occurred. This is, then, a technical, not a logical, difficulty and it in no way refutes the logical identity between

---

[18]Kaplan, *op. cit.*, p. 354.

explanation and prediction. Ernest Nagel has put it this way: "In many cases of physical inquiry we are ignorant of the pertinent initial conditions for employing established theories to make precise forecasts, even though the available theories are otherwise entirely adequate for this purpose."[19]

There is still another argument made by those who reject the logical identity of explanation and prediction. It is that we are often able to predict without being able to explain. This is, then, a reversal of the argument just considered. Abraham Kaplan has presented the following as a case in point. "Analysis of voting behavior, for example, may have identified certain counties or states as barometers but making predictions from them is very different from having an explanation of the vote."[20] The prediction proceeds in the following manner:

If X counties vote Democratic, the Democrats tend to win the national election.

X counties have voted Democratic.

Therefore, the Democrats will win.

This is a very rough prediction. If we apply it to a past Democratic victory, we have a very rough explanation relative to the findings of survey research. Thus the explanation and prediction are equally gross and neither is causal. Only mass election results can be predicted (and explained), and then without much confidence. The generalizations coming out of the voting studies allow for better explanations (accounting for more variance and explaining at more refined levels) and more accurate and inclusive predictions. The X-county findings either represent accidental correlations or indicate that there are deeper causal factors at work. If the former is the case, we will have learned something; if the latter holds, an attempt would be made to discover these factors, thus leading to the development of more refined explanations and predictions. For instance, if there are social characteristics, attitudes, or personality traits at work, it would be more fruitful to have laws relating them to voting behavior than laws showing a correlation between counties and national elections. But this goes for both explanation and prediction. What if the Democratic-type people make a mass exodus from the X-counties? The laws will no

---

[19]Nagel, *op. cit.*, p. 461.
[20]*Ibid.*, p. 350.

longer be useful for explanation or prediction since they were such low-level arguments in the first place.

THE COMPLETENESS OF EXPLANATIONS

In examining the nature of nomological explanation, we have not meant to give the impression that political scientists ought to sit on their hands until they have before them full-blown deductive or statistical explanations. At this stage such a requirement seems unrealistic and overly restrictive. Thus, the arguments against the possibility of a science of politics (and therefore the scientific explanation of political phenomena), which we attempted to refute on methodological grounds in Chapter 3, are often of practical significance. For instance, while the complexity of political phenomena presents no *logical* barrier to nomological explanation, it can create difficulties for the political scientist conducting research. No claim is being made that political science is simple and that complete nomological explanation is immediately achievable. On the other hand, we have argued that explanation in any science must meet certain requirements and it will only prove disillusioning to attempt to achieve explanation by drastically weakening these requirements. Taking a moderate position, one ought to realize that there are various degrees of completeness possible in explanation; one can make a series of logical distinctions between degrees of completeness and yet draw the line at inadequate explanations. In other words, if we are explicit, the class of incomplete but pragmatically acceptable explanation types can be distinguished from pseudoexplanations, arguments which have no explanatory value. The addition of one or several elements (usually laws) to an incomplete explanation makes it complete. But no addition could make a pseudo-explanation acceptable, short of complete revision. There are various degrees of incompleteness, and this allows one to construct a spectrum of potential explanations.

Carl Hempel has explicated this criterion of completeness for explanations rather thoroughly.[21] Using his analysis as a guide, we

---

[21]See especially, "Explanation in Science and History," in Robert G. Colodny, *Frontiers of Science and Philosophy* (Pittsburgh: University of Pittsburgh Press, 1962), pp. 7-33; and "The Function of General Laws in History," *Journal of Philosophy*, Vol. XXXIX, 1942, pp. 35-48.

can spell out a typology of completeness for political scientists. First, of course, are *complete* explanations, those that explicitly state all laws and initial conditions. Hempel points out that such perfectly complete nomological explanations are rarely achieved by scientists. In the natural sciences this is usually because the explainer assumes that certain laws will be presupposed, and so formally states only the necessary facts. "If judged by ideal standards, the given formulation of the proof is elliptic or incomplete: but the departure from the ideal is harmless; the gaps can readily be filled in."[22] In other words if asked to, the scientist could easily provide the missing laws (or initial conditions) that would completely account for the phenomenon in question. The number of *elliptical* explanations in political science is not great. This discipline is simply not well enough developed so as to allow a political scientist the luxury of assuming that others are aware of the laws he is implying. This is one reason for asking that political scientists explicitly formulate their generalizations.

Hempel's scheme has a category that can account for more explanations in political science. This he has called the *partial* explanation.[23] Like the elliptical type, it fails to explicitly formulate all the generalizations upon which it is based. But even when the generalizations are made evident, the explanandum is not completely accounted for. All that is demonstrated is that something in a particular general class is to be expected. Thus, suppose we want to explain why a certain presidential decision (*S*) was to send troops to nation Alpha (*W*). A partial explanation would only show (for example) that (1) *S* was an aggesssive act (class *F*); (2) in these circumstances an *F* is to be expected; and (3) *W* is in the class *F*. Thus the aggressive act would be explained completely, the sending of troops partially. As we have said, partial explanations are important for political science. An explanation is partial because its laws cannot completely account for its explanandum; this is the nature of most, if not all, laws about political phenomena.

One might have an explanation of sorts, but still not think it meets even the requirements of the partial explanation. In this

---

[22]Hempel, "Explanation in Science and History," *op. cit.,* p. 14.
[23]*Ibid.,* p. 15.

case, we might classify the argument as an *explanation sketch*. [24] Such an argument is characterized by a lack of explicitness and logical rigor; yet it seems to be pointing to an explanation. Thus, it serves as a sort of outline or sketch to direct one's attention toward possible relationships and ultimately a more complete explanation. The social sciences, including political science, abound with such explanation sketches. They are valuable if it is kept in mind that a complete explanation is still far in the future. Take, for instance, Nathan Leites' explanations of Soviet politics which begins with the maxim, "Character determines behavior." [25] They boil down to attempts at characterizing the Bolshevik-type personality and then relating it to political behavior (decision making, etc.). Leites' explanations are speculative and, like most psycholanalytic analyses, a bit short on scientific rigor. But as explanation sketches they are interesting and potentially useful, for they point out some possible explanatory factors—in short, a start is made. Once again we must admit that in its present stage of development, political science must often be satisfied with the explanation sketch. But that is an empirical, not a logical, shortcoming.

All of these incomplete explanation types can be distinguished from the pseudo or nonexplanation according to one main criterion. No matter how incomplete, it will be possible to test even an explanation sketch (admittedly, this may take some doing). That is, even in its rough state, the incomplete explanation makes some reference to empirical entities—to the world of experience. Such is not the case with nonexplanations. "In the case of nonempirical explanations or explanation sketches ... the use of empirically meaningless terms makes it impossible even roughly to indicate the type of investigation that would have a bearing upon these formulations...." [26] This distinction between incomplete and pseudoexplanations is important to our analysis. Many of the explanations that one comes across in political science are incomplete rather than pseudo. Thus, while they should be evaluated and criticized according to the standards of

---

[24]*Ibid.*

[25]Nathan Leites, *A Study of Bolshevism* (Glencoe, Ill.: Free Press, 1954), and *The Operational Code of the Politburo* (New York: McGraw-Hill, 1951).

[26]Hempel, "The Function of General Laws in History," *op. cit.,* p. 42.

sound scientific explanation, they ought not to be dismissed as useless. To the contrary, their explication should lead to more complete explanations when more sophisticated laws are available. A framework for such explication will be discussed in the next section.

PATTERNS OF EXPLANATION

The first part of this chapter described the nature of explanation in political science. We argued that only nomological explanations can account for political scientists' *why* questions. What might appear to be different types of explanation are actually variations on a single logical model; they share the basic characteristic of employing laws to explain. This section will describe a typology of patterns of explanation based on a survey of political science literature. If it is at all inclusive, then the argument that every sound explanation in political science contains at least one law becomes stronger, for the nomological character of each pattern will be demonstrated.

The patterns are six in number. The first three, dispositional, intentional, and rational, employ human characteristics as independent variables. The others are macroinstitutional, system-maintaining, and genetic. It will become clear that a single criterion has not been used to classify patterns. For instance, dispositional explanations are distinguished from macroexplanations mainly on the basis of content, that is, the different types of concepts used as independent variables in their generalizations. On the other hand a dispositional explanation and a genetic explanation have different structures. But we need provide no lengthy justification of this multiplicity of criteria, since our basic thesis is that all sound explanations are nomological. In this section we are interested in describing the methods (patterns) of explanation actually used by political scientists.

Before moving on to the patterns themselves, one more point needs clarification. Each of the patterns is an ideal-type of sorts. The explanations that one comes across in the literature of political science are often mixed. However, in most explanations either one pattern is dominant, or the two or more coequal patterns are distinguishable; therefore we are justified in speaking about six patterns and assuming that such discussion is useful for the practicing political scientist.

The dispositional pattern

The dispositional pattern in political science is so labeled because it uses dispositional concepts. A disposition is a tendency to respond in a certain way in a given situation. Included in the class of dispositional concepts are attitudes, opinions, beliefs, values, and personality traits. The dispositional pattern can be distinguished from the intentional pattern because the former makes no reference to conscious motives. In other words, the link between the disposition and behavior is not "out in the open."

The form of a dispositional explanation is X (the explanandum) because Y tends to do A in Z (the disposition). The Y can be either "all people" or "a certain type." In either case, the disposition is being used to explain an action, an event, an institution, or even another political disposition by indicating that people, groups, etc., with disposition X tend to behave in a certain way.

May Brodbeck has pointed out that the dispositional definition itself may be employed as the generalization in an explanation. [27] Thus we might explain an individual's electoral decision by stating the following definition: "A leftist is one who votes left" (voting left defines the disposition), and then claiming that the individual is leftist. However, the explanation is then, in May Brodbeck's words, "vacuous and circular."[28] That is, useful dispositional explanations which tell us something about the world will relate the disposition to another factor, the result being an empirical generalization. Such an explanation is not vacuous and circular. Thus the pattern's nomological nature becomes evident. Dispositions are antecedent conditions, independent variables which must be linked to resulting actions by covering laws before they can explain anything.

There are as many types of dispositional explanation as there

---

[27]May Brodbeck, "Explanation, Prediction and 'Imperfect' Knowledge," in Feigl and Maxwell, *op. cit.,* p. 268.

[28]*Ibid.*

are kinds of dispositions. Some of these we have already mentioned. However, there are several other dimensions according to which dispositional explanations can be classified. The dispositions may be attributed to individuals, decision makers, groups, types of people, classes, nations, or all men. The laws or relationships can be explicitly stated, consciously assumed, or unconsciously implied; and based on controlled analysis of statistical evidence, observation and experience, or commonsense speculation. A succinct statement of these dimensions can be made in the form of a series of questions, the answers to which provide a clear categorization of any dispositional explanation:

1. What kind of dispositional concept?
2. Who has the disposition?
3. How is it related to behavior (how well developed and articulated are the laws)?
4. What kind of evidence is provided (how scientific)?

The last two questions can be asked of any pattern, of course.

Let us consider an example. Lewis Dexter has attempted an explanation of the proposed fact that congressmen believe the mail they receive from their constituents is valuable and worthy of consideration.[29]   The explanation is based on a number of attitudes and beliefs that Dexter thinks lead to the general disposition (the belief). He discusses five such dispositions. Included are values: "Most congressmen *genuinely treasure* the right of petition and the opportunity of the individual citizen to complain about mistreatment";[30]   and beliefs: "Some congressmen actually *believe* and many others *like to feel* that on any issue of national significance rational communication between them and any constituent is possible."[31]   Dexter characterizes these as dispositions peculiar to congressmen. In order to use them in explanations, they must be related in the form of generalizations to the phenomenon being explained.

Dexter also uses another kind of dispositional concept. This is a general psychological attitude attributed to all or most people.

[29]Lewis Dexter, "What do Congressmen Hear?" in Nelson Polsby *et al., Politics and Social Life* (Boston: Houghton Mifflin Co., 1963), pp. 485-95.
[30]*Ibid.,* p. 487.
[31]*Ibid.*

"Most people seem to prefer to know what they are supposed to do"[32] helps explain the congressman's desire for indications of constituents' wishes. It is clear that the statement containing dispositions concerning most people can be considered a generalization about most people. And since congressmen are people, the generalization applies to them. We can conclude, then, that dispositions employed in explanations must be found in generalizations. For this reason, the dispositional pattern has explanatory power.

The intentional pattern

The existence of a dispositional pattern in our typology indicates that much political behavior is not intentional. Still, there is a class of actions which do seem to manifest such purposive behavior. This, then, is the basis for the inclusion of an intentional pattern. The term "intention" refers to all actions (not necessarily successfully carried out) that are consciously purposive. And as a matter of fact, political scientists often attempt to explain political phenomena by showing that the explanandum is the result of some sort of intentional action.

The simplest kind of intentional explanation can be schematically presented: "*X* does *Y* because he intended to do it." But this is not a complete explanation of *Y*, because no grounds are given for expecting its occurrence. Just because *X* intended to do *Y* doesn't mean *X* will actually do it, unless of course we have a law, based on empirical evidence, that such a person as *X* acts upon his intentions. Thus it can be seen why at least this simple law is necessary: intentions need not result in actions. Some sort of statement is required which provides grounds for explaining the action. Thus, for instance, saying that Senator Smith lent his support to the Civil Rights Act of 1969 because that was his intention doesn't explain anything unless we include the very general law that "When a senator intends to support a bill, he usually does." Thus even in this overly simplified case, a generalization is necessary for sound explanation.

Usually, however, what we have called an intentional or

------

[32]*Ibid.*, p. 486.

purposeful explanation includes more justification of its explanandum than "because he wanted or intended to," and "he who intends to, does." For if we want an intentional explanation of a political phenomenon X that goes beyond this trivial argument, we will probably have to refer to goals or objectives. It can be asserted, then, that another important characteristic of most intentional explanations is that there is some reference made to goals, purposes, or objectives. The structure of the pattern then becomes, "X did Y because he wanted G," based on the generalization "people who want G tend to do Y under these particular conditions." There is also a kind of variation on the intentional goal-seeking explanation that is often called "functional" or "teleological." Its strategy is to account for certain political phenomena by showing that agents believe them functional either for themselves or for a system, and so pursue them—make them their objectives.

We have now noted two kinds of intentional explanation based on two kinds of intentional generalizations. The second clause is important because, as we have argued, intentional explanations, whether of the simple ("because he intended to") or more important goal-seeking (because he had X-goal) type, require laws that relate the intention to the explanandum phenomenon and therefore demonstrate why it is as it is. The mere stating of an intention or a goal does not explain (unless, of course, there are laws implied and we accept it as a partial or elliptical explanation).

Lewis J. Edinger's explanation of why the nonpolitical elite in postwar Germany was not anti-Nazi is intentional because it is based on the proposed fact that the costs of a purge of pro-Nazi officials would have been more than the Allies were *willing* to pay.[33] In effect, Edinger explains the lack of a purge by setting forth the conditions for the decision to carry one out—i.e., recruiting an entirely new group of anti-Nazi nonpolitical leaders. His explanatory law is, "The more extensive the purge the more it will cost....On the other hand, the less the victor is willing to pay one or the other price, the more difficult it will be to carry

---

[33]Lewis J. Edinger, "Post-Totalitarian Leadership: Elites in the German Federal Republic," *American Political Science Review,* Vol. LIV, 1960, pp. 58-82.

through such a purge."[34] Clearly, the term which makes this a variation on the intentional theme is "willing." If X is not willing to pay the price, it will not carry out the purge. The explanation is not, "X failed to carry out the purge because it didn't want to," but, "because it didn't want to pay the price required." The lawful relationship exists between *purging* and *willingness to pay the price*. In short, goals are cited to explain the action.

So intentional explanations, like all other sound explanations, are nomological. They differ from the other patterns only in the type of concepts used and the way in which generalizations are arranged. However, some philosophers of social science see in intentional explanation a unique way of accounting for social phenomena—a method of explanation logically distinct from the nomological model. The basis of this position is a belief that a citing of intentions explains by showing the meaningfulness of the behavior under question. "The explanatory force of learning the agent's intention depends upon the author's familiarity with intentional behavior; the explanation must solve a puzzle and in order for the puzzle to exist there must be a 'previous stock of knowledge and beliefs' with which the perplexing event is at variance."[35] This interpretation of intentional explanation is based upon an assumption that we tried to refute in the first section. We contended that the psychological fact of familiarity has nothing to do with the logical requirements of explanation. There does seem to be an added attractiveness in viewing intentional explanation as being somehow more "meaningful" than other kinds. Going along with this interpretation is the argument that correlation does not really explain. "Our assertion of cause and effect in human behavior depends in addition on certain intuitive notions which are not derived simply from observation of correlations."[36] Knowing an agent's intentions or goals provides the meaningfulness. Our reply, besides the refutation of the "explanation from familiarity" argument, rests on the nomological nature of intentional explanation. An intention explains a political fact only insofar as it is lawfully related,

34*Ibid.*, pp. 80-81.

35Brown, *op. cit.*, p. 66.

36Runciman, *op. cit.*, p. 92.

directly or indirectly, to it. That the fact is thereby made psychologically meaningful is neither a necessary nor sufficient condition of the explanation.

The rational pattern

A rational-type explanation is based on the presumed or demonstrated rationality of men (all or types of men). This pattern may be considered as a special case of intentional explanation in the most general sense. However, it is sufficiently distinct and in wide enough use among political scientists to justify separate consideration. We will consider the most sophisticated use of "rationality" in political science, namely, game theory, in Chapter 11.

A rational explanation has the form, "*X* because *Y* is rational," or, bringing out its nomological nature, "*X* because *Y* is rational and in situation *S* a rational man does *X*." There are obviously many points in this basic characterization that require explication, but perhaps first a preliminary definition of rationality is in order.

Most definitions talk about rational behavior or action; thus, a man is rational insofar as he behaves rationally. Robert Dahl and Charles Lindblom have stated what seems to be the consensus definition of rational behavior: "An action is rational to the extent that it is correctly designed to maximize goal achievement, given the goal in question and the real world as it exists."[37] So an individual is rational if his pursuit of goals is as efficient as possible. The importance of goals to rationality indicates why we could say at the outset that rational explanation is, in a way, a special kind of intentional explanation. According to the definitions we have been considering, all rational behavior is goal-seeking. The only difference between it and the intentional pattern is the claim that rational action is the *best* way to achieve a goal. An intentional explanation makes no such claim; it merely states that *X* has goal *Y* and in situation *S*, people with *Y* tend to do *W* to achieve it—*W* is not necessarily the *best* method. J. W. N.

---

[37]Robert Dahl and Charles Lindbolm, *Politics, Economics and Welfare* (New York: Harper Bros., 1953), p. 38.

Watkins has succinctly made his point: "If we define purposeful behavior as trying ... to do or achieve something, it follows that fully rational behavior is a limiting case of purposeful behavior."[38] So we can now see why the rational pattern is often confused with intentional explanation.

We have referred to the nomological nature of rational explanation. Let us now show in more detail why this pattern shares the basic logical structure of all adequate scientific explanations. Saying that "A man, M, voted for candidate X because M was rational," while providing the outline of an explanation, does not really account for the behavior—show why it happened. It lacks the information that relates the initial condition, "M is rational" to the explanandum, "M voted for candidate X." This is provided by the generalization that, "A rational man, in situation S (the available candidates) would vote for X (or an X-type candidate)." Given the condition that M is indeed rational, the direction of voting is explained (or predicted). If we adopt the consensus definition of rationality—the rational seeking of given goals—then the explanation takes the form: "M has goal G (to have his interests acted upon); M is rational; in situation S, a rational man with goal G will vote for an X-type candidate; X is an X-type candidate; therefore, M will vote for X." The structure of the two is the same, the second case is simply more refined.

According to Carl Hempel's formulation of the rational pattern, "rationality" becomes a sort of dispositional concept, for it presents A's action, as it were, as a manifestation of his general disposition to act in characteristic ways—in ways that qualify as appropriate or rational—when in certain situations.[39] The law that accounts for the behavior asserts: "If M is rational, then in situation S he will do V." In other words, men with the disposition of being rational respond in *this* manner, under *these* conditions. To have the disposition of being rational then is not *logically* different from identifying with the Democrats (attitude) or being authoritarian (personality trait). We have previously

---

[38]J. W. N. Watkins, "Ideal and Historical Explanation," in Feigl and Brodbeck, *op. cit.,* p. 742.

[39]Hempel, "Reasons and Covering Laws in Historical Explanation," *op. cit.*

classified rational explanations as a special case of the intentional pattern. Now "being rational" has been characterized as dispositional. These two ideas can be integrated, with the result being an interesting formulation of the rational pattern. We can say that explaining "rationally" consists of stating an agent's goal (this conforms to the intentional pattern); attributing a disposition, rationality, to the agent (introducing a dispositional concept); and, finally, formulating a law relating them to the explanandum, "If X has A goal and is rational, then he does C."

The macro pattern

We have now analyzed three patterns of explanation. Each accounts for political phenomena in a different way, on the basis of different types of independent variables. Yet all are similar in that (1) they are nomological, and (2) the concepts, and subsequently the generalizations containing them that account for the explananda explicitly refer to human characteristics, whether individual or group. The pattern of explanation which will be analyzed in this section parts company with the first three on the latter point. That is, the generalizations that a macroinstitutional explanation employs have as antecedent factors or independent variables institutional or physical concepts, so that in an institutional law $A \rightarrow B$, the A is such a concept. There are consequently two variations of the macro pattern, the institutional and the physical.

The dispositional pattern already analyzed includes some group properties—group dispositions—such as "public opinion" and "national character." These are properly considered as statistical averages of many individual opinions or individual personality traits. Thus, since we have classified such concepts as dispositional, they will not be included in this section. What we are saying, in effect, is that there is a difference between an institution (admittedly made up of individuals and properties of individuals) and a group property such as public opinion. The opinion of a group is a direct disposition of the individuals who make up the group. When an institution such as the party system is cited as the cause of a political phenomenon, a property of that institution, its decentralized nature for instance, is usually being referred to implicitly or explicitly. Thus one might want to call "decentralization" a disposition of a party, since its existence is determined by observing certain behaviors of political parties in given situations. This is not incompatible with our macro pattern, even when we add the additional assumption that such dispositions as party decentralization and group cohesion are ultimately reducible to laws about individual behavior. That is, we can give this interpretation of party decentralization and still opt for the usefulness (at least existence) of a macro pattern of explanation in political science because the decentralization of a party is not a direct characteristic of its members as is a public's opinion. While (according to methodological individualism) this concept is definable in terms of individual behavior, an individual is not cohesive; but, of course, an individual does have opinions or personality traits. Therefore, we talk about the decentralization of the *party,* of the *institution.* This is because, while the party's decentralized nature is in part a result of human dispositions, these interact in such a way as to give the institution a characteristic which none of the individuals possess.

One of the best-known explanations in the literature of political science is the accounting for of the American two-party system. One of the first formulators of such an explanation was E. E. Schattschneider.[40] The general hypothesis from which he operates is, "The American two-party system is the direct consequence of the American election system, or system of representation."[41] Two institutional features of the electoral system in particular are cited as antecedent conditions—single-member districts and plurality elections.[42] The French sociologist Maurice Duverger has stated his version of the law: "The simple-majority single-ballot system favours the two-party system,"[43] and says about it, "Of all the hypotheses that have been defined in this book, this approaches the most nearly perhaps to a true sociological law."[44] These arguments are important to us because they represent straight-

[40]E. E. Schattschneider, *Party Government* (New York: Holt, Rinehart & Winston, 1942), pp. 67-84.

[41]*Ibid.,* p. 69.

[42]*Ibid.,* p. 74.

[43]Maurice Duverger, *Political Parties* (New York: Science Editions, 1963), p. 217.

[44]*Ibid.*

forward institutional explanations. The fact of having a two-party system is adequately accounted for by laws relating it to institutional properties of the electoral system.

We have now sketched the general nature of the macro pattern and provided a justification for its consideration as a separate kind of explanation. One kind of macro explanation uses institutions and properties of institutions. There is another subclass of the macro category. Besides institutional explanations there are those employing physical characteristics of the environment. Thus David Easton identifies three categories of, as he calls it, "situational data": "(1) the physical environment; (2) the non-human organic environment; and (3) the social environment or patterns of human activity flowing from social interaction."[45] The latter is close to the institutional category we have just discussed, and the former refers, of course, to our present concern. Easton goes on to say that, "Our physical environment influences our activity, regardless of the kind of people we are. Our non-organic resources, topography, and spatial location, such as being near or distant from the seat of government, influences the kind of political lives we lead."[46] A physical explanation in political science in simplest terms takes the form "A; if A (a physical fact), then B; therefore B (explanandum)." Physical facts include geographical variables and characteristics of the political system; for instance, the type of electoral ballot can be considered as a physical explanatory factor.

Some students of politics have noticed a relationship between the type of ballot and the incidence of straight-party voting. Angus Campbell states the association in the following manner: "We find, in the states which make it relatively easy for the voter to mark a straight ticket, that the number of straight tickets marked is some 20 percent higher than in those states where the ballot requires a series of separate decisions among the candidates for each of the various offices."[47]

Enough has been said to indicate that the macroinstitutional pattern is, like all sound explanatory types, nomological. In fact,

---

[45]David Easton, *The Political System* (New York: Alfred A. Knopf, 1953), p. 194.
[46]*Ibid.*, pp. 194-95.

[47]Angus Campbell, "Recent Developments in Survey Studies of Political Behavior," in Austin Ranney (ed.), *Essays on the Behavioral Study of Politics* (Urbana: University of Illinois Press, 1962), pp. 31-46.

macro explanations are perhaps more readily recognized as such than many other patterns because they claim simply that a political phenomenon is associated with a certain institutional characteristic or physical fact. That this association has to be expressed in a law seems evident.

The system-maintaining pattern

There are many activities in political science called "functional" or "system-maintaining." Some of these will be examined in Chapter 14. Our pattern includes only those which attempt to provide sound explanations of political phenomena. Thus several types of "functional analysis" have been rejected for inclusion in this section because they are not explanatory.

An important case of presumably sound, but in fact invalid, explanation must be distinguished from the potentially sound variety of system-maintaining explanation. In it the behavior pattern, institution, etc., that is the explanandum is supposedly explained by showing that it is necessary for the performance of functions that in turn are required by the system. The application of the label "teleological" can be seen as justified, for in effect, the present existence of a political phenomenon is being explained by its end. As a matter of fact, this kind of functional-teleological explanation is not sound. It is difficult enough to demonstrate that a certain function is necessary for the maintenance of a system—for instance, the allocation of values. However, it is another thing to prove conclusively that a particular political institution or activity is the only thing that can perform the function. Thus we might be able to present evidence that a certain political function is necessary for the maintenance (continued existence) of the social system. But one cannot show that a particular political institution is the only one that could perform the function.

At this point, we can discuss the sound type of system-maintaining explanation. Its main feature is the assertion and perhaps demonstration of a causal relationship between variables and a system. "It should be apparent that functional explanation is essentially causal; if it is concerned with the effects of a given activity or practice on a system, its purpose must be the establishment of cause and effect relationships."[48] Based on the analysis in Chapter 6, it seems reasonable to assume that if the notion of causality has any significance at all, it is because "to show cause" means "to subsume under general laws"; the concept of cause is reducible to the covering-law model. It follows that to explain functionally or to use the system-affecting pattern is to employ laws; thus, there is no difference in this respect from other sound patterns of explanation. In explaining a certain change, state, or maintenance of a system, we show what factors help produce it. The causal relationship can only be accounted for by citing a law that indicates the resulting state of affairs is expectable under the circumstances. The distinctive feature of system-maintaining explanations is the dependent variable, system maintenance. Such an explanation attempts to demonstrate that certain functions are necessary for the maintenance of the system and that specific variables fulfill these functions.

The genetic pattern

Of the six patterns of explanation we have distinguished, the one that is the most distinctive structurally is the genetic pattern. Each of the other patterns can be reduced to the admittedly oversimplified schema, "If *A* (representing laws and initial conditions), then *B* (the explanandum.)" But, in Ernest Nagel's words, "The task of genetic explanations is to set out the sequence of major events through which some earlier system has been transformed into a later one."[49] Thus, a genetic explanation does not fit the above schema because it involves several stages. Its basic pattern (in its simplest form, involving only two stages) is, "If *A* (factors at time 1), then *B* (consequent factors); and if *C* (*B* plus other factors at time 2), then *D* (explanandum)." It is clear, then, that the factors in the schema occur or exist at different times. This is why we said the genetic pattern is characterized by stages. A simple causal explanation, "If *A* then *B*; *A*, therefore *B*," involves a time sequence; one might say that a causal law is a

[48]Vernon Van Dyke, *Political Science: A Philosophical Analysis* (Stanford, Calif.: Stanford University Press, 1960), p. 32.

[49]Nagel, *op. cit.,* p. 25.

universal law with a temporal feature. However, a genetic explanation is marked by at least two explanation stages, each of which can be considered a separate explanation, which together show why a political phenomenon is as it is or was what it was. [50] In other words, an explanation fitting the genetic pattern first explains a state of affairs X and then proceeds to explain, on the basis of X, another state of affairs, and so on.

Thus the genetic pattern accounts for the present state of a political phenomenon by showing how it developed over time from previous stages. It differs from other patterns because of this temporal element and the multiplicity of stages. From what we have said so far it seems reasonable to conclude that the genetic pattern is often identified with historical explanation. It is also interesting to note, in this regard, that much of the methodological analysis of the genetic pattern has been carried out by philosophers of history. [51]   And as a matter of fact, many of the explanations provided by political scientists that can be classified as genetic are actually historical. That is, in these instances, the political scientist functions as an historian in accounting for political events or situations. For instance, Wilfred E. Binkley traces the development of the office of the Presidency using a narrative style that mentions the key historical occurrences that Binkley believes influenced the formation of the office. [52]   But genetic and historical explanations are not identical. There are genetic explanations which are not historical in the technical sense, for instance, the explanation of the development of party identification in *The American Voter*. [53]

A main characteristic of many genetic explanations, then, is a narrative style or chronicling of events. However, it is obvious that in accounting for a political phenomenon, not every antecedent event is relevant. We can say, at this point, that genetic explanations account for political phenomena by describing a

---

[50]A genetic explanation can be cut off at any point, so that the origin at one time may be a stage at another, and a stage may become the explanandum if we push the analysis back in time.

[51]See, for instance, W. B. Gallie, "Explanations in History and the Genetic Sciences," in Patrick Gardner (ed.), *Theories of History* (Glencoe, Ill.: Free Press, 1959).

[52]Wilfred E. Binkley, *President and Congress* (New York: Vintage Books, 1962).

[53]Angus Campbell *et al., The American Voter* (New York: John Wiley & Sons, Inc., 1960).

series of *relevant* events which, in a chain-like fashion, determine the state of the explanandum.

However, there is more to genetic explanation than a listing of relevant stages in the development of a political phenomenon. We might say that each event or circumstance is a contingently necessary condition for subsequent events. This notion implies the nomological nature of genetic explanation. Let us attempt to justify this assertion. A genetic explanation accounts for a political phenomenon by showing how it was changed or influenced at various stages in its development. Now the important point is that each stage supposedly has some influence on the following stage, and so on until the explanandum is reached; this, of course, is why one talks about "necessary conditions." The question is, How can each stage be linked to the next? Our answer is, through the use of generalizations. That is, a law explains why the phenomenon changed from A to B, and then another law relates some part of B to C, and so on. Hempel has succinctly summarized the nomological nature of genetic explanation: "In a genetic explanation each stage must be shown to 'lead to' the next, and thus to be linked to its successor by virtue of some general principle which makes the occurrence of the latter at least reasonably probable, given the former."[54] Thus we see that if a genetic explanation is to be of any value, it must be nomological, for it depends on the demonstration that one stage has an effect on the next.

An example will help clarify our argument. William Riker's explanation of the decline of judicial review can be interpreted as a genetic explanation.[55] Taking some liberties with his analysis, we can present the following as an explanation of the phenomenon in question: (1) the Supreme Court's experience with the "Court-packing" bill of 1937 persuaded it to practice judicial restraint; (2) one manifestation of its judicial restraint was its periodic restriction of doctrines that had been used to justify striking down acts of Congress; (3) therefore, when acts of Congress that previously were affected by such doctrines come before the Court, it does not employ the doctrines. Thus, it does

---

[54]Carl Hempel, "Explanation in Science and History," *op. cit.,* p. 22.

[55]William Riker, *Democracy in the United States* (New York: Macmillan Co., 1965), pp. 260-64.

not practice judicial review. The explanation is genetic because the explanandum is the result of the relationships between three stages of the Court's history. And each relationship must be expressed in the form of a law; for instance, "a judicial body which is trying to divest itself of a power will give up devices that justify the exercise of that power."

In addition to laws, nomological explanations contain initial conditions. It follows that a genetic explanation, like all sound explanations (except those of laws), requires generalizations *and* initial conditions. The upshot of this fact is the realization that each stage of a genetic explanation is in effect a separate explanation. Thus, using the example from Riker, we see that the explanation of the Supreme Court's adoption of judicial restraint (because of the fear engendered by the attack of Roosevelt in 1937) is logically independent of the next step. And each of the consequent steps can be pulled out of context and made to stand as a complete explanation of a single development. The realization that initial conditions are a part of genetic explanations provides the foundation for an important caveat about the pattern. It is that the genetic pattern should not be thought of as an historical theory of society *a la* Spengler or Marx. That is, a genetic explanation merely states that, "At stage I, *A* happened, which because of events 1 and 2 at stage II, helped cause *B*, which because of events 3 and 4 at stage III, helped cause *C*." In other words, the explanation does not read, $A \rightarrow B \rightarrow C$, as it probably does in Marxian theory. This is because we are simply noting how a combination of conditions at each stage influenced the next stage. There is nothing inevitable about the outcome *C*, because events 1, 2, 3, and 4 did not *have* to happen (although of course they were caused).

COMBINATIONS OF PATTERNS

We have now identified six patterns of explanation and their subpatterns. Each was presented as an essentially pure pattern. That is, we analyzed a number of explanations as if each were only dispositional, only intentional, only system-maintaining, etc. However, practically speaking, one notices a great number of explanations in political science that are really combinations of patterns; in fact, perhaps most explanations are not pure, in the above sense. One could take the position that a pattern is characterized as dispositional, for instance, because dispositional laws are dominant but not exclusive; in other words, it is dispositional to a greater *degree*. In saying this, however, we should not overlook political science explanations that are "pure"; in short, this section is designed to refine or add to, not correct, the typology of patterns which has been presented in the previous section.

In discussing "combinations" of patterns, it should be realized that one of our patterns, the genetic, is naturally a mixture of sorts. We pointed out that the stages of a genetic explanation can be analytically viewed as a series of separate explanations. Thus, a dispositional explanation may account for the movement from one stage, and an intentional explanation the movement to the next. If a genetic explanation uses dispositional generalizations at each stage, it might be classified as both genetic and dispositional. The key point is, as we noted in the second chapter, that several criteria are being used to characterize patterns of explanation in political science. A dispositional explanation receives its label mainly because of the types of laws (and concepts contained in them) used to account for political phenomena; a genetic explanation, on the other hand, has a distinctive structure. This makes clear why the "combining" that characterizes the genetic pattern is somewhat different than the combination of, say, the dispositional and intentional patterns.

The system-maintaining pattern is distinctive in that it is characterized by the nature of its explananda or dependent variables, namely, the maintenance of systems. As we have seen, various sorts of laws can account for this phenomenon. Thus, for instance, dispositional or macro concepts can be cited as antecedent conditions for the maintenance of systems. It is trivial, then, to say that system-maintaining explanations employ different kinds of concepts. This is simply a reiteration of the assertion that our typology of patterns lacks a single distinguishing criteria.

If this last point is kept in mind, the discussion to follow will be more meaningful. We will examine several ways that patterns can be combined (in addition to the sequential combining which occurs in genetic explanations). First, and most obvious, the types of laws that characterize several patterns may be employed jointly to account for a single explanandum. Take for instance, V. O. Key's tentative explanation of the American two-party system. [56] He argues that instead of a single-factor explanation, "A more tenable assumption would be that several factors drive toward dualism on the American scene."[57] The factors he cites (with appropriate generalizations stated or implied) are: (1) the persistence of initial form—this implies both institutional and dispositional explanations; (2) the influence of institutional factors, such as the single-member district; (3) the existence of "systems of beliefs and attitudes"—this, of course, implies a dispositional explanation.

While disclaiming anything but a rough explanation sketch, Key has provided us with the structure of one type of combination-of-patterns explanation. Both dispositional and institutional factors lead to the explanandum. We should note at this point that several dispositional or institutional factors can be used in an explanation; in other words, a pure dispositional explanation can, and often will, cite several factors. But since we are talking about *combinations* of patterns, it seems legitimate to restrict the discussion as we have done. We are simply citing special cases of more general categories. More about this in a moment. The structure of an explanation such as Key's is, then, "Factor *A* (pattern *X*) and factor *B* (pattern *Y*) together account for *Z*." That is the combination of the factors is a sufficient condition for the occurrence of the two-party system.

Another way of combining patterns in an explanation is to relate several of them in one of several ways. That is, instead of showing how a number of factors independently come together to influence the explanandum, the political scientist often attempts to demonstrate how several variables *interact* to bring about the phenomenon to be explained. The simplest type in this category is characterized by a linking of several factors in a "causal chain." John H. Fenton and Kenneth N. Vines' explanation of why Negroes register more in southern than northern Louisiana is an

---

[56]V. O. Key, *Politics, Parties and Pressure Groups* (New York: Thomas Y. Crowell Co., 1958), pp. 227-31.

[57]*Ibid.*, p. 227.

example.[58] The explanandum is accounted for by the permissive-attitude differential between the two regions. The more permissive attitude of the southern area is in turn accounted for by an institutional property, the traditions of the Catholic Church, which is dominant in that area. The structure of the explanation is, then, "Registration because of attitudes; attitudes because of Catholic church." This might be thought of as a sort of genetic explanation, but it seems to us there is a difference. A genetic explanation is constructed of a series of distinct stages in temporal sequence. The "mixed" explanation under consideration is not characterized by such distinct stages. Correlations have been discovered between two sets of factors and they have been combined to explain the political behavior in question. Further-more, the implication is that the process continues to operate. In short there is structural difference between, "The Supreme Court is as it is today because *X* happened at stage I, which in turn caused *Y* to happen at stage II, etc." and "Negroes in southern Louisiana register more because the Catholic church lays the foundation for more permissive attitudes."

Besides "horizontal" causal chains, patterns may be combined in more complex arrangements. Thus dispositional, institutional, and intentional laws may interact in many complicated ways, determinable only by equally complicated statistical tests. A simple example of this sort is Robert Dahl's explanation of "why political influence is always distributed unevenly in political systems."[59] Dahl uses three factors, "the unequal distribution of resources, variation in the skill with which different individuals use their political resources, and the variations in the extent to which different individuals use their resources for political purposes." [60] These factors involve dispositions, intentions, and physical characteristics. While Dahl calls his explanation a causal chain, it differs from Fenton and Vines' in that it includes a notion of feedback. Thus, while differences in political skills and motiva-tions lead to differences in political influence, the latter in turn

---

[58]John H. Fenton and Kenneth N. Vines, "Negro Registration in Louisiana," *American Political Science Review*, Vol. LI, 1957, pp. 704-13.

[59]Robert A. Dahl, *Modern Political Analysis* (Englewood Cliffs, N.J.: Prentice-Hall, Inc., 1963), p. 17.

[60]*Ibid.*

helps determine the amounts of the former two factors. It can be seen, then, why such an explanation is more complex.

We have now distinguished three kinds of pattern-combination structures: the coming together of several independent variables; the arrangement of several variables in a causal chain; and the more complex arrangement of several variables, with provisions for interaction, feedback, etc.

8 Theories and models: Explanation and discovery

Among those activities which are probably essential to the development of a scientific discipline, two which seem especially interesting to political scientists are model-building and theory-construction. There are several reasons for analyzing them in the same chapter. On the one hand, models and theories are structurally and, up to a point, functionally similar. On the other hand, their similarity often leads to the, as we will argue, unwarranted conclusion that they are identical. For instance, the social scientist Herbert Simon once began a paper entitled "The Uses and Limitations of Models," with these words: "In contemporary usage the term 'model' is, I think simply a synonym for 'theory.' I am to speak, then, on 'Theories: Their Uses and Limitations.' "[1]

As a matter of fact, it is useful to make a methodological distinction between theories and models because, as they are used by political scientists, they have different purposes, and the failure to realize this difference can lead to confusion and perhaps even disillusionment. Thus, in addition to analyzing the nature of models and theories, each important in its own right, this chapter will attempt to demonstrate that the student of politics is aided in his studies if he understands the difference between them.

The distinction between models and theories is in many ways

---

[1] L. D. White, *The State of the Social Sciences* (Chicago: University of Chicago Press, 1956).

135

not a hard-and-fast one. However, given the normal activities of political scientists—all scientists, for that matter—the following proposition seems in order: theories are used *primarily* to *explain* political facts, models to *discover* then, This implies a more basic distinction between scientific *explanation* and *discovery*, a distinction which will be analyzed in more detail later in the chapter. At this point, let us simply keep in mind that how a political scientist develops a hypothesis (discovery), and how he goes about confirming and explaining it, are logically distinct activities.

THEORY

It might be useful to begin an analysis of scientific political theory with two distinctions, one important but often ignored, the other misleading yet widely circulated.

The first distinction points out that the "political theory" now under consideration is not the same as that venerable activity which often goes under the same name but which in Chapter 1 was labeled "political philosophy." Let us recall the normative character of political philosophy, its emphasis on *ought* questions; What *should* be the goals of the political system? What is the *best* political system? These activities can be contrasted with the scientific-empirical nature of political theory, that is, theory has to do with *is* questions. Confusion arises from the traditional interchangeability of "political philosophy" and "political theory." While an ever-increasing number of political scientists are accepting one form or another of the distinction we have mentioned here, the confusion lingers on. This is attributable not so much to the failure of political scientists to understand the nature of scientific theory, although this is one source of difficulty, as to the continued substitution of "theory" for "philosophy," based on the unquestioned assumption that the two refer to the same activity. It is our point that they don't; the subject of this section is *empirical* political theory not *normative* political philosophy.

A second distinction, the misleading one, is often made between "theory" and "practice." As manifested in the widely heard statement, "That's fine in theory, but it won't work in practice," it assumes that theory or theoretical thinking is false or unrealistic.

The student of political theory Arnold Brecht has put it another way: "The relation between practice and theory is well indicated in the popular saying that we learn best through 'trial and error.' Trial is practice; error refers to theory. When theory miscarries in practical trials it needs correction..."[2]

This chapter will attempt to demonstrate that there is no divorce in the above sense between theory and practice. Rather than being unrealistic or false, a *sound* theory is the basis for reliable knowledge of politics. Theories help us explain and predict political phenomena, and therefore, ultimately, to make well-founded practical decisions.

A second related and more sophisticated interpretation of the "theory vs. practice" distinction views the former as the result of speculation. Its catch-phrase is, "That's fine in theory, but will it work in practice?" The distinction is still a fundamental one, but "theory" is given a higher status. Now, at least, a theory is not necessarily false, for according to this interpretation it is in effect an elaborate hypothesis, a set of guesses to be tested. Thus to be theoretical is to be hypothetical, *potentially* true. While this view is more generous than the first, it too is misleading, in ways which will become more evident as we move along.

The nature of political theory

Having discussed what political theory is not, it is time to discuss what it is. There seem to be several variations on "theory" which are popular among political scientists. Quentin Gibson has given a definition of theory which is indeed basic: "Sets or systems of statements logically inter-connected in various complex ways."[3] In a similar vein, Nelson Polsby *et al.* have written that, "A scientific theory...is a deductive network of generalizations from which explanations or predictions of certain types of known events may be derived."[4] The simplest interpretation of theory,

---

[2]Arnold Brecht, *Political Theory* (Princeton, N.J.: Princeton University Press, 1959), p. 19.

[3]Quentin Gibson, *The Logic of Social Enquiry* (London: Routledge & Kegan Paul, 1960), p. 113.

[4]Nelson Polsby *et al* (eds.), *Politics and Social Life* (Boston: Houghton Mifflin Co., 1963), p. 69.

then, views it as a set of related empirical generalizations. Therefore, several generalizations about a particular area of politics can be classified as a theory. Take, for instance, the laws which have come out of the voting studies.[5] Since each law describes the relationship between a social, economic, political, or psychological variable and a type of voting act (men tend to vote more than women), the conjunction of several can explain in a more general way the voting behavior of Americans. Or one may view David Braybrooke's "miniature axiomatic system" as a theory, at least a potential theory, of party behavior.[6] It is an attempt to organize and relate a number of generalizations from the literature of party behavior, the objective being the development of a systematic theory.

The notion of political theory as a collection of empirical generalizations about a particular field or subject is a popular one among many political scientists. To others it represents a simplified version of that interpretation of theory which is more commonly accepted by the scientific community at large. According to this interpretation, a theory is characterized by the use of theoretical constructs about which we have spoken in Chapter 5. Thus, a theory might be defined as, "A set of generalizations containing concepts with which we are directly acquainted and those which are operationally defined; but in addition, and more important, theoretical concepts that although not directly tied to observation are logically related to those concepts that are." This provides the basis for a distinction between theories and empirical generalizations. While the latter can be empirically tested (confirmed or rejected), because their concepts are directly tied to observation, we can't test *in the same way* a generalization which contains theoretical (or, by definition, nonobservable) concepts. However, this is not to say, as we will see, that theories cannot be tested and evaluated.

Despite their characteristic use of theoretical concepts, sound

---

[5]See, for instance, the list of propositions in Bernard R. Berelson *et al., Voting* (Chicago: University of Chicago Press, 1954), Appendix A. This, of course, does not include the significant generalizations developed in Angus Campbell *et al., The American Voter* (New York: John Wiley & Sons, Inc., 1960).

[6]David Braybrook, "An Illustrative Miniature Axiomatic System," in Polsby, *op. cit.,* pp. 119-29.

theories are empirical. We can say that a scientific theory has two features, one structural, the other substantive; one referring to the relationship between its concepts, the other to its empirical content. Carl Hempel has provided a more technical description of the elements of scientific theory: "Any...scientific theory may be conceived of as consisting of an uninterpreted, deductively developed system and of an interpretation which confers empirical import upon the terms and sentences of the latter."[7] We might begin, for instance, with a purely formal logical system such as Euclidean geometry, in which concepts are implicitly or internally defined, and then directly define (tie to observables) *some* of its concepts. This would then give the other concepts, those we have labeled theoretical, indirect empirical import. There is a difference, then, between an uninterpreted mathematical or logical system and a scientific theory, and the difference is the latter's empirical nature. Ernest Nagel makes this point, along with several other significant points, in the following passage: "It is clear...that if a theory is to explain experimental laws, it is not sufficient that its terms be only implicitly defined. Unless something further is added to indicate how its implicitly defined terms are related to ideas occurring in experimental laws, a theory cannot be significantly affirmed or denied and in any case is scientifically useless."[8]

The functions of theories

Since theories are empirical, they can be evaluated according to their soundness. A close analysis of a proposed theory should indicate whether it is properly constructed and empirically based. But perhaps a more fruitful approach to the nature of scientific theory is through an examination of the functions it performs, for one way to evaluate a theory is to determine how well it is doing what it is expected to do. Several comments have already suggested that a theory's major function is explanation—to explain singular facts and occurrences, but perhaps more importantly to

[7]Carl G. Hempel, *Fundamentals of Concept Formation in Empirical Science* (Chicago: University of Chicago Press, 1952), p. 34.

[8]Ernest Nagel, *The Structure of Science* (New York: Harcourt, Brace & World, Inc., 1961), p. 93.

explain empirical generalizations. This latter function is what gives the scientific theory its power.

Very briefly, a theory can explain empirical generalizations because it is more general, more inclusive than they are. The great power of Newtonian mechanics, demonstrated over the centuries, is based upon the ability of a rather small set of theoretical laws to explain a great number of empirical laws about bullets, missiles, and other moving objects. "Explain" here means, following the logic of the last chapter, that the empirical generalizations are deductively implied by the theory. The same situation could exist in political science, although at the present moment it is misleading to talk about an existing theory of politics (in the second, more sophisticated sense of theory). Let us suppose that general stimulus-response learning theory[9] is able to explain a wide range of empirical laws, all the way from the voting behavior of individuals to the military activity of nation-states. The point is, once again, that if learning theory were a sound theory of political behavior, a set of general laws using such theoretical concepts as "demand" and "habit" would explain or imply a number of generalizations which previously had appeared to be independent, or at least not closely related.

This implies that in one sense a theory is not to be judged true or false, but more or less useful as an explainer of empirical laws. Since laws describe our knowledge in a particular field, the sound theory explains the knowledge more generally and completely, indicating to us the interconnection between seemingly isolated facts.

In taking this position, we cannot overlook a controversy which exists among philosophers of science over the status of theories.[10] Some say they are true or verified in the sense that empirical laws are. That is, they are real descriptions of the world of observation. This position, usually labeled the *realist,* recognizes no logical or philosophical distinction between theoretical and nontheoretical concepts since they both refer to *real* entities. The opposing school of thought, the *instrumentalist,* takes another position, closer to one we adopted in the last paragraph. Briefly, it argues

---

[9]See Chapter 10 for an analysis of learning theory.

[10]For a thorough discussion of this controversy see Abraham Kaplan *The Conduct of Inquiry* (San Francisco: Chandler Publishing Co., 1964), Chapter 8.

that there is no point in trying to determine whether a theory is true or false, since it is neither. It does not describe the world, but rather explains or predicts worldly phenomena. A theory is tested according to how well it performs its major functions; thus the label "instrumental." This is approximately how we characterized "theory." However, the strict instrumentalist's complete rejection of the reality of theories is questionable. For while a theory contains theoretical concepts, it is also tied to observation through an empirical interpretation. Thus it *more or less* describes the world. The theoretical concepts fill in the gaps and allow the theory to explain in more general terms that which has been explained by individual empirical laws.

Lurking behind explanation is another function of theories. Scientists use theories to organize, systematize, and coordinate existing knowledge in a particular area or field. According to the first notion of theory, a set of related empirical generalization, a theory is in itself a systematization. A theory of voting behavior would be a set of relevant generalizations which have been collected and put into logical juxtaposition. According to the higher level notion of theory, a theory organizes as it explains. As several diverse generalizations are accounted for by the theoretical propositions of the theory, they are also related and made parts of a system of knowledge. "Lurking behind" was an appropriate choice of words because the organizational function is a consequence of the explanatory function.

Theories explain and organize existent knowledge. They also suggest potential knowledge by generating hypotheses. A theory can, on the basis of its highly abstract generalizations, often predict an empirical generalization—predict that a particular relationship holds. The hypothesis can then be tested and accepted or rejected. Thus it can be said that in addition to its explanatory and organizational functions, theory has an heuristic one—to suggest, to generate hypotheses.

The place of theory in political science

In determining the role of theory in political science, we ought to keep in mind the two notions of theory, for a different conclusion may be arrived at in regard to each. The first question which confronts us is, Do we have any scientific theories in political science? From what has been said in this chapter, the answer would appear to be no, if we are talking about the higher level notion of theory. But if this is the case, is there any point in spending time talking about theories? There are probably other methodological topics more significant to contemporary political scientists, is one reply. While, because of limited resources and time, there is some wisdom in this position, it is perhaps too restrictive. For even without a sound scientific theory in hand, the political scientist is not wasting his time if he takes an interest in theory-construction. That is, there is a payoff in asking such questions as, What would we have if we had a sound high-level theory? What would be its structure and what functions would it perform? And then, given the characteristics of scientific theory, are there any potential or near-theories awaiting further development in the literature of political science? The first set of questions has been touched upon in this chapter; the last question is one which will be of some relevance to the more substantive analyses contained in Part Three.

If "theory" means a collection of empirical generalizations, then our answer to the original question about the existence of political theories can be more generous. For there are theories, or at least near-theories, of certain kind of political behavior— consider once again our knowledge of voting behavior. Finally, let us recall the relationship between the lower and higher level notions of scientific theory. The implication is that a collection of laws can serve as the foundation of an abstract theory. Thus, if the higher level notion is accepted as the standard of theory, the collected laws of voting behavior can be legitimately classified as a near-theory. In any case, the condition of theory in political science is not as bleak as might appear, although at this point in the discipline's development the political scientist's time and effort might be more profitably spent on pretheoretical activities, such as those discussed in Chapters 5 and 6.

MODELS

The philosopher of science May Brodbeck notes in answer to the question, "What exactly is a model and what purposes does it serve? I venture to suggest that ten model builders will give at least five different, or at least, apparently different answers to this question."[11] It is probably the case, then, that definitions of "model" are so numerous that we cannot mention all of them. However, there is one notion of "model" which does merit initial consideration. It is more rigorous than the others and usually serves as their foundation, often in a very indirect way. However, as we will see, in its fully developed form this notion of "model" is not the most widely accepted (or even recognized) in political science.

The technical, or what might be called the professionally acceptable, meaning of model is based on the notion of "isomorphism," which in simplest terms refers to the similarity between one thing and another (its model). More technically, isomorphism requires: (1) that "there must be a one-to-one correspondence between the elements of the model and the elements of the thing of which it is the model," and (2) that "certain relations are preserved."[12] Models of this sort are found in all areas of life (i.e., scale-model airplanes); in science the isomorphism is usually thought to hold between two theories, or more explicitly, their laws. This is what we will take as the core meaning of "model." If the elements (generalizations or concepts) of one theory are in one-to-one correspondence to those of another theory and the required relations hold, the one may be called a model of the other.

This meaning of "model"—an isomorphism between two empirical theories—is for all purposes nonexistent in political science; the reason is clearly the lack of any sound scientific theories of politics. However, following May Brodbeck, we can mention another notion of "model" that also involves isomorphism, this time between an empirical theory (in the sense of a set of empirical generalizations) and a set of purely arithmetical truths. "If this is the case, then the latter is called an arithmetical

---

[11]May Brodbeck, "Models, Meanings and Theories," in Leonard Gross (ed.), *Symposium on Sociological Theory* (Evanston, Ill.: Row & Peterson, 1959), p. 374.
[12]*Ibid.*

representation of the empirical theory."[13] This meaning may be more relevant to political science, largely because of the increasing use of game theory, which may be considered as such an "arithmetical representation." We will have more to say about this later in this chapter and in Chapter 11.

Besides these isomorphic models, there are, as Brodbeck notes, several other common usages of the term, none of them directly involving isomorphisms.[14] (1) "Any as yet untested or even untestable theory may be dubbed a 'model.'"[15] (2) "Model" may also be used to refer to abstracted theories, like those about "economic man." (3) Theories making use of "ideal" entities such as perfectly straight lines are often called models. (4) When numbers can be attached to the concepts of a theory, it is often called a model. Brodbeck calls these uses of "model" unnecessary. However, it would seem that they, or combinations and variations of them, are what political scientists have in mind when they use the term "model." For instance, in speaking of the model-building activity, William Riker writes, "The essential feature of this method is the creation of a theoretical construct that is a somewhat simplified version of what the real world to be described is believed to be like."[16] Riker's idea of model doesn't appear to emphasize an isomorphic relationship; this is the key point. Rather, he, along with many other political scientists, uses "model" in the idealizing and abstracting sense mentioned by Brodbeck (usages two and three).

The basic argument of this section, that models are unlike theories in that they do not explain, assumes that "model" means either arithmetical representations or idealized or abstracted theories in the general sense we just described. Isomorphism of theories will not be considered because, as we have already noted, there are few if any theories in political science. Some might say we are subverting the "real" meaning of model. However, we are primarily interested in what political scientists attempt to do with models. Furthermore, even the "subverted" notions of model are

---

[13]*Ibid.*
[14]*Ibid.*, p. 381ff.
[15]*Ibid.*, p. 381.
[16]William Riker, *The Theory of Political Coalitions* (New Haven, Conn.: Yale University Press, 1962), p. 7.

remotely based on isomorphisms. An idealization or simplification of something is in a sense a rough isomorphism, because the former resembles the latter to a greater or lesser degree. Perhaps a way out of this controversy is to substitute another word for "model"; "conceptual scheme" is one in widespread use. Thus "model" would be saved for those cases in which there is an isomorphism between theories. However, because most political scientists continue to use "model," we will also.

The use and misuse of models

Our argument begins with the realization that those political scientists who construct models often characterize them as unrealistic or idealized. In fact, this seems to be the most popular use of "model" or "conceptual scheme" in political science (although it diverges from the more technical meaning). While asserting its idealized nature, the political scientist will often attempt to use his model to explain phenomena. Or, more accurately, the creator of a model will realize its limitations as an explanatory device, but those who come after and use the model for their own purposes are prone to make more extravagant claims about its explanatory usefulness. Our point is that these claims, in their extravagance, are unfounded.

We will now attempt to show why the function of models is not to explain. Let us first consider arithmetical representations. Our primary example will be game theory, since it is one of the most popular and promising models in political science. Game theory is arithmetic because it defines rationality—maximizing one's gains and minimizing one's losses—in terms of the probability calculus and set theory. It is supposedly isomorphic because the political scientist attempts to connect it to laws about political behavior. In this regard, Anthony Downs has provided a model of party politics,[17] William Riker of coalition formation,[18] and L. S. Shapley and Martin Shubik of power in a committee system.[19] However, as May Brodbeck has noted, "The trick for the social

---

[17]Anthony Downs, *An Economic Theory of Democracy* (New York: Harper & Row, 1957).

[18]Riker, *op. cit.*

[19]L. S. Shapley and Martin Shubik, "A Method For Evaluating the Distribution of Power in a Committee System," *American Political Science Review*, Vol. XLVIII, 1954.

scientist...is to find appropriate descriptive terms which when coordinated to the arithmetical ones result in true empirical laws of human behavior."[20] We would argue that, thus far, the confirmed empirical laws have not been discovered. But more importantly, the model-builders usually admit that their models are unrealistic. For instance, Anthony Downs says of his model of rational decision making, "The model is not an attempt to describe reality accurately. Like all theoretical constructs in the social sciences, it treats a few variables as crucial and ignores others which actually have some influence."[21] Notice that besides the model's isomorphic nature (not obvious from this quote) there is reference to idealizing and abstraction. Returning to our central point, even while admitting that his model is unreal, Downs claims that, "It proposes a single hypothesis to *explain* government decision-making and party behavior in general."[22] And at another point he argues that, "Theoretical models should be tested primarily by the accuracy of their predictions rather than by the reality of their assumptions."[23] Our criticism of Downs' argument is a statement of our rejection of models' (as the term is used by most political scientists) explanatory powers. It is that in admitting that his model is ideal, unreal, etc., Downs has articulated its inability to explain political phenomena. Constructing a theory of rational behavior and then stating that no one really behaves rationally undercuts the model's explanatory value.

At this point we can draw several preliminary conclusions about models and explanation. In the first place, attempts to make arithmetic theories, such as game theory, models of actual political behavior force the political scientist to frame unrealistic assumptions. In admitting that his model does not fit the real world, the model-builder admits, consciously or not, its lack of explanatory power. A mathematical model such as game theory can explain only if the actual political world operates in accordance with it—if the two are isomorphic.

Furthermore, models such as game theory contain *idealizations* referring to "rational" political behavior. Insofar as they are

---

20Brodbeck, *op. cit.,* p. 391.
21Downs, *op. cit.,* p. 3.
22*Ibid.,* p. 33.
23*Ibid.,* p. 21.

unreal—because they leave out variables—they cannot explain. May Brodbeck has said of such ideal types in economics, "The better the theory, the more knowledge we have about the conditions under which the neglected variables do or do not make a difference. If there are no economic men or if the ideal type of capitalism does not exist, then certain suggested theories are false. Calling them models will not make them truer."[24] Here we reach the heart of the matter. As Brodbeck implies, the formulators of such models often use them as if they were theories; in other words they confuse models with theories.

Let us recall the nature of scientific theory. If a theory is viewed as a system of related empirical generalizations, then we must conclude that models are not theories, for the former are not constituted of confirmed empirical generalizations. And since confirmed generalizations are essential to explanation, models cannot be granted the same explanatory status as theories. However, what about the more refined and probably more widely held conception which views a theory as a system of generalizations containing directly observable and operationally defined concepts, but in addition theoretical concepts which although not observable are logically related to those that are? Are the idealizations and speculations of models logically similar to theoretical concepts? This is the crux of the issue; for if they are, then it would seem that theories are not entitled to a superior explanatory status.

Our answer is that idealized concepts which are admittedly unreal cannot be equated with theories which contain theoretical concepts. A theoretical concept is so labeled, not because it is divorced from reality, but because it is derived from observational terms within a theory: "Theoretical notions cannot be understood apart from the particular theory that implicitly defines them."[25] Furthermore, to be explanatory, such a theory must have some empirical content, so that the theoretical constructs are linked, at least indirectly, to observational phenomena. In this sense, the theoretical concepts are not nonempirical, idealized, or admittedly unreal, but instead not observable; they fit within the empirical theory.

---

[24]Brodbeck, *op. cit.*
[25]Nagel, *op. cit.*, p. 87.

Thus we see that a model (in the idealizing sense) is not an empirical theory. Idealized concepts are not equivalent to theoretical concepts. Insofar as they are ideal they are unreal. Note, also, that an unreal assumption about political rationality is not analogous to a theory such as the ideal gas theories, which use the zero point of a variable. For in the case of the latter, the laws of the theory are extrapolated for the zero value of a variable; variables are not intentionally left out. "The scientist uses these imaginary 'zero' notions when theorizing in order to predict how *other* properties of such entities...are connected, assuming the one is absent."[26] The gist of all this is that empirically sound theories refer to experience; thus they can explain experience. If a mathematical model is truly isomorphic with a segment of political phenomena, then it will have empirical referents, and so be able to explain; at this point, following our usage, it becomes a theory.

We have now argued that models, as they are usually construed by political scientists, do not explain as theories can; this includes both notions of theory—a set of related observational-empirical laws, or a set of theoretical laws. But, in criticizing the assumption that models in political science explain, we have not meant to detract from their overall scientific value. For models such as game theory can be of heuristic value. It is not difficult to see how. If the political scientist is trying to accumulate basic knowledge in his field, it probably helps to have something available which stimulates his imagination and sharpens his insight. These functions are admirably performed by some models. If the model is a simplified interpretation of reality, the researcher is forced to consider what the situation would be like if the model did describe reality and to what extent the model is unreal. If the model is based on a formal theory such as game theory, he has a host of relationships suggested which can be tested. If a model of politics is based upon a structure or theory in another area, a biological model for instance, the researcher has a potentially rich supply of hypotheses generated as he compares his field with the other.

The reason for our earlier assertion that all models are basically isomorphic now comes to the surface. Actually, models in political

---

[26]Brodbeck, *op. cit.*, p. 382.

science are suggestive primarily because they are representations of something else. The heuristic use of models generally takes the following form: we observe theory or system A; we see certain similarities between it and our own area of interest, B (they appear to be isomorphic to some extent); so, we begin to wonder if some of the relationships which hold in A also hold in B. We recognize that certain adjustments and additions are probably necessary, but at least the model we derive from A will provide a basis for the formulation of hypotheses and the organization of our study of politics. It is at this point that the "familiarity" argument which we rejected in Chapter 7 as a sound criteria for explanations becomes relevant. If we use a familiar system, let us say the game of poker, to organize our study of an unfamiliar situation or area, international politics for instance, then progress has been made. The model, in this case simple game theory, opens the door.

The distinction between the explanatory and heuristic value of theories and models is based upon the more fundamental distinction between scientific justification and discovery. Let us explicate the latter a little more fully in order to demonstrate its relevance to our main thesis. Throughout our analysis of the nature of generalizations and explanation and the function of theories in political inquiry, we have been dealing with scientific justification, the relationship of evidence to explananda. As we have seen, this is amenable to logical analysis. There are methods of distinguishing between a good and a bad explanation or no explanation at all, between a sound or unsound theory, and between an acceptable and unacceptable generalization. Scientific discovery, on the other hand, has to do with how scientists find out about scientific facts. This has to do to a large extent with the psychology of scientists, and is therefore an activity which emphasizes creativity. Hans Reichenbach has succinctly summarized the character of discovery: "The act of discovery escapes logical analysis; there are no logical rules in terms of which a 'discovery machine' could be constructed that would take over the creative function of genius."[27] It is clear, then, in which context heuristic models are the most at home.

---

[27]Hans Reichenbach, *The Rise of Scientific Philosophy* (Berkeley: University of California Press, 1951), p. 231. Reichenbach analyzes the two scientific activities in greater depth in *Experience and Prediction* (Chicago: University of Chicago Press, 1938).

If models are mainly of heuristic value, if their primary function within the scientific enterprise is to suggest relationships between concepts—to generate hypotheses—then they belong in the realm of scientific discovery and not explanation. This is our major conclusion. The objective of our analysis has not been to question the importance of models but only to point out that they have a different role to play in the development of scientific knowledge. And given the fact that there are few if any developed theories of politics, the significance of any device which does suggest possible relationships cannot be exaggerated.

Models and other heuristic devices in political science

We have evaluated game theory in very general terms as a model of politics. But there are others less explicit and more speculative. Part Three, which begins with the next chapter, is a discussion of some of the more popular and promising models, conceptual schemes, or approaches used in the study of politics. But we will consider a few models here to make the argument more meaningful. Several are rough attempts at isomorphism, while others are idealized models or conceptual schemes. Their inability to explain, often realized by their creators, will become obvious, but their possible heuristic value will also be noted.

Kenneth Boulding has examined several models of social conflict. He labels two of them the "ecological" model and "epidemiological" model.[28] The former draws attention to "the similarity between the conflict of groups in human society and the competition of species in biological ecosystems."[29] The latter compares the spread of contagious diseases through a population to certain types of group conflict, such as conversion.[30] Boulding cites parts of Lewis F. Richardson's "process model" of international conflict to illustrate the epidemiological model.[31] The

---

[28]Kenneth Boulding, *Conflict and Defense: A General Theory* (New York: Harper & Row, 1962), especially Chapters 6 and 7.

[29]*Ibid.*, p. 123.

[30]*Ibid.*, p. 124.

[31]*Ibid.* Richardson's main published works are *Arms and Insecurity* (Pittsburg: Boxwood Press, 1960), and *Statistics of Deadly Quarrels* (Chicago: Quadrangle Press, 1960).

chapters that Boulding devotes to these models are, in the main, provocative discussions of suggestive similarities between different systems of phenomena. No explanations or potential explanations are forthcoming. This Boulding admits. "In applying simple mechanical models such as we have explored in this and in previous chapters to the enormously complex dynamics of conflict in society, we should look for insights rather than for exact correspondences."[32] The key word is "insights," for it manifests the heuristic emphasis of model-building.

More ambitious claims have been made by some social scientists interested in "general systems theory."[33] The comparing of systems of social behavior with chemical systems and biological systems, for instance, seems to some to lay the foundations for explanations. "As we observed earlier, models and theories are never perfect but simply approach the limit of correct explanation..."[34] But we would argue that the mere noting of similarities between "systems" explains nothing. Analogies and metaphors are often enlightening, but they account for no facts. Once again, we return to the heuristic value of models. Anatol Rapaport has written in this regard, "Metaphor and analogy, although they cannot be accepted as scientific 'explanations' are sometimes important aids in the sense that they prepare the mind to make more precise investigations."[35] This applies as well to the much more sophisticated systems analyses of political scientists such as David Eston.[36]

There is another kind of model-building in political science that is seemingly remote from isomorphic analysis. It is characterized instead by idealized sets of assumptions about given areas of political phenomena. As we implied at the beginning of this section, this activity is perhaps the most prevalent of those that go under the name of "model-building." A sophisticated example, the

---

[32]Boulding, *op. cit.,* p. 137.

[33]One attempt to apply general systems theory to the study of society is James G. Miller, "Toward A General Theory for the Behavioral Sciences," *American Psychologist,* Vol. X, 1955, pp. 513-31.

[34]*Ibid.,* p. 531.

[35]Anatol Rapaport, "Various Meanings of 'Theory,' " *American Political Science Review,* Vol. LII, 1958, p. 984.

[36]David Eston, *A Framework of Political Analysis* (Englewood Cliffs, N.J.: Prentice-Hall, Inc., 1965).

decision-making approach of Richard C. Snyder and Glenn D. Paige, will be discussed in Chapter 10.[37] Less elaborate models, this time of party systems, are analyzed by Samuel Eldersveld. [38] He clearly uses them in a heuristic fashion to suggest relationships that can be tested.

As we already implied, some political scientists call the kind of model we have just been discussing a "conceptual scheme." The term seems to imply a set of ideal assumptions about a given subject area. Thus William C. Mitchell has said in introducing his own "structural-functional" conceptual scheme: "A conceptual scheme or framework is an essential tool in all scientific investigation for it provides the elementary concepts, assumption, ideas, and directives that guide the selection and interpretation of facts."[39] Once again it can be seen that models or conceptual schemes are more important for their suggestiveness than their explanatory power.

In addition to idealized or speculative models, there are other heuristic techniques, strategies of discovery in political science which are sometimes thought to be explanatory. We will conclude this chapter with a brief discussion of some of these. This will, hopefully, clarify the heuristic nature of models and indicate that there are alternatives available. A popular heuristic device is *Verstehen* or empathic understanding.[40] According to its users *Verstehen* suggests possible relationships by somehow "getting into" other people's heads in order to speculate about how others would behave in certain situations. There are several related techniques of discovery in political inquiry. Consider, for instance, the method of constructing "alternative futures" practiced by Herman Kahn.[41] Kahn has sketched out several realistic world societies of the 1970's in order to examine the possibilities

[37]Richard C. Snyder and Glenn D. Paige, "The Decision-Making Approach to the Study of International Politics," in James N. Rosenau (ed.), *International Politics and Foreign Policy* (New York: Free Press, 1961), pp. 186-92.

[38]Samuel Eldersveld, *Political Parties: A Behavioral Analysis* (Chicago: Rand McNally, 1964), especially Part III.

[39]William C. Mitchell, *The American Policy* (New York: Free Press, 1962), p. 3.

[40]For a methodological critique, see Theodore Abel, "The Operation Called *Verstehen*," in Herbert Feigl and May Brodbeck (eds.), *Readings in the Philosophy of Science* (New York: Appleton-Century-Crofts, 1953), pp. 677-87.

[41]Herman Kahn, "Alternative World Futures," (Hudson Institute, 1964). Also see *On Thermonuclear War* (Princeton, N.J.: Princeton University Press, 1960).

of nuclear war and other types of international behavior. This "as if" speculation is clearly not predictive, but rather suggestive.

A strategy which is somewhat similar to "as if" speculation but probably more empirically grounded has been described by Alexander George: "The analyst rehearses in his mind the different possible versions of a missing piece, trying to decide which version is more plausible, given the values of the pieces already known to him."[42] This might be interpreted as the first step toward theory *building*, but note that it has to do with the *discovery*, not justification, of facts.

A more sophisticated yet less widespread heuristic technique is the mathematical and logical demonstration that a given type of political behavior is logically possible. This is usually done in regard to rational political behavior. For instance, William Riker has shown, by means of mathematical reasoning, that "Congress may act irrationally and probably does so occasionally."[43] Riker defines rationality as transitivity of preferences and then presents a mathematical proof that shows how congressional preferences can be intransitive.[44] Thus, this scientific technique indicates to the political scientist that certain political outcomes are logically possible and so are potential explananda.

We will consider one more heuristic strategy in political inquiry. It is the increasingly employed technique of simulation.[45] In a "simulation" run, an artificial political situation is fabricated or an actual situation is reproduced, and either individuals act out political roles or a computer makes a series of decisions based on data and decision-criteria that have been programmed into it.[46] The result in either case is a possible outcome, given the data.

---

[42]Alexander George, "Prediction of Political Action by Means of Propaganda Analysis," in Polsby *et al.,op. cit.,* p. 850.

[43]William H. Riker, "Voting Methods and Irrationality in Legislative Decisions," in John C. Wahlke and Heinz Eulau (eds.), *Legislative Behavior* (Glencoe, Ill.: Free Press, 1959), pp. 97-108.

[44]The basic work in this area is Kenneth Arrow, *Social Choice and Individual Values* (New York: John Wiley & Sons, Inc., 1951). Also see Robert A. Dahl, *A Preface to Democratic Theory* (Chicago: University of Chicago Press, 1956), pp. 41-42.

[45]A good book of readings on simulation is Harold Guetzkow (ed.), *Simulation in Social Science: Readings* (Englewood Cliffs, N.J.: Prentice-Hall, Inc., 1962).

[46]For an example of the latter type of simulation study see Ithiel deSola Pool *et al.,Candidates, Issues and Strategies* (Cambridge, Mass.: M. I. T. Press, 1964).

Simulation is important both in producing such possible outcomes and in providing hypotheses about how decisions are made.

The analysis of this chapter has attempted to draw a distinction between explanatory theories and heuristic models, a distinction based on the difference between scientific justification and discovery. Part Three will devote more time to the latter. The next few chapters will examine a number of approaches, ways of organizing our study of politics, which are to some extent more or less sophisticated models and to some extent potential theories of politics.

Part Three

APPROACHES TO THE STUDY OF POLITICS

9 Approaches to the study of politics

An approach, in political inquiry, is a general strategy for studying political phenomena. The next seven chapters examine some of the most important approaches in contemporary political science. This chapter introduces that examination. Approaches are formulated and used for a number of reasons. They can function at both heuristic and explanatory levels. That is, an approach might provide the framework for, or even take the form of, a model or conceptual scheme or it might serve as the impetus for the development of a theory of politics. Thus, in evaluating an approach, we will consider its promise as an explanatory or potentially explanatory device.

A tentative answer which anticipates our analysis of specific approaches is that they are of more heuristic than explanatory value. That is, an approach is probably used most often to suggest hypotheses which can then be tested. Approaches to the study of politics are therefore more an aspect of scientific discovery than of explanation. Part Three, then, meshes with the second section of Chapter 8 because of the close *functional* ties between models and approaches. In many instances, the two labels are synonymous.

However, this does not mean that approaches are never of explanatory value. As we have already suggested, they may stimulate the formulation of theories. There is, in addition, a lower level explanatory function of approaches which is related to their heuristic functions. In suggesting hypotheses, an approach might be instrumental in generating an explanation sketch or perhaps even a partial explanation of a political phenomenon without providing the foundation for a theory.

In this regard, it is clear that approaches and patterns of explanation overlap to some extent. This is not surprising when we realize that both approaches and patterns attempt to deal with the world as it is. If, for instance, dispositions are *as a matter of fact* a significant kind of political variable, then we would expect there to be dispositional approaches and a dispositional pattern of explanation.

However, while there is overlap in content and function, the notions of pattern and approach refer to different methodological entities. A classification of patterns describes the kinds of concepts political scientists use to explain and the forms nomological explanation can take. Approaches, on the other hand, are attempts to develop strategies for directing the research activities of the political scientist.

What is an approach to the study of politics? We have given some general answers, but now a few more specific ones can be suggested. But it must be noted that a full-blown answer is possible only after a more thorough examination of actual approaches has been made.

An approach may involve the attempt to locate an organizing concept or set of concepts that can orient research and coordinate empirical data from several sources. We might say that an approach is designed to include as wide a range of political phenomena as possible within a single set of concepts. The political scientist then has to determine how much scope his conceptual scheme has and how much revision is required if it is to include an even wider range. Or he may realize that it applies only to a limited range. This activity involves both conceptual analysis and empirical research, as the conceptual scheme is refined and expanded upon or reduced in scope. In the process the political scientist will be able to organize his study and will hopefully have hypotheses suggested to him. The ultimate success would be the generation of an empirical theory.

There are certain characteristics which all approaches have in common: all make assumptions which to some extent shape the political scientist's analysis and research. In addition, every approach assumes and makes use of nomological relationships.

These can take several forms. In the most general sense, they are either verified or verifiable empirical generalizations, or intentionally unrealistic assumptions used to generate hypotheses which are verifiable.

Let us now describe the substance of Part Three in light of what we have just said. Some of the approaches to be examined are more highly developed than others. Some are broad conceptual schemes, while others are narrower models revolving around a single central concept. Some are to a large extent sets of empirical generalizations, while others are formal models. In every case we will use the dual criteria of suggestive and explanatory usefulness to evaluate them.

The organization of Part Three can be viewed as a continuum of levels of analysis. The idea is one of cutting into politics at a number of points in order to examine different slices of political life. Thus, on the face of it, no approach is right or wrong; but some may be more useful than others. Because we do not have a finely honed knife available, there is some overlap between the approaches. But there are differences to be drawn which are meaningful for the political scientist.

We begin with those approaches which make the individual and his psychological characteristics the center of attention. Chapter 10 deals with approaches which emphasize dispositional, and those which emphasize intentional, behavior. The most highly developed variety of each, learning theory (dispositional) and decision-making theory (intentional) are analyzed. Chapter 11 considers approaches based on the concept of rationality viewed as a characteristic of individuals in a political system. This includes an analysis of the most fully formulated rational model of politics, game theory.

The discussion then moves to an approach which considers the individual in political roles. Chapter 12 analyzes role theory. The concept of role is viewed as a link between individualistic and group approaches.

Chapter 13 analyzes the group approach, and so moves away from the individual to the group as the central concept of political science.

Approaches which stay at the level of political systems are the topic of Chapter 14. The main part of the analysis focuses on the most important offshoot of systems theory, functionalism, which bases its approach to the study of politics on the functions of political systems.

Chapter 15 considers an aspect of political systems which is attracting the attention of more and more political scientists, namely, communication. Communications theory asserts that any approach to the study of politics is incomplete without a consideration of how political information is transmitted within and between political systems.

One of the most important concepts in political science is the topic of Chapter 16. Power is viewed both as one significant aspect of political systems and as a centralizing concept for organizing the study of politics.

10 *Individualistic-psychological approaches*

Vernon Van Dyke has written: "The basic point about political phenomena is that they consist of or result from the actions of human beings."[1] It would seem difficult to deny, no matter what one's philosophical position, individualism or holism, that humans are the fundamental stuff of politics. Groups are composed of individuals; so are political institutions. Whether he is working at the macro or micro level, with individual political actors or large nation-states, the political scientist will be concerned with human behavior in one form or another. Therefore, it seems proper to consider first those approaches which focus upon concepts referring directly to human characteristics.

This kind of approach is perhaps more closely identified with behavioralism than most others, because it deals with behavior through the use of psychological and sociological concepts. Furthermore, it probably grounds more than its share of low-level, narrow-gauged theories of politics.

Speaking in the most general terms, there are three individualistic approaches to the study of politics. The first concentrates upon those human characteristics which are usually called *dispositions:* included in this category are attitudes, opinions, and personality traits. The second bases its examination of politics upon *intentional* behavior, that is, the conscious seeking of goals

---

[1] Vernon Van Dyke, *Political Science: A Philosophical Analysis* (Stanford, Calif.: Stanford University Press, 1960), p. 23.

161

by political actors. One type of intentional action can be characterized as *rational*, that is, attempting to achieve a goal in the most efficient manner possible. This constitutes a third type of approach.

Dispositional and intentional approaches—including the most highly developed representative of each, learning theory and decision-making theory, respectively—will be analyzed in this chapter. The rational approach, with its increasingly popular offspring, game theory, is the subject of the next chapter. We will examine and evaluate the basic assumptions and methodological foundations of each approach. The critical questions underlying this evaluation are, How suggestive is the approach as a heuristic device? and, What are its prospects as an explanatory theory, or at least as the core of a theory of politics? These, of course, are questions we will ask of every approach.

DISPOSITIONAL APPROACHES

Political thinkers of the past, including Plato, Aristotle, and Hobbes, recognized that if one is to understand political phenomena he has to study human nature. They consequently spent much time speculating about the nature of man and its relationship to politics. But it was not until 1908, when the English political thinker Graham Wallas refuted rationalism and intellectualism in political analysis and emphasized unconscious attitudes, that the groundwork was laid for dispositional approaches to political phenomena.[2] While primitive, his work is all the more important because it provided an impetus to the scientific study of politics. But of primary relevance here are his insightful remarks about the dispositional approach. If one were able, Wallas argues, to photograph a man's activities for an entire day and then present him with the film, "He would, of course, see that much of his activities consisted in the half-conscious repetition, under the influence of habit, of movements which were orginally more fully conscious. But even if all cases of habit were excluded he would

---

[2]Graham Wallas, *Human Nature in Politics* (Lincoln: University of Nebraska Press, 1962).

find that only a small proportion of the residue could be explained as being directly produced by an intellectual calculation."[3]

This plea to emphasize dispositions in political analysis did not fall upon deaf ears. Since Wallas wrote his groundbreaking book *Human Nature in Politics*, social scientists have done much to advance our understanding of dispositions, and many have opted for their use in the explanation of political phenomena. For instance, the political scientist Robert Lane has written: "Explanations of political decisions which rely wholly upon analyses of the social environment, while they may have high predictive value, neglect a vital link; they never explain why an individual responds to the environment the way he does."[4] It is this link which interests us here.

The nature of dispositions

A disposition is a tendency to respond in a certain way in a given situation. To say that a man has the attitudinal disposition, that is, the attitude "Democratic" means that when asked, "With which party do you identify?" he answers, "the Democratic." In this case, the situation is the asking of a question and the response is a particular answer. There is another feature of the disposition which distinguishes it from its relation, the intention. What we are here calling dispositions can be thought of as psychological characteristics or factors which are unconsciously related to other political phenomena. For instance, the individual voter with attitude X doesn't perceive its influence on the direction of his vote. He doesn't say, "I voted for candidate Y because I have attitude X," although empirical research may discover a strong relationship between the attitude and the type of voting decision. If he says, "I voted for Y because I want Z to happen and I think Y's party also wants Z to happen," we have a case of intentional behavior.

Dispositions can be more or less unconscious. Thus, we are completely unaware of many dispositions which influence our behavior. We would probably place personality traits in this

---

[3]*Ibid.*, p. 47.
[4]Robert Lane, *Political Life*, (Glencoe, Ill.: Free Press, 1959), p. 98.

category. On the other hand, we might know we have attitude X—we are certainly aware of our Democratic or Republican leanings. The important distinction between intentions and dispositions is that the *relationship* between the latter and behavior is not "out in the open," even though we are aware that we have the disposition. Note that an acceptance of this distinction does not require one to advocate a mentalistic psychology which proposes looking into people's heads to find unconscious motives. Dispositions are defined behaviorally, that is, in terms of observable actions. Once again, it is the link between the disposition and relevant political phenomena which is below the surface, and not necessarily the knowledge that one has the disposition.

A discussion of dispositions in general is useful only up to a point. We have now reached that point when some of the major types of dispositional concepts ought to be described. The conclusion one comes to after reading the literature of political science which analyzes and uses dispositions is that there are several types in widespread use. These are opinions, attitudes, values, and beliefs. We will also consider personality traits as dispositions, although there are some who would question this classification.

An opinion has been defined as "an implicit verbal response or 'answer' that an individual gives in response to a particular stimulus situation in which some general 'question' is raised."[5] An opinion is usually distinguished from an attitude on the basis of generality. That is, an opinion has to do with a specific issue, for instance, price supports for farmers, while an attitude is broader; carrying through the example, one would have an attitude toward the government's role in the economy. Thus an attitude can be thought of as being manifested in a number of opinions.[6] The political scientist Lewis Froman has defined attitude in this manner: "A predisposition of an individual to evaluate some aspect of his world in a favorable or unfavorable manner, that is, a predisposition to approve or disapprove, like or dislike, some

---

[5]Carl I. Hovland, Irving L. Janis, and Harold H. Kelley, *Communication and Persuasion* (New Haven, Conn.: Yale University Press, 1953), p. 6.

[6]This distinction between opinions and attitudes is made in H. J. Eysenck, *The Psychology of Politics* (London: Routledge & Kegan Paul, 1954), pp. 111ff.

social or physical object."[7] An attitude is probably more stable and durable than an opinion; one would expect an individual's opinion toward government aid to farmers to change more often than his attitude toward governmental regulation of the economy.

There is one more dispositional level directly related to opinions and attitudes. This is usually labeled "ideology." Perhaps the best way to think of an ideology is to imagine a cluster of attitudes. Eysenck has called it a super-attitude.[8] Thus a person's attitude toward the government's role in the economy might be part of his overall conservative ideology. Ideologies are usually identified impressionistically or historically by political scientists, psychologists, and sociologists, although more rigorous techniques have become increasingly popular.[9] Thus, Eysenck identifies an ideology by statistically correlating a number of attitudes.[10] We have, then, three important dispositional levels. A quick survey of political science literature tends to indicate that opinions, attitudes, and to a lesser extent ideologies are used extensively to orient the study of politics and explain political behavior. Furthermore, explaining the dispositions, that is, treating them as dependent variables, is becoming an important task of political scientists.

Closely related to attitudes and opinions are values. "A value is a statement of 'good' or 'bad,' 'right' or 'wrong,' something which is desired or thought desirable."[11] A value is less specific than an attitude. Political scientists have often emphasized the importance of political values (values pursued politically) when explaining political behavior. For instance, Harold Lasswell has identified a number of values that men seek in politics: power, wealth, well-being, skill, enlightenment, affection, rectitude, and respect. [12] There is a methodological point about values which should be

---

[7]Lewis Froman, *People and Politics* (Englewood Cliffs, N.J.: Prentice-Hall, Inc., 1962), p. 20.

[8]Eysenck, *op. cit.,* p. 113.

[9]For studies employing the latter, see David E. Apter (ed.), *Ideology and Discontent* (New York: Free Press, 1964); and Robert E. Lane, *Political Ideology: Why the American Common Man Believes What He Does* (New York: Free Press, 1962).

[10]Eysenck, *op. cit.,* Chapter 4.

[11]Froman, *op. cit.,* p. 18.

[12]Harold Lasswell, *Psychopathology and Politics* in *The Political Writings of Harold D. Lasswell* (Glencoe, Ill.: Free Press, 1951) pp. 74-77.

mentioned. In Chapter 1 the distinction between fact and value was drawn. We emphasized that our analysis of the scientific study of politics deals only with how we know facts; description and explanation, as we understood their relevance for political inquiry, have to do with empirical, not normative, questions. However, while "values" are not true or false, it is a fact that people have one value or another; an assertion attributing the holding of a value to someone can be empirically tested (if it is properly formulated). Thus values in this empirical sense are fair game for political *scientists*.

Beliefs have to do with matters of fact. "Beliefs are defined as cognitions with an extra feeling of credibility which distinguishes them from cognitions which are not believed."[13] Thus a belief can be true or false. But a false belief is no less a belief, for its truth or falsity is logically independent of the psychological certainty of its believer. The relevance of beliefs to political behavior is obvious. What a man believes is often the main determinant of what he does and what his attitudes are. But, of course, there need be no logical consistency among attitudes, values, and beliefs. Values and beliefs might seem to differ from attitudes and opinions in that the former are less obviously dispositional. But while an opinion is clearly a response to a situation, so too is a value. An individual responds to certain objects or ideals with approval or disapproval. We characterize them as dispositional because their existence is determined (by definition) by measuring responses—if X does Y in situation Z, he has disposition D.

Another important class of characteristics that we have included in the dispositional category are personality traits. Many social scientists make much of the distinction between attitudes and personality traits. This is often based on a conclusion derived from a model that makes attitudes the result of learning and personality, of heredity. The available evidence seems to blur this distinction, so that it is probably more realistic to consider personality traits as simply more deeply seated dispositions. In other words, this latter model sees both attitudes and personality traits as products of the learning process. "Personality

---

13Lester W. Milbrath, *Political Participation* (Chicago: Rand McNally, 1965), p. 31.

as we know it is an essentially social product, inconceivable in the completely isolated human being."[14] But, whatever the source of the personality, it can be legitimately considered as a dispositional concept. A politician is labeled politically aggressive if he responds in a certain way in a certain situation.

Scientific techniques of personality measurement, such as projective tests and questionnaires, can be used with some degree of reliability and validity. In any case, the dispositional nature of personality traits seems well established. Although we have taken the position that personality traits are actually more permanent (than attitudes) dispositions, and are probably the result of the learning process, there is a reason for distinguishing them from attitudes. Several social scientists have found meaningful correlations between the two.[15] Thus, while they may not be different in kind, there is enough of a difference in degree to justify studying them independently.

Our classification of dispositions has up to this point been one of individualistic concepts. Thus we have mentioned the attitudes, personality traits, etc., of individuals. A brief presentation of the methodological individualist's position in opposition to emergence can be found elsewhere in this book. In accepting the idea that, in principle, all group characteristics can be reduced to the individual level or all group phenomena are explainable in terms of individualistic properties, one does not have to close his eyes to the existence or usefulness of group properties. While such a property is logically reducible, it is often more practical for the political scientist to continue working at the group level (realizing that the property is not emergent). This prepares us for the inclusion in our schema of group dispositional properties. We might say, the Democratic party is more liberal than the Republican; and, the Senate opposes a tax increase. This is justifiable as long as we realize that the attitudes of the

---

[14]M. Brewster Smith, Jerome S. Bruner, and Robert W. White, *Opinions and Personality* (New York: John Wiley & Sons, Inc., 1956), p. 31.

[15]See, for instance, *ibid.,* Chapter 10; Eysenck, *op. cit.,* Chapters 6 and 7. The ground-breaking work in this area is Theodore W. Adorno *et al., The Authoritarian Personality* (New York: Harper, 1950). For a direct application to political phenomena, see Herbert McClosky, "Conservatism and Personality," *American Political Science Review,* Vol. LII, 1958, pp. 27-45.

Democratic party and the Senate refer to the attitudes of individual party members and senators.

Finally, on the most general level are those dispositional concepts which are summarized by the notion of "national character." That there are two interpretations of national character is evident. It is viewed as "the set of values and other personality traits distributed among the *individuals* who make up the society...."[16] National character then describes the typical dispositional makeup of a nation. The second meaning or approach does allow for emergence. It refers to national character as if it were a single personality—as if something called "the state" had a set of dispositions independent of its citizens'.[17] This interpretation is in many ways not as useful as the first. But both represent group dispositional concepts that can be employed in models, conceptual schemes, and theories of politics.

The nature and uses of the dispositional approach

Having described the main varieties of concepts used in the dispositional approach to the study of politics, we can examine the nature of the approach itself. Actually, there are several ways political scientists use dispositions in the discovery and explanation of political phenomena; thus we can talk about variations on the dispositional approach.

Perhaps the most straightforward, and as a potential theory of politics the most promising, dispositional approach views dispositions as antecedent conditions of political phenomena. In other words, the assumption is made that it is possible to formulate hypotheses which express such relationships, and that these generalizations can then provide a foundation for useful models and, hopefully, explanatory theories of politics.

It is not difficult to find examples of low-level dispositional models or potential theories of politics. We will examine only two, one constructed by Lewis Froman, the other by Seymour Martin

---

16For a thorough discussion of national character and political analysis, see Alex Inkeles, "National Character and Modern Political Systems," in Nelson W. Polsby *et al.* (eds.), *Politics and Social Life* (Boston: Houghton Mifflin, Co., 1963), pp. 172-89. A useful bibliography is included.

17This is, of course, a holistic position and goes back at least to the philosophy of Hegel.

Lipset. Froman has speculated about the differences between leaders and nonleaders in interest groups; for instance, in regard to their group loyalty.[18] Starting from a dispositional approach, he hypothesizes that there are relationships between interest group leaders' behavior and their attitudes, values, and beliefs.[19] In effect, a behavior differential is related to a dispositional differential. For instance, Froman argues that, "Non-leaders have fewer values relating to why they are in the group."[20] Thus the group is more important to the leaders. A number of similar generalizations are suggested by the dispositional assumptions of Froman's model. Together they explain (or provide an explanation sketch of) the membership differential.

Another explanation based upon the dispositional approach has been provided by Lipset.[21] He is interested in the fact that extremist movements are very often backed by the lower classes. After supporting this fact with much empirical evidence, he attributes a psychological trait, a disposition, to the lower classes. "The social situation of the lower strata ... predisposes them to view politics as black and white, good and evil. Consequently, other things being equal, they should be more likely than other strata to prefer extremist movements which suggest easy and quick solutions to social problems and have a rigid outlook."[22]

There is always the danger of giving ex post facto explanations. It is especially tempting to use dispositions to account for political phenomena *after the fact.* And, in a sense, this is what Lipset has done. Noticing the relationship between lower classes and extremism, he speculates and formulates a disposition which, if possessed by the lower classes, would account (at least partially) for their extremism. An ex post facto explanation should not be condemned as long as its creator realizes that he is speculating, playing

---

[18]Froman, *op. cit.,* pp. 43-48.

[19]It should be made clear that we are not drawing a logical distinction between dispositions and behavior. By definition, a disposition is a type of behavior, that is, a response to a situation. But when using dispositional models there are practical reasons for such a distinction. These boil down to the need to emphasize that the dispositions are being used as independent variables and so are antecedent conditions of political behavior (which might include other dispositions).

[20]Froman, *op. cit.,* p. 43.

[21]Seymour Martin Lipset, *Political Man* (New York: Doubleday, 1959), p. 97.

[22]*Ibid.,* p. 100.

with his data, and not producing a substantiated explanation. In the present context, the significance of such analyses as Froman's and Lipset's lies in their demonstration of how a general dispositional approach to politics can (1) lay the foundation for an explanatory theory; (2) generate hypotheses to be tested, and in general act as an impetus for discovering new relationships. That is, the dispositional approach fulfills one of the classic functions of the scientific heuristic device. It directs the political scientist's attention toward certain variables which might account for the facts that interest him, and at the same time suggests hypotheses which can be tested.

A more highly developed model based upon assumed relationships between dispositional concepts and political behavior has been presented in *The American Voter.*[23] The authors of this highly praised voting study argue that in order to describe, explain, and predict electoral behavior, a sound and economical approach is needed. The attitudinal approach which they use can be considered dispositional because it places primary emphasis upon attitudes. It assumes that although past experiences and situations influence an individual's political behavior, the most efficient method of accounting for voting and voting preference is through the measurement of dispositions which are, in effect, directly related to the final decision. Their model does not fail to take into account sociological and economic factors. It only, in the author's words, "maximizes explanatory power while dealing with a minimum number of variables."[24] These variables are attitudes toward such factors as "the issues of domestic policy; the issues of foreign policy; and the comparative record of the two parties in managing the affairs of government."[25] The attitudes serve as a link between socioeconomic factors and the voting act. We see, then, how a general dispositional approach can suggest a strategy of explanation, and if reasonably successful, as in this case, provide the basis for a low-level theory of political behavior.

---

[23]Angus Campbell *et al.,* The American Voter (New York: John Wiley & Sons, Inc., 1960).

[24]*Ibid.,* p. 33.

[25]*Ibid.,* Section Two. They are able to explain and predict the voting decisions of 86 percent of their sample, using a law which is the multiple correlation of six attitudinal factors with voting choice.

An alternative interpretation is sometimes made of the dispositional approach. It is nonnomological in that it rejects the assumption that a dispositional model deals with generalizations relating dispositions and other political phenomena. Instead, this interpretation suggests that dispositions refer to the characteristics of specific individuals and thus do not require generalizations. The philosopher of history William Dray has argued along these lines in claiming that the dispositions of material things (the breaking of glass) are different from human dispositions (such as the trait "ambition"). "For ambition is not a general characteristic of men (or even perhaps, of politicians) in the way being brittle is of glass."[26] According to this reading of the dispositional approach, the political scientist works with the normal behavior of *individuals*.

There are several ways of showing the weakness of this position. Perhaps the simplest is to first admit that, practically speaking, political scientists usually do explain individual actions with descriptive statements about the individual—particular statements describing the general behavior of one person. However, the very use of dispositions indicates that one is employing general concepts which ultimately imply laws about all men, or, more likely, a class of men. May Brodbeck makes this point in regard to the explanation of action by means of personality characteristics. Referring to the social scientist or historian engaged in such explanatory activities she says, "He just uses laws about his particular man. It would be odd, though, if he were to say that another man of similar character in similar circumstances would nevertheless behave very differently. 'Character' after all, refers to a certain *kind* of man though possibly, just possibly, there might be only one of the kind."[27] While one may speak of one man, he must ultimately refer to all men of a particular type. While political scientists continue to analyze the President's, a senator's, or Hitler's personality or attitudes, each disposition is ultimately useful as a heuristic or explanatory

---

[26]William Dray, *Laws and Explanation in History* (Oxford: Oxford University Press, 1957), p. 146.

[27]May Brodbeck, "Explanation, Prediction and Imperfect Knowledge," in Herbert Feigl and Grover Maxwell (eds.), *Minnesota Studies in the Philosophy of Science*, Vol. III (Minneapolis: University of Minnesota Press, 1962), p. 270.

device only insofar as it can be related to other variables in generalizations.

LEARNING THEORY

The assumptions of the dispositional approach can be expressed more theoretically in the language of psychological learning theory. As a matter of fact, there are good reasons for viewing it as the most promising dispositional model currently available to political scientists. In addition, learning theory seems to be able to explain the formation of dispositions.

First of all, psychologists have accumulated an extensive body of experimental data on learning and have subjected this data to some rigorous methodological analyses. The result has been the development of a rather well-honed scientific tool. Political scientists thus have available to them a useful model if, and this is the crucial question, learning theory is related to the behavior of political actors. That an impressive model exists is one thing; to be able to use it is another. Indications are that political scientists can make use of learning theory. The matter of relevancy, then, is the second reason for a political scientist's taking an interest in learning theory.

This section examines each of these reasons. The next several paragraphs describe some of the major elements and assumptions of learning theory. We hope that a foundation of sorts will be laid for the evaluation of attempts to apply learning theory to politics which follows.

What is learning theory?

The scientist and philosopher Anatol Rapaport defines learning as the "selective accumulation of behavior patterns."[28] Let us begin our analysis of learning by unpacking Rapaport's definition. "Accumulation" refers to the fact that the learner comes out of the learning process with something which he doesn't have when

---

28Anatol Rapaport, "Mathematical, Evolutionary and Psychological Approaches to the Study of Total Societies," in Samuel Z. Klansuer (ed.), *The Study of Total Societies* (New York: Doubleday, 1967), p. 136.

he goes in. But what? The obvious answer is "behavior patterns," including dispositions, or in the more technical language of learning theory, associations between stimuli and responses—upon receiving a particular stimulus, a public opinion question, for instance, the individual gives a particular response, a "no" answer. But why is accumulation selective? This gets to the heart of learning theory, for it is simply another way of asking why only some behavior patterns are learned; it is at this point that a systematic presentation of the basics of learning theory seems in order.

There are two varieties of learning theory—two ways to account for stimulus-response connections.[29] The first, which we can call *association* theory, says simply that people learn through observing or experiencing associations or relationships of various kinds. A child watches its parents behave or react to situations and thus he learns to behave in a similar manner. An example from political science might clarify the process. We know that there is a strong correlation between the American voter's party identification and that of his parents.[30] How might we go about explaining this? Association learning theory tells us that a child observes his parents' political activities, listens to their political discourse, and becomes aware of their attitudes. If they identify with the Democratic party, he will come to associate "Democratic" and "political party." There need be no attempt, and there usually is none, by the parents to instill in the child their own political attitudes. Instead, because of the observed relationship, it is second nature for the child to think of "Democratic" whenever it hears "party."

A second brand of learning theory begins with the assumption that a connection between stimulus and response usually requires reinforcement if it is to be established. Mere association is not enough, in most cases. *Reinforcement* theory argues that we learn to make certain connections when we are rewarded and not to make others when the result is punishment. The first is an example of positive reinforcement. Psychologists know that rats can be

---

[29]For a survey of learning theories, see Winfred F. Hill, *Learning* (San Francisco: Chandler Publishing Co., 1963).

[30]Angus Campbell *et al., op. cit.,* pp. 146-47.

taught to push (response) a lever (stimulus) if the response produces food (reinforcement). Conversely, they can be taught not to push the lever if the result is an electric shock (negative reinforcement).

We know less about the relevance of learning theory to human behavior. But we can, based on some fairly sound data, speculate about its potential value and at the same time make the distinction between association and reinforcement theory.[31]

We have already considered how association theory accounts for the learning of party identification. The point was that the child forms the association between "party" and "Democratic" without any overt attempt on the part of his parents to instill in him a particular disposition through reward and punishment. That is, if a mother buys a toy for her six-year-old son every time he calls himself a Democrat, or if a favorable response to his father's question, "Which party is the best?" leads to a trip to the zoo, the learning which takes place is based on reinforcement. This example is absurd, because few parents would resort to such strategies simply to teach their children a party identification. Political attitudes, in most cases, are simply not that important. The learning of party identification is incidental, then, to the main experiences of childhood. But because of the pervasiveness of the parents' influence, the association is formed.

Are there, however, dispositions relevant to political science which can be explained by reinforcement theory? The answer is probably yes; in fact it is very likely the case that most political behavior can be accounted for in this way. Once again, an example might prove useful. An interesting question is, Why do some people change their attitudes, including party identification, after they become adults? There is, for instance, the case of the moderately strong Democrat, Smith, who enters a business corporation, works his way up to a fairly responsible administrative position, moves out of the central city, and buys a house in the suburbs. At each point in his new environment our Democrat is subjected to Republican influence. As he advances, Smith finds that an increasing number of his business associates and friends are

---

[31]For behavioral applications of learning theory, see Eysenck, *op. cit.;* and Neal E. Miller and John Dollard, *Social Learning and Imitation* (New Haven, Conn.: Yale University Press, 1941).

Republican. And when he finally moves to the suburbs, he discovers that his neighbors are predominantly Republican.

A dispositional approach to political behavior based on reinforcement theory would probably predict a shift in Smith's party identification. Let us see why. First of all, Smith will no doubt talk about politics with his new friends and neighbors. He soon discovers that any favorable comment about the Democratic party is met with ridicule, criticism, or at best an uncomfortable silence. In addition, Smith begins to notice that while there are a few Democrats at the lowest occupational levels of the corporation, as status and income increase they become fewer and fewer, until upon reaching the middle levels there are none to be found. At this point the long-standing Democrat begins to wonder if Republican identification is an unwritten requirement for advancement in the company.

Given these conditions, it would not be surprising if Smith became a Republican. For in terms of reinforcement theory, there are many reinforcing agents at work which tend to teach Smith to make the association between the stimulus "party" and response "Republican." He discovers that he is rewarded—he forms friendships, is treated cordially by associates and neighbors, and finds it easier to climb the occupational ladder—if he responds correctly. On the other hand, an unfavorable response leads to punishment.

What can this oversimplified but not unrealistic example tell us? First of all, because humans are far more complex than rats, it follows that reinforcement theory must be more subtle and flexible in its approach to political behavior than to the behavior of rats. Even our simplified example describes a situation in which the possible reinforcing agents are numerous and intertwined. As a model of politics, reinforcement theory must, of course, simplify—reduce the variables to a manageable few. But this is the strategy of any conceptual scheme. Its success is evaluated on the basis of how suggestive it is, or, if it is proposed as the rough draft of a theory, how it might go about explaining political phenomena.

The same could be said of association theory. Let it be made perfectly clear that neither brand of learning theory has all the "good" on its side. At this early stage, it seems prudent to think of general learning theory with its two variants, each with its own areas of applicability. So there is reason to speculate that in some situations—the learning of party identification by children, for instance—a mere association is at the root of the learned response. On the other hand, there are dispositions more effectively accounted for by reinforcement theory; probably many of the more highly developed dispositions—attitudes, personality traits—ought to be included in this category. One preliminary conclusion is that a parochial interpretation of learning theory as an approach to the study of politics is counterproductive. The political scientist, keeping the general principles of learning theory in mind, ought to first see how his model fits the world—how useful it is in generating hypotheses and how it might at some future time explain and predict—before refining it to a "reinforcement" or "association" theory.

The uses of learning theory

It is clear that we are evaluating learning theory on two levels: first as a heuristic device which organizes our thoughts and suggests that we look for particular factors and relationships. We have seen, for instance, how reinforcement theory focuses our attention on reinforcing factors when the phenomenon being considered is attitude change. There seems to be no doubt, then, that learning theory can function as a useful *model* of politics, if, as we have been assuming, the value of a model stems from its suggestiveness.

But how would we evaluate learning theory on the second level, as an explanatory theory of politics? That it does not, at this point, constitute a sound theory seems noncontroversial. Thus, a more sensible question asks if the learning approach provides the basis for a theory of politics yet to be developed but in the offing. In order to answer this, we have to distinguish two theoretical-explanatory functions which learning theory might perform.

First, learning theory can perhaps explain dispositions, that is, account for attitudes and opinions in terms of association and reinforcement. But the explanatory scope of learning theory is potentially much broader. Thus it is not unrealistic to look forward to the development of a theory of general politics based on stimulus-response connections which could, in addition to explaining dispositions, account for such phenomena as political change, and stability, and conflict, to name only a few.

Those who occasionally become interested in the application

of learning theory to the study of politics usually use it to study political dispositions. Thus, the English psychologist H. J. Eysenck sees in learning theory the basis of a theory which can explain political attitudes and link them to other kinds of political behavior.[32] Since available empirical data primarily describe individual learning, this emphasis is understandable.

However, some social scientists have argued for a more extensive use of learning theory in the analysis of larger social and political systems. Kenneth Boulding has made the following observation and suggestion: "Up to this point in the development of the social sciences, learning has been treated largely on an individual basis. The time now seems to be ripe for the development both of theoretical systems and of empirical studies of learning on the scale of the large society, or what might be called the 'macrolearning' process."[33] In other words, it might be fruitful to begin thinking about learning done by communities, cities, or interest groups, and how to measure the accumulation of behavior patterns by such large-scale political systems. As a matter of fact, several political scientists have directed their attention toward this significant question.

Richard M. Merelman has examined the relationship between "learning and legitimacy" in political systems.[34] He analyzes the nature of the moral support which a people gives its political regime—how legitimate the regime is perceived to be—through the assumptions of reinforcement theory. He conceptualizes the problem and justifies his use of the approach in the following manner: "This process of learning, in which the government acts as the provider of a learning stimulus to a population and the population responds, is possible because the government attaches a series of sanctions or, in learning theory terms, reinforcements to each policy."[35] Merelman goes on to argue that material reinforcements are replaced by symbolic ones, which become symbols of legitimacy. In other words, the support which is given the system is ultimately based on, and therefore explainable in

---

[32]Eysenck, *op. cit.*

[33]Kenneth Boulding, "The Learning Process in the Dynamics of Total Societies," in Klansuer (ed.), *op. cet.*, p. 111.

[34]Richard M. Merelman, "Learning and Legitimacy," *American Political Science Review*, Vol. LX (1966), p. 548-61.

[35]*Ibid.*

terms of, the rewards and punishments allocated by the decision-making process. There is nothing surprising about the hypothesis that the legitimacy of a political system is a function of the policies it makes and enforces. It surely has prima facie validity. What makes the hypothesis significant to us is the way it was generated; by the principles of learning theory.

Another application of learning theory at the macrolevel has been made by Henry Teune.[36] He is interested in "the learning of integrative habits" by political systems, all the way from the city to the nation-state. The key concept is "integration." So we might say that Teune is interested in the integration of political communities, which, by the way, is the title of the more general work of which his article is a part. The basic assumption is that integration—the tendency of people to psychologically identify with a particular political unit, or even of nations to identify with an international or regional community—is learned. "The major point of this presentation is that known facts about political integration can be explained by a psychological theory—learning theory. These psychological factors will be similar for political integration at any level."[37] Teune mentions explanation, thus implying that the propositions about learning constitute an empirical theory. On the other hand, he talks about the use of learning theory "to prompt some insights into the process of political integration" and "to piece together some seemingly isolated bits of knowledge into a more general framework."[38] The implication seems to be that learning theory is being viewed first as a heuristic device to suggest hypotheses about integration and second, hopefully, as a future theory which can explain integration.

INTENTIONAL APPROACHES

It is often tempting to think of all human behavior as purposive, that is, intended. The political scientist Vernon Van Dyke has

---

36Henry Teune, "The Learning of Integrative Habits," in Philip E. Jacob and James V. Toscano (eds.), *The Integration of Political Communities* (Philadelphia: J. B. Lippincott, 1964), pp. 247-82.

37*Ibid.*, p. 248.

38*Ibid.*

articulated this outlook: "The action of human beings ... usually relates somehow to their desires. Human beings are purposive." [39] On the face of it, this probably goes too far. If the first section of this chapter demonstrated anything, it was that much political behavior can be accounted for by dispositions of various sorts that are not consciously linked to the behavior. And if an intention has the characteristic of being conscious, in the sense that objectives are intentionally pursued and therefore consciously linked to behavior, it follows that much political behavior is not intentional.

This conclusion goes against the grain of a tradition in political thought which views political phenomena as explainable largely in terms of human intentions. For instance, Thomas Hobbes bases much of his political philosophy upon the egoistic (intentional) nature of man. From this assumption, the political system itself is viewed as the result of intentional behavior. John Locke argues that men leave the state of nature in order to find more effective methods of protecting their natural rights. Perhaps the clearest example of a general political philosophy based on intentional behavior is the utilitarian calculus of Jeremy Bentham, which assumes that political behavior is ultimately a conscious calculating of needs and wants and the means necessary to satisfy those needs and wants.

The nature of intentional behavior

A preliminary conclusion is that in order to understand fully the limited utility of the intentional approach, we ought to distinguish it from the dispositional approach. That is, the difference between unconsciously and consciously motivated political behavior must be kept in mind. Perhaps a brief analysis of the concept "motive" would help at this point, for it seems that this is what we are talking about, or at least around. "Motive" is being viewed as the label of the class of all factors which influence or lead to behavior. This definition, it is clear, includes both dispositions and intentions. Robert Brown has classified motives into three categories: intention motives, impulse motives, and

---

[39] Van Dyke, *op. cit.*, p. 23.

dispositional motives.[40] Our own distinction follows Brown's rather closely, if, that is, an impulse is viewed as a sort of innate or unlearned disposition.

A motive classification, this time a dichotomous one, has been formulated by Richard W. Snyder, H. W. Bruck, and Burton Sapin.[41] Because they are political scientists, their scheme is perhaps more relevant to our analysis. They label all intentions "in order to" motives, and what we have called dispositions, "because of" motives. In their own words, "*In order to* motives refer to an end state of affairs envisaged by the actor," while, "On the other hand, *because of* motives refer to the actor's past experience, to the sum total of factors in his life-history which determine the particular project of action elected to reach a goal."[42] This, then, gets at the basic distinction between unconscious dispositions and conscious intentions.

We should, however, be aware that an overzealous application of this distinction can lead us astray. For, to some, it implies that dispositions are explainable while intentions are not—that dispositions are general tendencies while intentions are *free* creations, "off the top of the head," so to speak. This position usually comes down to an application of the philosophical doctrine of free will to political behavior: there are some actions, namely, intentions, which are born in the minds of men with no antecedent conditions. From this assumption is derived a fairly common criticism of psychological and sociological explanations of political behavior, especially voting behavior. There are certain mental activities, such as the decision to vote Democratic, so the argument goes, which cannot be explained by general tendencies yet are accountable for by an assumption of free will.[43]

This clearly conflicts with the assumption of determinism, a principle which we have argued is basic to any scientific activity.

40Robert Brown, *Explanation in Social Science* (Chicago: Aldine Publishing Co., 1963), p. 83.

41Richard W. Snyder, H. W. Bruck, and Burton Sapin, "Motivational Analysis of Foreign Policy Decision-Making," in James N. Rosenau (ed.), *International Politics and Foreign Policy* (New York: Free Press, 1961), pp. 247-53.

42*Ibid.*, p. 252.

43See, for instance, the chapter by Walter Berns on voting studies in Herbert J. Storing (ed.), *Essays on the Scientific Study of Politics* (New York: Holt, Rinehart & Winston, 1962).

To one who accepts it as an operational rule, the belief in undetermined intentions is unfounded and overly restrictive. Why exclude, on a priori grounds, the possibility of scientific knowledge of intentions? If it is assumed that intentions are unexplainable, if they do spring newly born from the minds of men, then the argument might be advanced that they cannot be related to other factors—they cannot be placed in generalizations. But given the nomological nature of scientific knowledge, it follows that intentions are of scientific value only if they can be placed in generalizations. In effect, then, we are assuming that a "unique" intention is actually the result of a *combination* of general tendencies, including dispositions, which is unique.

This assumption provides the basis for our inclusion of intentional behavior in this chapter. Both dispositions and intentions are the result of general tendencies. The difference between them is not logical but pragmatic. Even though we make a distinction between conscious and unconscious factors, let us remember that the characteristic of consciousness has to do with the relationship between behavior and its determinants. This does not preclude the possibility of demonstrating that the intention which is cited as the reason for a particular action is itself the result of other factors; in fact, this is what we would expect to be the case. In other words, if intentional behavior is to serve as the foundation of an approach to political inquiry, the "free seeking of goals" must be viewed as behavior which is designed (intended) to satisfy a particular need, want, or desire, which in turn can be explained. Thus, an act of free will is not, in principle, unexplainable.

A related reason for not exaggerating the distinction between intentions and dispositions is based upon the fact that an intention (defined as we are defining it—a conscious act) often becomes a disposition. That is, a conscious intention may in time be transformed into an unconscious response. Take, for example, the case of a new legislator who performs certain acts consciously in order to build a foundation of power within his legislative body, but who after several years makes many of the same moves— responses out of habit; he has learned certain patterns of behavior. What was once intentional behavior could now without contradiction be labeled dispositional.

There is an important characteristic of intentional behavior which, while lurking near the surface of this section's discussion, has not yet been straightforwardly stated. If we equate *in order to* motives with intentions, then the thrust of the definition seems to be that intentional behavior is goal-directed. To say that a presidential candidate gave a speech because he intended to is not necessarily incorrect; nor is it very enlightening. What we probably want to add is, the candidate gave the speech because he wanted to *(in order to)* influence voters. Thus, intentional behavior usually involves the seeking of goals or objectives. While there is nothing illogical about replying, "Because I wanted to," to the question, "Why did you do that?" it would seem more reasonable to cite the objectives which motivated the action. This is usually the beginning assumption of the political scientist who uses the intentional approach to suggest, explain, and predict.

The uses of the intentional approach

Used heuristically, an intentional approach to politics can be very suggestive. More than most other approaches, the intentional seems to make political phenomena meaningful and thus susceptible to coherent analysis. However, at the point when the political scientist begins visualizing the intentional approach as a potential explanatory and predictive theory of politics, certain limitations must be kept in mind.

Let us repeat the observation which began this section. While some political behavior seems to be explainable in terms of intentions and goals, there is a large portion that is not. Several reasons can be discerned. (1) Not all intentions are acted upon. If we are trying to predict behavior, the single assertion by Smith that he intends to start a riot will not be enough; Smith might be a liar or braggart whose speech is impressive but not indicative of behavior. (2) Those intentions which are acted upon do not always realize successful completion. As we all know, it usually takes more than strong resolve to achieve a goal. The most dedicated and purposeful candidate does not always win the election. (3) Or, the results of intentional behavior are not always intended. Political strategies have been known to backfire. (4) And finally, as we have already pointed out, much political behavior is the result of unconscious dispositions.

For these reasons, there is no place in political science for an all-inclusive theory that explains everything on the basis of intentions. One of these, the conspiracy theory, appears to account for all kinds of political behavior on the basis of the intentional seeking of objectives by behind-the-scenes leaders. Because it has been a popular and at times respected explanatory device within political science, it deserves mention and requires refutation. In Karl Popper's words, "The conspiracy theory of society cannot be true because it amounts to the assertion that all results, even those which at first sight do not seem to be intended by anybody, are the intended results of the actions of people who are interested in the results."[44] This, then, summarizes what has already been said several times, namely, that intentions and goals by themselves do not usually account for political phenomena.

Something else is needed in conjunction with intentions. In any intentional theory or model there will also be statements referring to other factors besides the intention itself, such as the intender's beliefs about how best to achieve his goals, his capabilities, and relevant environmental conditions.

DECISION-MAKING THEORY

We can tie up some of the loose ends which are still dangling by describing the most highly developed model of intentional political behavior. Our brief analysis of *decision-making theory* will help us understand the general nature of the intentional approach, while at the same time indicating what can be done by way of suggesting and explaining when the basic assumptions of intentionality are worked into a systematic model.

Decision-making theory focuses upon the decision maker as the fundamental unit of political analysis. The basic assumption is not that every political act is intentional—this assumption has, we trust, been laid to rest—but that ultimately, politics involves the

---

[44]Karl Popper, *The Open Society and Its Enemies* (New York: Harper Torchbooks, 1962), Vol. II, p. 96.

making of decisions which are in effect judgments about how to gain a particular objective in a given situation. Thus the decision-making theorist does not claim his model accounts for all political phenomena; rather, he assumes that decision making is the most important aspect of the political system and is therefore of primary interest to the political scientist.

While the decision maker is the focal point, he is not viewed as operating within a vacuum. His environment, the situation in which he finds himself, is recognized as an important factor, both as a shaper of the objectives which he is trying to achieve and as a set of limits which help determine what he can and cannot do in seeking his goals.

Decision-making theory is a refined version of the general intentional approach. It emphasizes the intentional seeking of goals, but does not fail to recognize the influence of environmental or situational factors. In addition, the decision maker's dispositions can be included in the model, although as decision-making theory is used by political scientists they are sometimes de-emphasized. Thus, even though the President has his objective clearly in mind, his decision about how to achieve it may be colored by his attitudes, opinions, beliefs, and personality, and this latter kind of influence will probably operate without his being aware of it. In short, political decision makers are no less subject to the influence of their dispositions than other people.

We can begin to see the heuristic value of decision-making theory. In focusing upon the decision maker and his activity, the researcher has his attention directed toward those factors which might be related to the focal points. The model provides an overall framework for analyzing certain basic aspects of politics and is the foundation for a potential theory of politics.[45]

Let us examine how decision-making theory can be used to explain a particular policy or event through an example from the literature of political science. Richard C. Snyder and Glenn D. Paige have provided an explanation of the decision by the United States to resist the invasion of South Korea by North Korean

---

[45]For an evaluation of the uses of decision-making theory, see James N. Rosenau, "The Premises and Promises of Decision-Making Theory," in James C. Charlesworth (ed.), *Contemporary Political Analysis* (New York: Free Press, 1967), p. 189-211.

forces.[46] From decision-making theory comes their basic assumption: "Acts of a nation-state result from more or less deliberate and conscious choices by someone at some time, and a course of action is followed to serve certain purposes."[47]

Snyder and Paige argue that the decision to resist aggression in Korea was made by our decision makers because of several basic objectives, including protecting our national security and avoiding World War III. While admitting the influence of other factors—environmental conditions, etc.—their argument boils down to the following: The United States intervened in Korea because President Truman and his advisers decided that certain basic values were worth protecting and these objectives have to be related to military intervention by way of generalizations. Perhaps the most generally appropriate law would be: if a national leader wishes to preserve his nation's security, he will intervene in any conflict which threatens this security. It can be seen that other factors—beliefs and capabilities, for instance—would have to be included. Snyder and Paige can then show that the specific objective-values are variations on the theme of national security and so included in the generalization. The result is an explanation using laws which relate goals and action taken. In other words, an explanation is generated by the principles of decision-making theory. The assumption of intentionality is especially important, for it suggests directly or indirectly the other relationships which might be significant: Assuming that President Truman has objectives A and aims to achieve it, and given that action X was taken, what other factors would have to be present if A is to lead to X?

---

[46]Richard C. Snyder and Glenn D. Paige, "The United States Decision to Resist Aggression in Korea: The Application of an Analytical Scheme," in Rosenau (ed.), *op. cit.*, pp. 193-208.

[47]*Ibid.*, p. 195.

11 The rational approach and game theory

There is a particular kind of intentional behavior, usually called rational, which grounds another approach to the study of politics. The approach assumes that all political actors, or a particular class of them, are rational. From this premise other characteristics of individuals or political systems are deduced; in other words, hypotheses are generated. If some of them are verified, then the indication might be that a rationalistic theory of politics is in the offing. Thus rational approaches can be both heuristic and potentially explanatory.

We will begin our analysis of the rational approach to the study of politics with a discussion of rationality in general, its meaning and significance in political inquiry. Then we will consider the most highly developed rational model, game theory.

THE CONCEPT OF RATIONALITY

The first thing to do is to consider some proposed definitions of rationality. Most of them are behavioral in the sense that "rational" implies a certain kind of activity. Robert Dahl and Charles Lindblom have summarized what many political scientists have in mind when they talk about rational behavior: "An action is rational to the extent that it is correctly designed to maximize goal achievement, given the goal in question and the real world as it exists."[1]

---

[1] Robert Dahl and Charles Lindblom, *Politics, Economics and Welfare* (New York: Harper & Row, 1953), p. 38.

187

To be rational, then, is to be efficient in the pursuit of goals; in the words of economist Anthony Downs, "maximizing output for a given input, or minimizing input for a given output."[2] A politician is rational if, given a particular objective and situation, he chooses that course of action which is most likely to achieve the objective. The influence of economic theory on this notion of rationality is obvious. But it is not surprising when one realizes that many of its developers and users are or were originally economists.

There are other ways to characterize rationality. The philosopher of social science Quentin Gibson has equated "considering the evidence" with rational behavior.[3] If in a given situation an individual, in seeking an objective, bases his choice of means on all the available evidence, he is rational. This notion of rationality is perhaps more applicable to political situations, for it takes into consideration the possibility of a decison maker's having incomplete or imperfect evidence. Herbert Simon has been among the handful of political scientists who have attempted to work out usable concepts of rationality. He has advocated a move away from the concept, most often identified with economic theory, which revolves around the assumption of *ideal* rationality. Simon states that his task "is to replace the global rationality of economic man with a kind of rational behavior that is compatible with the access to information and the computational capacities that are actually possessed by organisms, including man, in the kind of environments in which such organisms exist."[4] With a more "realistic" notion of rational, a greater number of social and political phenomena can be included within a rational model of politics.

At the heart of any definition of rational behavior lies some notion of using the best means to achieve a given goal. So far we have been talking about rationality in general—any type of means to achieve any type of goal. But our central interest is rationality in politics. This can be conceptualized in two ways: rational action

---

[2]Anthony Downs, *An Economic Theory of Democracy* (New York: Harper & Row, 1957), p. 5.

[3]Quentin Gibson, *The Logic of Social Enquiry* (London: Routledge & Kegan Paul, 1960), p. 46.

[4]Herbert Simon, *Models of Man* (New York: John Wiley & Sons, Inc., 1958), p. 241.

designed to achieve *political ends,* or rational *political action* directed toward any ends. Anthony Downs has clarified this refinement with the following example: "Let us assume a certain man prefers party *A* for political reasons, but his wife has a tantrum whenever he fails to vote for party *B*. It is perfectly rational personally for this man to vote for party *B* if preventing his wife's tantrums is more important to him than having *A* win instead of *B*."[5] In Chapter 2 we examined representative definitions of politics, and these should help us single out that particular kind of rational behavior which interests us here.

Let us backtrack a bit. The definitions we have considered say that one is rational if he uses the best means to achieve his goals. This implies that while *means* are rational or not rational, there can be no such evaluation of what is being sought. We never label ends rational, only means. Thus, one can seek any goal—order or disorder, for instance—rationally.

However, after having identified rational behavior and *means* activity, we must recognize that some political scientists have formulated notions of rational *ends*. That is, they claim or imply that an act is rational if it is designed to achieve certain ends.

The national-interest theory of Hans Morgenthau is a case in point.[6] Morgenthau states that nations seek their rational interest. Then he goes on to imply that this type of behavior is rational. A major difficulty with such an approach is its ambiguity. In making a political end rational, it is not quite clear if the basic assertion—all rational nations seek their national interest—is an empirical generalization of a definition of rationality.

Furthermore, it can be argued that in postulating an *end* as rational, the political scientist moves into the realm of normative political philosophy. That is, he is recommending that men or nations pursue an objective that is "good" or "best." It is not unfair to interpret Morgenthau's argument in this manner. For he is, in effect, saying that it is morally right for a state to seek its national interest. In other words, he makes seeking its national interest the ultimate moral good of a state; since it is rational to protect one's national interest, it is good-for the state, "rational"

---

[5]Downs, *op. cit.,* p. 7.
[6]Hans J. Morgenthau, *Politics Among Nations* (New York: Alfred A. Knopf, 1960).

is equivalent to "morally right." To be fair to Morgenthau, we must add that he makes this the good of politics while at the same time arguing that there are different moral values in other spheres of human activity.

If our basic distinction between facts and values has any validity, then it seems fairly clear that this kind of rational analysis has no place in the empirical study of politics. In fact, one can probably trace this sort of normative rational argument back to theories of the "good order" which have always had an important place in political philosophy. William T. Bluhm has, in characterizing such theories, made evident their similarity to the contemporary rational-ends theorists. "Investigating the "rational' or 'best' order, the theorist first of all seeks to determine the rational or 'right' order of human ends or values."[7] We can conclude, then, that in political science, rational models and theories deal with the means that are appropriate for a given end. And those theories which postulate an end as rational have probably moved into the realm of normative political philosophy.

How the rational approach is used

Rational approaches can be used both to suggest and to provide potential explanations of political phenomena, usually decisions. As the basis of a potential explanatory theory, the concept of rationality must be related to other variables in generalizations. As we saw in Chapter 7, the basic explanatory premise in rational theories takes the following form: "A rational man in situation S would perform act A." Or, more completely, a rational man with goal C and faced with alternatives $A...Z$ will choose A. So, being rational or having the disposition of rationality is related to a particular decision. The useful rational theory of politics would, of course, expand upon this simple hypothesis as it added variables and relationships. But its basic nomological structure would remain intact.

In evaluating the usefulness of rational theories, one should begin by noting that on the face of it much political behavior is not rational. Thus, rational theories are limited in their scope.

---

[7]William T. Bluhm, *Theories of the Political System* (Englewood Cliffs, N.J.: Prentice-Hall, Inc., 1965), p. 5.

This implies that it is incumbent upon the political scientist who contemplates employing a rational theory to substantiate the claim that a political actor is rational. This calls for a clearly defined concept of rationality with empirical import. Before we can determine whether or not the President is rational, we have to have in mind what it means to be rational. If the concept is not properly defined, then, in Kenneth Boulding's words, "it can easily collapse to the empty proposition that people do what they do, for what they do is by definition the best choice."[8] Many political scientists are guilty of this tautological activity, despite its obvious shortcomings. The result is the unthinking attribution of rationality to everyone, which obviously doesn't take us very far.

But an even more significant question, especially in regard to theory construction, is, Are there empirical laws about rational men? Or, at least, are there well-constructed hypotheses which can be tested?

So we must have two kinds of knowledge to use the concept of rationality in theories and explanations; generalizations relating rationality to other variables, and evidence that relevant political actors are rational to demonstrate that the generalizations and theories encompass them.

At this point, mention should be made of a strategy which is apparently not bothered by the empirical limitations and methodological requirements of the rational approach. An appropriate label is the "commonsense rational" theory of politics. Take, for instance, the following argument of W. G. Runciman: "There is nothing, in a sense, that needs to be explained about a South Wales miner voting Labour or an executive of General Motors voting Republican. The simplest model of rational self-interest is enough to explain these cases without being in defiance of Graham Wallas, exaggerating the 'intellectuality' involved."[9] The basis of Runciman's "explanation" is either the assumption that everyone is rational until proven nonrational or that when behavior conforms to our expectations it is rational and thus requires no further explanation.

Because of the limited time and resources available to political

---

[8]Kenneth E. Boulding, *Conflict and Defense* (New York: Harper & Row, 1962), p. 9.

[9]W. G. Runciman, *Social Science and Political Theory* (Cambridge: University of Cambridge Press, 1963), p. 94.

scientists, such arguments may be of temporary usefulness. In addition, the assumptions might be of some heuristic value. However, both assumptions are empirical assertions, and if they are to serve as explanatory premises their particular manifestations must ultimately be tested against the world. In addition the assumptions require that evidence be collected which demonstrates the rationality of the particular class of political actors being referred to. So Runciman's argument might be valid in certain instances, but he is misusing the rational approach if he assumes that the burden of proof is on those who believe there is nonrational behavior. A rational theory does not have privileged status relative to other theories. It, too, must be evaluated according to how well it organizes and explains the world of politics.

The building of rational theories of politics is no easy task. And their formulation and verification does not guarantee that more than a narrow range of political phenomena will be accounted for, because so much political behavior cannot be included within a concept of rationality.

Although theories of politics based on rationality may be difficult to develop and limited in scope, the concept may serve as a foundation for models or conceptual schemes of politics. In short, while the explanatory power of rationality seems to be limited, its usefulness as a suggestive device for discovery is probably greater.

There is a heuristic gambit which some take. It revolves around the assertion that the "rational political man" like the "rational economic man" is, after all, only an ideal. However, even though there are no rational men, a model making the unrealistic assumption that there are is useful in suggesting what men would do *if they were* rational. On the basis of this kind of information, the political scientist begins to formulate generalization about the kinds of situations in which men (or certain kinds of men) act rationally. In other words, the strategy generates data which can be used to map out the limits of rational theories—to see just how far one can go in developing rational explanations. Karl Popper has suggested such a strategy, which he labels the "zero-sum method." He means by this, "the method of constructing a model on the assumption of complete rationality...on the part of all the individuals concerned, and estimating the deviation of the actual behavior from the model behavior, using the latter as a kind of zero co-ordinate."[10] A concept of rationality, then, at least serves as a focal point or standard against which behavior can be measured.

GAME THEORY

The most highly developed rational model of politics is game theory. Thomas Schelling has defined it as "the formal study of the rational, consistent expectations that participants can have about each other's choices."[11] Game theory seems relevant to the study of politics because it analyzes conflict situations–situations in which two or more actors are competing for values. A decision maker might use game theory to help formulate the best strategy in a particular situation. A political scientist might use it to suggest the possible behavior of political actors or explanations of various kinds of political decisions.

At the heart of game theory is an assumption of rationality. That is, it is assumed that in a game situation, the players or decision makers are trying to maximize their gains or minimize their losses–putting it in simpler terms, they want to get as much as they can out of the game. The assumption applies to poker, football, and political situations.

The elements of game theory

All games have a common set of characteristics.[12] First, and most obvious, there are *players* or participants, each with *goals* and *resources*. A gambler without money cannot play at cards, and

---

[10]Karl Popper, *The Poverty of Historicism* (New York: Harper & Row, 1964), p. 141.

[11]Thomas Schelling, *The Strategy of Conflict* (New York: Oxford University Press, 1960).

[12]For discussions of the elements of game theory, see Richard C. Snyder, "Game Theory and the Analysis of Political Behavior," in *Research Frontiers in Politics and Government* (Washington: Brookings Institution, 1955), pp. 70-103; and Martin Shubik, "Game Theory and the Study of Social Behavior: An Introductory Exposition" in Martin Shubik (ed.), *Game Theory and Related Approaches to Social Behavior* (New York: John Wiley & Sons, Inc., 1964), pp. 3-77.

a nation without military forces cannot play at war. But in addition to resources, the players have goals or objectives which indicate what they want to get out of the game. In the most general terms, this is to win. But to be meaningful, the goals in any particular game situation must be specified, for they may differ from game to game, and within a game, from player to player. For instance, imagine an election in which one candidate runs because he sincerely wants to help his country while his opponent seeks office for the prestige it will bring him. They are playing in the same game, for the same prize, but with different values in mind.

A game involves players with goals and resources. Game theory, then, makes the assumption that the players are rational. This leads to the formulation of another important concept, *strategy*. Strategy in game theory has much in common with the term we use in everyday conversation. It has something to do with planning, working out methods for success. In game theory it refers, more specifically, to the plan of action which a rational player develops, telling him what to do given the possible moves of his opponent(s). In most games a number of strategies are open to each side. The objective is to choose the one which maximizes gains and minimizes losses. The best strategy is not always the one which, if successfully completed, will lead to the biggest payoff; it is often the case that one will be chosen which offers a good chance for modest gain and slight chance of loss. The big-payoff strategy might have as another possible payoff the disastrous loss.

So it is up to each player to select the most rational strategy. This is what the football quarterback does when he decides whether to run or pass from his own one-yard line; what the baseball pitcher does when he throws a fast ball rather than a curve ball; and perhaps what the Presidential candidate does when he chooses to campaign only in the largest states. In each case, the rational player keeps in mind the possible strategies of his opponents. The defense has a number of formations it can employ in its effort to cover all the moves of the quarterback. The batter may be expecting either a fast ball or curve ball. The opposing candidate *B* can meet candidate *A* head-on or campaign unchallenged in the smaller states.

We have been referring to another basic element of game theory, the *payoff*. Each set of strategies has a set of values attached to it which constitute the outcomes of the game—so much won or lost, given the combinations of opposing strategies. These are the payoffs. In a general sense, they describe, in mathematical terms—dollars, votes, runs—the goals of the players. It is the tallying of payoffs at the end of the game which determines the winner.

There is one element of game situations which we have not mentioned. It has to do with the framework, the environment within which the game is played. This framework is usually described in a set of *rules*—a set of propositions indicating what the players can or cannot do. In poker, chess, and football, the rules are specific and unambiguous. In politics, they are more complicated. What are the rules of an election or a negotiation between two nations? There are, no doubt, rules, but they are not neatly summarized in a rule book. Instead we have to look at customs, traditions, legal codes, constitutions, and in addition geographical, biological, sociological, and psychological limitations on the players' behavior. It is clearly more difficult to ferret these out. But this is simply one way of saying, "Politics is more complex than poker."

Types of game theory

When we think about game theory and its possible applications to politics, it becomes more and more obvious that there are actually several game models. They can be classified according to how many players the game has and what kinds of payoff the game provides.[13]

The two-person zero-sum game is the simplest type. It involves two participants competing in a game with rules which allow only strategies which lead to payoffs of the all-or-nothing variety. That is, the winnings and losses always cancel each other out. Two-handed poker is of this sort: if player A wins $50, then player B has to lose $50 (50 + - 50 = 0). There are probably political situations which can be made to fit zero-sum conditions,

---

[13]For a discussion of various kinds of games see Shubik, *op. cit.;* for a detailed discussion of two-person games see Anatol Rapaport, *Two-Person Game Theory* (Ann Arbor: University of Michigan Press, 1966).

if certain variables are left out. A two-man election can be so conceptualized. If we assume that each candidate is rational and is simply trying to win, then clearly it is a zero-sum game, for one will win, the other will lose. This kind of a game involves head-to-head conflict; and while there are political situations which can be analyzed within a two-person zero-sum framework, there are probably more which require a more complex game model.

One such model defines the two-person nonzero-sum game. In this game, the gains and losses of the two players do not cancel out, do not equal zero. This allows a wide variety of possible payoffs, including situations in which both players gain and those in which both players lose. It is not difficult to think of political situations which might fit this model—certain situations in international relations come immediately to mind. What of negotiations between two nations in which the payoff results in a gain, let us say, in territory for both, even though they are in conflict; or the converse situation of nuclear war, in which neither nation wins?

An even more complex game model includes those games in which more than two players participate and in which gains and losses do not cancel out. Thus it is labeled the n-person nonzero-sum game. Take, for instance, the very common situation in which a number of states are competing for a large federal atomic energy plant. If there are ten states involved, then clearly one will win and the other nine will lose; the sum of all their gains and losses will equal minus eight. This game model is probably applicable to a number of political situations including interest group behavior, international bargaining, and many coalition situations.

Because it is more complex than two-person games, the n-person game is probably applicable to a wider range of political phenomena. But its complexity, the greater number of variables and relationships it uses, calls for a high degree of mathematical sophistication on the part of its user, and in general makes it extremely difficult to employ. Thus political scientists are faced with a dilemma: the game models which are the least complex and easiest to use are probably the least applicable to politics.

Using game theory

This leads to a more general observation about the use of game theory in political science. Richard Snyder has warned against the premature application of mathematical models such as game theory to social and political phenomena.[14] He sees the possible prematurity stemming from two sources: first, the fact that game theory, or at least certain kinds of game theory, might not yet be sufficiently developed. In this case the political scientist should be aware of the limitations of the mathematical model itself. But, second, it is much more likely that the reverse is true. That is, political science is not yet ready to use many of the sophisticated models developed by mathematicians and economists. Before they are used, the political scientist must be ready to approach his data in a particular way, making assumptions which are often foreign to traditional political analysis. And of course, even if he does prepare himself, there is no guarantee that game theory will be applicable to more than a narrow range of political phenomena.

The indications are, however, that game models are of more significance than this. Their main function for the present and near future seems to be heuristic: suggesting explanatory hypotheses. Let us examine one highly respected example.

William Riker bases his *Theory of Political Coalitions* on an assumption of rationality. From this starting point he develops a game model which he attempts to adjust to empirical realities. He then uses his modified game model to generate a hypothesis which can explain a relationship discovered by V. O. Key between the existence of a Republican minority in Southern states and the continuance of organized factions in Democratic parties.[15] The hypothesis which Riker labels the "size principle" states that, "In social situations similar to *n*-person, zero-sum games with side payments, participants create coalitions just as large as they believe will ensure winning and no larger."[16] This principle can be

---

14Snyder, *op. cit.,* p. 72-73.

15V. O. Key, *Southern Politics in State and Nation* (New York: Alfred A. Knopf, 1949), p. 300.

16William Riker, *The Theory of Political Coalitions* (New Haven, Conn.: Yale University Press, 1962), p. 32.

translated into the following hypothesis about party behavior: political parties try to win by the *smallest* possible margin. This is rational, because then the winnings have to be divided among a minimal number of party members.

Riker provides some empirical (both experimental and historical) evidence in support of the hypothesis which has been generated by his game model. He is then able to use his generalization to explain Key's discovery. "When the Democratic party is a coalition of the whole, it is worth nothing. But when an opposition exists, the coalition is worth something. Hence, a majority faction inside the Democratic party appears to take charge of the winnings. It then expels some of these not necessary to win in order to divide the gains among fewer persons."[17]

This example demonstrates the usefulness of game models. Their rigor and sharpness make them a significant source of hypotheses. Game models will probably not be applicable to politics exactly as they come from the mathematician or economist. We noted that Riker modified the model to make it more relevant. But the basic assumptions remain the same. If game theory is to be fully exploited by political scientists, they will have to become familiar enough with its nature and limitations to be able to decide when it can and when it cannot be used, or how it might be adjusted to meet the complexities of particular political situations.

---

[17]*Ibid.*, pp. 95-96.

12 Role theory

Political scientists approach the study of political behavior in several ways. Chapters 10 and 11 examined approaches which focus upon the psychological characteristics of political actors and so hypothesize relationships between independent variables, such as attitudes, opinions, and intentions; and dependent variables, referring to political phenomena of various kinds. This chapter considers *role theory,* an approach which accepts the validity of psychological models but argues that they don't go far enough.

To the role theorist, the reason is clear enough. As Heinz Eulau puts it, "Political behavior...is always conduct in the performance of a political role."[1] The strong implication is that political scientists will never develop sound explanations of political phenomena if they view political actors only as individuals, or even individual members of groups. Instead, role theory suggests that political behavior is to a large extent the result of the demands and expectations of the role or roles which a political actor happens to be filling. Surely, the personality and attitudes of the man who is President influence his decisions, but the decisions are made as he fills a role or set of roles and this fact, the role theorist argues, is of primary interest.

Most role theorists emphasize the difficulties inherent in a

---

[1]Heinz Eulau, *The Behavioral Persuasion in Politics* (New York: Random House, 1963), p. 40.

purely individualistic approach to politics, and therefore the advantages of role theory. John Wahlke, in the introductory essay of an application of role theory to legislative behavior writes, "No legislature or other institution could be seen by the analyst if the human actors did not exhibit behavior in conformity, to at least some minimal extent, with the norms of behavior constituting their roles."[2] Thus one attractive feature of role theory is its attempt to place political activity in a social context; that is, a conceptual framework is provided which views the individual as someone who depends upon and reacts to the behavior of others. More about this in a moment.

Another selling point of role theory, according to proponents, is its ability to describe institutions behaviorally. To the role theorist, a political institution is a set of behavior patterns associated with roles. Let us quote Wahlke again: "The chief utility of the role-theory model of the legislative actor is that, unlike other models, it pinpoints those aspects of legislators' behavior which make the legislature an institution."[3] An institution is, in effect, a number of interrelated roles. Role theory thus bridges the gap between individualistic and group approaches. One can still talk about individual behavior, but now it is in terms of roles, which in turn are the basic components of institutions.

The nature of role theory

Role theory begins with the assumption that political actors find themselves in various positions, from President to voter, with certain behavior patterns associated with them. Putting it another way, there are certain expectations about how someone in a particular position is supposed to behave. These expectations constitute a role, or roles.

There are two kinds or sources of expectation. First are those which "outsiders" have. That is, a society has certain notions about what the President should and should not do. The "notions of society" include the expectations of private citizens, of groups,

---

2John Wahlke, Heinz Eulau, William Buchanan, and LeRoy C. Ferguson, *The Legislative System* (New York: John Wiley & Sons, Inc., 1962), p. 10.

3*Ibid.,* p. 9.

and of governmental officials and are manifested in constitutions, legislative statutes, public opinion, and deeply seated cultural norms. To the extent that he is aware of them, these expectations influence the behavior of anyone filling a particular role. Thus, there is a two-way psychological relationship in every role. On the one hand there are the expectations that outsiders have. On the other hand are the perceptions the "insider" has of the outsiders' expectations. The President knows there are legal restrictions on his power, and if he is an astute politician he also realizes that various publics, including other professional politicians, conceive of the role of the President in terms of particular duties, responsibilities, and sanctions. The accuracy of the President's reading of these expectations is one important ingredient of presidential effectiveness. So the first kind of influence proposed in role theory stems from the relationship between the expectation of those outside the role and the perception of these expectations by those filling the role.

This suggests a second kind of influence. It is the way the role occupant, the insider, interprets his role; that is, his *own* expectations about what he should and should not, can and cannot do. The man who is President considers the expectations of outsiders, but he also comes to the office with his own ideas about the role he must play. These ideas reflect, to a large extent, attitudes, ideology, and personality traits developed before his movement into the role. But, in addition, they will be conditioned by the expectations of outsiders. We have already noted that the role filler consciously considers such expectations. Now we are suggesting that the outside expectations influence his own interpretation of the role. It is, in short, a case of *learning;* this is why the word "conditioned" was used. The President, to continue our example, *considers* what other politicians think he should be doing, and adjusts his behavior accordingly. But there is also a strong possibility that he will begin to adopt some of these ideas and attitudes *as his own.* He will learn, through association or reinforcement, to have a particular interpretation of the role of President. It is clear, then, that while for purposes of analysis, role theory can make the distinction between outside expectations and internal interpretations of a role, as a matter of fact they are closely intertwined; the difference between considering outside expectations and having your own interpretations shaped by these expectations is often difficult to see. The important point to keep in mind is that in either case, behavior is affected by the role.

A role does not exist in isolation. Role theorists therefore use the concept "role network" to describe the relationships among roles. Heinz Eulau provides an example: "A legislator is 'colleague' to his fellow legislators, 'representative' to his constituents, 'friend' (or enemy) to lobbyists, 'follower' to his party leaders.... Whatever role is taken, simultaneously or seriatim, what emerges is a very intricate structure of relations in which one role is implicated in several other roles."[4] Several important points are suggested by this passage. First, role theory deals with complex social situations. Any conceptual scheme or model that is developed from the approach will have to simplify the situation, in emphasizing a particular set of role relationships, and deemphasizing others.

A second implication is that many of the most visible roles are really made up of a number of subroles. Eulau's "legislator" is a case in point. But so, too, are "President," "politician," "citizen," and most other role concepts in widespread use. In fact, some include so many subroles as to be ambiguous and nearly indeterminate; consider the roles of "citizen" and "politician" as they are commonly used. Another problem for the political scientist using role theory is the sorting out of political roles from other kinds; or more accurately, the sorting out of political role networks. A legislator performs a number of political roles, but at the same time these are probably tied to roles that we would identify as social or economic. That is, in addition to being a "representative" and "colleague," a senator might be a "father," "church member," and "union member."

This leads to another important phenomenon suggested by role theory. It is the concept of *role conflict*. It is not difficult to visualize a situation in which two or more of a political actor's political roles come into conflict, or a political role comes into conflict with a social or economic role. An example of the first would be the dilemma faced by a legislator who, in order to satisfy his constituents (who favor extensive federal spending in the

---

[4]Eulau, *op. cit.,* p. 41.

cities), must work against the party's policy of cutting such spending, or vice versa. An example of the second would be the problem faced by the conscientious senator-father who believes his children should be back in the wide open spaces of their home state rather than in Washington, where the senator can be of some use to his state and his country. In both kinds of situations the expectations attached to the several roles pull in different directions. How the role occupant resolves the dilemma is an important question for role theory.

The uses of role theory

The most obvious, and as a tool of political analysis the most important, use of role theory is as an explainer and predictor of political behavior. It is not difficult to see how role theory might accomplish this objective. Knowledge of the expectations attached to a role by a society provides us with a basis for predicting the behavior of a particular occupant of the role. This is the starting point of an explanatory and predictive role theory of political behavior. We might say, then, that President Johnson did not veto congressional act A because this would have violated the accepted norms of his role as chief legislator.

But, of course, there is more to a role than outside expectations. Therefore, an empirical role theory must include the concepts of perception of outside expectations and internal role interpretations. In short, the theory would be based on the three factors we discussed in the last section. If we know the societal expectations, internal perceptions of the expectations, and interpretation of the role by the role occupant, we should be able to predict and explain the behavior of the role occupant with some degree of confidence. At least this is a primary objective of role theory.

The concept of role conflict might also be of some use to the political scientist. It might explain, for instance, the seemingly erratic behavior of a particular governmental official. The discovery of conflict between several roles could suggest hypotheses relating role conflict and resulting behavior designed to resolve the conflict. As the number of roles increases, the likelihood of developing accurate generalizations decreases. But even in these situations, the assumptions of the approach—that political actors fill roles and that because they often fill several roles, conflict is possible—have focused the political scientist's attention on certain kinds of potentially relevant phenomena.

The point was made in the last section that role theory provides a framework for analyzing institutions in behavioral terms. According to role theory, institutions are neither groups of individuals nor rigid structures, but systems of interrelated roles. This gives the role theorist the ability to treat an institution such as the Senate or the Democratic party as a dynamic process which nevertheless has some continuity. There is some stability in roles—all modern Presidents have filled the same set of roles—and yet because role expectations change, and different individuals occupy roles, there is also a change in the nature of the role. All Presidents are chief legislators, but because of shifting outside expectations and different Presidents, the role has had several connotations throughout the history of our political system. In addition, change and development in the political system is provided for by the element of role learning on the part of the role occupant. His interpretation upon entering the role may not be the same as the one he has when he leaves it.

In addition to providing a foundation for explanations of the behavior of role occupants, role theory suggests an approach to the study of political recruitment. It is not difficult to comprehend. If a role has certain expectations attached to it, then it seems reasonable to assume that individuals meeting the requirements proposed by these expectations will be more likely to fill the role than those who don't. If a city (its political leaders) expects its mayor to be unaggressive and subservient to the city council, then it is unlikely that an aggressive initiator will move into the position. The limits of this kind of analysis are obvious; we might be able to predict that certain types will *not* be recruited into certain roles, but it is much more difficult to predict who the occupants will be because other factors are involved. In addition, role expectations may change, and the competitors for the position may be instrumental in changing them. This, then, is another kind of role learning, by the outsiders. We have already mentioned its opposite number, learning by the role occupant.

Our discussion of role theory would be misleading if we did not articulate the problems that every political scientist will become aware of as he uses this approach. First of all, given the complexity of most role networks, the question must always be asked, Can the roles in a particular situation be reduced to a manageable number which still describes with some accuracy the behavior involved? This leads to a second question. Are there other kinds of nonrole variables that might influence behavior and which cannot be included within a role approach? In other words, can role theory do the job by itself?

13 The group approach

Most approaches to the study of polities have been borrowed by political scientists from other disciplines. Systems theory and functional analysis are largely the products of sociology and anthropology; game theory was developed by economists and mathematicians; and psychologists are responsible for learning theory. Group theory, on the other hand, is primarily "home grown." Beginning with the ground-breaking work of Arthur Bentley in 1908, group theory has been developed and applied almost exclusively by political scientists or social scientists interested in political phenomena.[1] Thus one question that seems relevant in the analysis of many approaches—Is it applicable to politics?—is on its face not quite so significant when evaluating group theory. As the authors of a recent methodological analysis of political science put it, "Emphasis on the group takes us right to the heart of the discipline."[2]

THE SIGNIFICANCE OF THE GROUP IN THE STUDY OF POLITICS

We needn't spend much time working out a definition of "group," for there seems to be a fairly widespread consensus

---

[1]Arthur Bentley, *The Process of Government* (Chicago: University of Chicago Press, 1908).

[2]Robert T. Golembiewski, William A. Welsh, and William J. Crotty, *A Methodological Primer for Political Scientists* (Chicago: Rand McNally, 1968), p. 121.

among political scientists about what they are referring to when they use the term. Most agree that a political group exists when men with shared interests organize, interact, and seek goals through the political process. The key notions are "interaction" or "relationships"; "interest"; and "process" or "activity." In fact, David Truman, in his modern reinterpretation of Bentley, argues that such interactions *are* the group.[3]

Assuming that there is basic agreement in regard to the question, What is a group? let us see how group theorists line up on the methodologically more important questions: What is the significance of the group in the political system? and the derivative, How useful is group theory to the study of politics? Answers to these questions can be placed into one of two categories. On the one hand are those who say that group activity *is* politics. The founding father, Arthur Bentley, takes this position. After stressing the importance of a research concentration on groups, Bentley writes: "When the groups are adequately stated, everything is stated. When I say everything I mean everything. The complete description will mean the complete science, in the study of social phenomena, as in any other field."[4] The argument is clear. A description of group activity is a description of politics. It follows that an approach to the study of politics must be based on the concept of group; hence the indispensability of group theory.

The second kind of group theorist is less parochial in characterizing his approach. He retains the basic assumption that group behavior is at the center of politics, but he is not ready to view a description of political groups as equivalent to a description of all politics. The following statement of David Truman is similar to Bentley's, but one senses a shift toward a more moderate position. "We have argued, in fact, that the behaviors that constitute the process of government cannot be adequately understood apart from the groups, especially the organized and potential interest groups, which are operative at any point in time."[5] This implicitly asserts that not all political behavior is group behavior, although

[3]David Truman, *The Governmental Process* (New York: Alfred A. Knopf, 1951), p. 24.
[4]Bentley, *op. cit.,* pp. 208-9.
[5]Truman, *op. cit.,* p. 502.

the activities which we identify as political can ultimately be explained by facts about group behavior.

Truman, for instance, does not completely dismiss the significance of the individual and individual characteristics in politics. "We do not wish...to deny that individual differences exist or that there is evidence to support the notion of individuality."[6] This, however, does not imply that the completely unaffiliated individual has much impact on political decisions. What Truman seems to be saying is that different individuals behave differently in the same group. Thus, the assumption is being made that groups are the basic stuff of politics and individualistic factors are important only in a group context. "It follows that the personality of any reasonably normal individual is not wholly accounted for by any single group affiliation. This proposition not only must be accepted; it must be a central element in any satisfactory explanation of the political process in group terms."[7] Individuals exist, and they are not described solely in terms of their membership in a group. It is more realistic to view the individual as an entity with a distinctive character moving in and out of several groups or being a member of several groups simultaneously. Thus Truman can allow for the individual and at the same time develop a group theory of politics without contradiction, because while the individual is important, the basic stuff of politics is the group.

Bentley, on the other hand, rejects the usefulness of individualistic concepts in the study of politics. Since there is no way to get at them, attitudes, beliefs, and other psychological traits are mere "soul stuff."[8] We can only study political processes, and the only processes we can observe are those of groups. Once again we reach the conclusion that politics is group behavior.

Another way to look at the difference between interpretations of group theory is in terms of the individualist-holist controversy which we have referred to several times in earlier chapters.[9] Truman is clearly an individualist in that he does not view the properties of groups as emergent. A political group is made up of

---

[6]*Ibid.*, p. 49.

[7]*Ibid.*

[8]Bentley, *op. cit.*

[9]See especially Chapter 2.

individuals and relationships between individuals. This is a point which should be stressed, for it leads to the realization that one need not be a holist to advocate a group approach to politics. The philosophical position that a group is no more than the sum of its parts is compatible with the research strategy that views group behavior as the most useful unit of analysis.

Bentley, on the other hand, is closer to the holist position, and therefore represents those group theorists who view the group as the stuff of politics both philosophically (methodologically) and strategically. It seems that few contemporary political scientists who employ the group approach make the holistic assumption. They are not necessarily conscious individualists, but at least they would probably react negatively to Bentley's position that "there are no political phenomena except group phenomena."

The major question which concerns the group theorist is, How do groups behave in the political system? He is not methodologically interested in the internal makeup or processes of groups except insofar as they influence the behavior of groups in the political process. Since politics is ultimately explained in terms of relationships between groups as they make claims on each other and compete for the values of the society, only those characteristics of groups which are relevant to this kind of activity are studied. The resulting model of politics might be labeled "macroatomic" or, perhaps more accurately, "molecular," for the political process is viewed as a system of bounded and somewhat compact groups attracting and repelling each other in neverending competition.

While this characterization of the group approach catches its basic shape, it does not take us very far. Are we to assume, for instance, that group theorists fail to include the governmental decision-making process in their models of politics? The answer is, they do talk about government; but they view the role or functions of the government (defined as the legal institutions of the state) in the political system in a number of different ways.

There seem to be two basic positions in regard to this question. The first, and the one which Bentley advocates, claims that government is a mere register of group pressures. "The official procedures of government are techniques through which interest groups operate rather than independent forces in the political process."[10] Thus, groups compete, pursue their interests, and government rings up the results indicating who has won and who has lost. It is obvious, then, that the significance of government is deemphasized in this interpretation. At best, a congress or a parliament is one group among many. And this Bentley admits. From it he concludes that perhaps governmental institutions have interests of their own.

This realization, which Bentley clearly feels is of no great importance, opens the door to the second interpretation of the role of government in a group model of politics. The fact that Congress or the Presidency or a court is as much a group as an interest group is stressed; each is a part of the competitive political process. But this significant assumption leads to a perhaps more significant assertion about the role of government. If, let us say, the Senate has its own interests, then it follows that it is not merely a political cash register, an inert mechanical computer recording the interests of other groups or the balance of power among them. Government instead takes an *active* role in tipping the balance. In fact, most group theorists today would probably argue that the governmental decision-making apparatus is the most powerful group or set of groups in the political system. The resulting model of politics is the same molecular one, but now there is a dominant central moelcule, government. That David Truman views government and interest groups as significantly different is evident in the following passage: "An interest group is a shared-attitude group that makes certain claims upon other groups in the society. If and when it makes its claims through or upon any of the institutions of government it becomes a political interest group."[11]

A political group is characterized by its contact with government. This, of course, implies that not all groups are political. A labor union bargaining with industry is not political until it leaves the bargaining table and appeals to Congress, the President, or the courts. Thus, referring back to the discussion of politics in Chapter 2, we can conclude that a group theorist like Truman limits the scope of political science to group activity taking place around the

---

[10] Bentley, *op. cit.*
[11] Truman, *op. cit.,* p. 37.

official institutions of government. This is broader than it might seem, for two of the institutions that groups work through are elections and public opinion. But some group activity lies outside politics.

Governmental institutions are groups, but nevertheless groups of a special kind. They are groups because they have interests and compete with other groups. Consider the struggle that takes place among the branches of government. On the other hand, they stand out in relation to other groups because of their position and role in the political process. Government regulates the group struggle and in effect determines the balance of power within the system. But in addition government formulates the rules which to some extent determine the shape of the struggle. This all assumes that governmental decisions result from the interplay of the demands and objectives of interest groups and governmental institutions.

If politics is primarily the activity of groups as they make claims on government, then a group model of politics should be able to include or account for most political phenomena. Let us now examine some of the major concepts and relationships from which a model might be built.

To begin with, the group theorist assumes that the primary objective of every political group is the successful realization of its objectives, namely, the satisfaction of its demands. This implies that a group theory must be able to identify the interests of groups if it is to account for the outcomes of the political process.

An equivalent way of saying, "All groups try to achieve their objectives," is, "All groups attempt to acquire power—to influence decisions in their favor." But however one phrases it, this is only a beginning. Concepts must be formulated and hypotheses generated which describe how power is sought and exercized and how, in consequence, decisions are made.

THE CONCEPT OF "ACCESS"

The central concept is "access." As Truman argues, no interest group can influence decisions unless it gains access to decision points within the government. Thus Truman concludes that access "becomes the facilitating intermediate objective of political interest groups. The development and improvement of such access is a common denominator of the tactics of all of them."[12] This is a commonsensical notion: if a group has nowhere in government to go to make its demands, it is difficult to imagine it influencing decisions. "Access" seems to have a sound empirical basis. For as it is used by a group theorist such as Truman, we are able to tell when and at what point an interest group has access. In order to achieve its objectives an interest group will seek to influence decisions. To do this, it will have to work with, on, or through governmental decision makers. If it is successful, it has gained access, and the point of contact between the group and the decision makers is the access point.

But if access is to serve as the central concept of a model of politics, it must be more than empirically sound. It must also be useful in organizing, describing, and perhaps explaining political phenomena. There seems to be prima facie evidence that access is useful or, in terms we have used before, has *systematic import.*

Let us note some of the functions which "access" can perform in a group model of politics. In the first place it provides the all-important linkage between groups and government (realizing, of course, that governmental institutions are groups). This function must be performed in a group model because of the model's emphasis on the influence of groups on political decision making.

If the model is to generate hypotheses, access must be related to other concepts. One kind of relationship might make access the antecedent condition or independent variable in a generalization which makes power or influence the dependent variable. Thus, we might be able to explain why interest group A has more influence than interest group B by demonstrating that A has more access to government.

On the other hand, access is a dependent variable to be explained. We would like to know why some groups have more access than others. Group theorists usually cite such factors as *group cohesion* (how much of its individual members' total loyalty it commands) and *organization* as important determinants of access. The more cohesive and highly organized a group is, the more access it has. Another crucial factor in group models of

---

[12]*Ibid.,* p. 264.

politics is the *status* of the group. David Truman says, "Perhaps the most basic factor affecting access is the position of the group or its spokesman in the social structure....The deference accorded a high-status group not only facilitates the acceptance of its propaganda but also eases its approach to the government." [13] Other factors which might be cited are the group's *leadership,* its *wealth,* and its *geographical distribution.* As one proliferates the list of variables which might influence access, we see more and more its usefulness as a central concept. In effect, most of the important concepts used in the group approach seem to be related to access. It is truly a centralizing concept in the sense that it is the connecting link between independent variables, such as status, and dependent variables, such as influence and, ultimately, political decisions.

Implicit in all that we have said is the fact that "access" is a comparative concept. Remember that Truman calls it a common denominator. This clearly means that all interest groups will at least have the seeking of access in common. This opens the door to the possibility of comparing or ranking groups according to how much access they have. And if access is a central concept, then in comparing access we will also be indirectly comparing influence and effectiveness. And this, after all, is the objective of the group approach.

EVALUATING THE GROUP APPROACH

While group theory seems a useful (in terms of suggestiveness) approach to the study of politics, it does not go without criticism. Let us conclude our analysis of the approach by evaluating several of these criticisms. We have already mentioned one in a different context. It claims that group theory leaves out one important set of variables, namely the characteristics of individuals. But as we pointed out then, the political scientist does not have to be a holist assuming the existence of emergent group properties to base his study of politics on the group. In short, most group theorists do not reject the importance, let alone the existence of individuals in politics. They only point

---

[13] *Ibid.,* p. 265.

out that it is a wise strategy to stay at the group level. This criticism, then, probably misses the mark.

There is another criticism which argues the other side of the coin. It claims that the group approach is wrong and misleading in not considering the nation, the state, or society. Instead, the argument goes, group theory studies a limited range of political phenomena, never thinking about the supergroup of which they are all a part. This often leads to the closely related claim that group theory cannot properly handle the notion of "public" or "national interest." One reaction to this criticism is well articulated by David Truman: "In developing a group interpretation of politics...we do not need to account for a totally inclusive interest because one does not exist."[14] Instead, that which we call the public interest is the result of the group struggle. So most group theorists would reject the idea that a public interest exists apart from or independent of the political process. Groups compete, governments make decisions, and the output can be labeled the public interest. But we should realize that this is a derivative concept with no emergent status of its own. Thus, as Truman suggests, one should not be criticized for ignoring a nonexistent entity.

---

[14]*Ibid.*, p. 51. For an analysis of various interpretations of "public interest," see Glendon Schubert, *The Public Interest* (New York: Free Press, 1962).

14 *Systems theory and functional analysis*

Two of the more popular methods of organizing thought in social science are *systems theory* and *functional analysis*. As a matter of fact, the latter is an offshoot of the former, and so they can be placed in the same methodological category. The basic point is that functional analysis assumes the existence of a system, and therefore it is reasonable to begin with a brief consideration of systems theory. Then we will devote more time to its perhaps more sophisticated and impressive relative, functional analysis.

SYSTEMS THEORY

Like many approaches in social science, systems theory has a commonsensical appeal. It is natural to think of phenomena as parts of wholes. For many people it is difficult to conceive of the entity which does not fit somewhere.

This is, in effect, the starting point of the political systems theorist. He begins by assuming that political phenomena can best be analyzed by viewing them as parts of a systematic whole. Morton Kaplan, one of the foremost users of systems theory in the study of international politics, asserts that "a scientific politics can develop only if the materials of politics are treated in terms of

217

systems of action."[1] This may be a bit strong for those who are not themselves systems theorists. But even they might admit the utility of a rudimentary notion of system as a starting point for theory construction in political science.

The commonsensical appeal of systems models is not a phenomenon unique to contemporary social science. Plato and Aristotle viewed the polis as a political system made up of interrelated elements. And more than 300 years ago Thomas Hobbes wrote: "By systems I understand any number of men joined in one interest or one business."[2] While this is a primitive and perhaps unacceptable definition, at least it demonstrates the historical pervasiveness of the concept of system.

The components of systems

Systems theorists agree that every system has several components. First of all, it has elements which are clearly identifiable. The planets and the sun are the elements of the solar system. If we are treating the family as a system, the individual members would be its elements. The elements of a political system could be individuals, groups, or nations, depending on the scope of the system.

We don't, however, call every set of elements a system. Something else is clearly needed. This something else is a set of relationships among the elements. A family is not a system because it is made up of identifiable elements but because the elements interact, because they are interdependent. The characteristic of interaction prevents us from labeling every set of elements a system. Systems theory then allows us to make a methodological distinction between, let us say, all the people who happen to be in a department store at the same time and an interest group made up of a set of interacting and interdependent people.

If we are going to talk about a system we had better be able to

---

[1]Morton Kaplan, *System and Process in International Politics* (New York: John Wiley & Sons, Inc., 1957), p. 4. Other basic expositions of the systems approach can be found in David Easton's works: "An Approach to the Analysis of Political Systems," *World Politics*, Vol. IX, 1957, pp. 383-400; *A Framework for Political Analysis* (Englewood Cliffs, N.J.: Prentice-Hall, Inc., 1956); and *A Systems Analysis of Political Life* (New York: John Wiley & Sons, Inc., 1965).

[2]Thomas Hobbes, *Leviathan*, Chapter 22.

indicate its extent—where it ends and other systems begin. In other words, every system has *boundaries* which ought to be specifiable by the systems theorist. It makes little sense to speak of a system developing or changing or influencing other systems if its boundaries are not at least roughly described.

In general, then, we can say that every system has three characteristic components: identifiable elements, relationships among the elements, and boundaries. In addition, most systems will have subsystems. That is, the elements and relationships of a system will, in effect, break themselves down into smaller systems. For instance, the Congress is a subsystem of the American political system, the Senate a subsystem of Congress, and the Foreign Relations Committee a subsystem of the Senate. One implication of this analysis is that systems exist at a number of levels. In addition, the indication seems to be that every system has an environment—there are always other systems "on the outside," so to speak. The political scientist slices the conglomeration at the level he wants to study, treating smaller systems as subsystems and the larger ones as possible environmental conditions.

The systems theorist who adds some substance to this rather bare frame usually does so by talking about the inputs and outputs of political systems.[3] These concepts are significant because they describe how a systems model accounts for linkage between the system and its environment, or between systems. For instance, we might view the decision-making apparatus of the United States (legislatures, executive, and courts) as a political system, and then study its inputs—demands and supports—from the larger social system and its outputs—rule making, rule enforcement, and rule interpretation—for the social system. Or the entire set of elements—inputs, decisions, and outputs—could be viewed as a system having certain relationships (inputs and outputs) with its environment, which in this case would be the international society. Or one could move in the other direction, viewing, let us say, a congressional committee as a system with inputs from, decisions, and outputs for the larger political system. The point we

---

[3]These notions are developed in Easton, "An Approach to the Analysis of Political Systems," *op. cit.*

want to make is that input-output analysis provides the conceptual basis for the notion of linkage between systems.

There is one other concept that is basic to systems theory. It is the notion of "feedback." Feedback refers to the influence of outputs on inputs and so, ultimately, on decisions. An interest group makes demands (inputs) on Congress, asking for the passage of a particular bill. Despite these demands, Congress defeats the bill (output). There will be feedback in the form of the reaction of the interest group to Congress' decision. The result will probably be new inputs, perhaps even the withholding of support, including civil disobedience. Congress then learns of the results of its decision through the change in inputs, and perhaps modifies its behavior. In the next chapter we will see that communications theory has just been anticipated.

"Feedback" is important to systems theory because it provides a kind of continuity. That is, it builds into the approach a method for handling the two-way relationship between inputs and outputs. The behavior of systems then can be viewed as a continuous process in which outputs are reactions to inputs and inputs are in turn influenced by outputs.

The uses of systems theory

For political scientists who use it, systems theory is primarily a way of looking at phenomena—it is in many ways a state of mind. The commitment is made to concentrate on the system and its behavior, including the interaction of its elements, but not the characteristics of the elements. Systems theory is most accurately placed within the category of macro, as opposed to micro, approaches to politics. Now, as it is used by political scientists, systems theory seems to be of heuristic, not explanatory, significance. Thus the label "theory" is a misnomer; it is much more accurate to think of the systems approach as a conceptual scheme, perhaps even more realistically, as we just pointed out, as a state of mind or general orientation which serves as a jumping-off place for more specialized political research.

It seems that the systems approach generates two basic sets of questions: First, how does the system handle inputs and outputs? In other words, what are the relationships between inputs and outputs? Secondly, how does a system cope with its environment? What kinds of system behavior lead to system survival or maintenance, what kinds to system deterioration or death? The second set of questions is the major concern of functional analysis, the more highly developed, and it would seem more useful, relative of systems theory.

FUNCTIONAL ANALYSIS

Ernest Nagel has said that, "In the judgement of many students a comprehensive theory of social phenomena is most likely to be achieved within the framework of systematically 'functional' analyses of social phenomena."[4] While not yet the major school of thought in political science that it is in sociology and anthropology, functionalism has nevertheless come into its own as an important approach to analyzing political phenomena.[5] The label "functional analysis" is applied to a number of activities and styles of analysis. Functional analyses are used to generate hypotheses and organize existing knowledge of the political system, and at times a functional explanation is proposed to account for political phenomena. The feature which characterizes all of them is a primary focus on the functions of political systems.

Strictly speaking, the functional approach is concerned with system maintenance—how political systems survive over time. This is how functionalism ties in with the more general systems approach. However, while an assumption of system maintenance may underly all functional analyses, practically speaking many of them go no further than a consideration of the effects that certain variables have on a system. Thus, we should not expect every functional analysis to explain why a system is maintained. However, since this is the ultimate objective, we can legitimately criticize a proposed functional explanation if it is going in the

---

[4]Ernest Nagel, *The Structure of Science* (New York: Harcourt, Brace & World, 1961), p. 520.

[5]The main influence on functional analysis in political science has been the work of the sociologist Talcott Parsons. His basic theoretical work is *The Social System* (New York: Free Press, 1951). For an application to politics see " 'Voting' and the Equilibrium of the American Political System," in Eugene Burdick and Arthur Brodbeck (eds.), *American Voting Behavior* (New York: Free Press, 1959).

wrong direction or no direction at all, even though it is not yet dealing directly with system maintenance.

In its simplest form functional analysis contains the following elements: a system; variables; arguments demonstrating the effects of the variables on the system. The fully developed system-maintaining variety has the additional feature of arguments showing how the variables contribute to the maintenance of the system by performing certain necessary functions. Thus, the analysis is called functional because of an assertion that certain conditions (functions) are necessary for the continuance of the system.

The major methodological requirements of this approach are rather simple, commonsensically so. First, the system being referred to must be explicitly defined and its boundaries clearly indicated; otherwise, it will be impossible to determine if the system is in fact being maintained or changed. Looking at it from another standpoint, if one wants to examine the influence of a variable on a system, he has to first have the nature and extent of the system clear in mind. This leads to a second requirement. The influencing variables must be empirically conceptualized; they must be defined in terms of testable properties of the world. Finally, in the case of system-maintenance explanations, the necessary conditions or functions that the variables are supposed to perform must be empirically defined.

Types of functional analysis

Having made these general comments about the methodological foundations of functional analysis, let us examine several of the activities which are commonly assigned this label. The first has been labeled "simple-functional" or "eclectic" by William Flanigan and Edwin Fogelman.[6] It is probably the most widespread of those activities that, lumped together, constitute "functional analysis." Eclectic functionalism involves the listing of activities that an institution, individual, or nation engages in. Thus, Clinton Rossiter has enumerated the functions of the

---

[6]William Flanigan and Edwin Fogelman, "Functional Analysis," in James C. Charlesworth (ed.), *Contemporary Political Analysis* (New York: Free Press, 1967), pp. 72-73.

President,[7] Herman Finer the functions of the legislator,[8] and Frank J. Sorauf those of political parties.[9] "Function," then, is equated with "action." Ernest Nagel has characterized this activity as an attempt to "denote a more or less inclusive set of processes or operations within (or manifested by) a given entity, without indication of the various effects these activities produce either upon that entity or any other."[10] When the functional approach is used in this manner, its intention is not to explain the maintenance of a political system. Eclectic functionalism is more a descriptive enterprise. The central concept of "function" is used to organize the behavior of political actors and institutions.

However, eclectic functionalism sometimes becomes inter-mingled with a more promising activity. For instance, Sorauf's *listing* of party functions carries with it the implication that they have some effect on the political system—i.e., they politically educate and socialize the public. Now we can call this kind of functional approach "system-affecting" to distinguish it from the more basic and important "system-maintaining" variety. For there is no mention of the activity or function, X, contributing to the maintenance of a system. It may, in fact, be doing just that. But there is no claim that the system needs X to survive; only that X has some effect on it. Of course, it is clear that system-affecting arguments can often become system-maintaining if further analysis is carried out. Perhaps another example will clarify this point.

In his study of political party behavior in Michigan, Samuel Eldersveld makes much of the functional consequences of parties; in our language, this means the effects the parties have on the political system of Michigan.[11] Thus Eldersveld concludes a section of his analysis with these words: "We have seen how party effort is associated with increased voting turnout, strengthening party identifications and loyalties, and developing attitudes

---

7Clinton Rossiter, *The American Presidency* (New York: Harcourt, Brace & World, 1960), Chapter 1.

8Herman Finer, *The Theory and Practice of Modern Government* (New York: Henry Holt, 1949), pp. 379-84.

9Frank J. Sorauf, *Political Parties in the American System* (Boston: Little, Brown & Co., 1964), pp. 2-6.

10Nagel, *op. cit.,* p. 523.

11Samuel Eldersveld, *Political Parties: A Behavioral Analysis* (Chicago: Rand McNally, 1964).

favorable to working for the party operation. In addition, our analysis revealed that exposure to the party results in greater interest in foreign affairs, national domestic affairs, and local public affairs."[12] These seem to be the findings of a study that is based upon the system-affecting functional approach. The activities of the parties have an effect on the nature of the political system. And in the body of his study, Eldersveld presents statistical evidence, often in the form of generalizations—"party exposure, combined no doubt with other influences and interlinked with them, seems to be related to high voting participation"—to substantiate such claims.[13] Thus we see that the generalizations generated by the system-affecting approach are not very unique. They differ from other hypotheses only in that the dependent variable is "the nature of the system" (in Eldersveld's case, a political system with high voting participation).

We said that system-affecting arguments often become, implicitly or explicitly, system-maintaining arguments. That is, the initial demonstration that element X has Y effects on system S frequently results in the claim that X contributes to S's maintenance. Thus, we find Eldersveld making such statements as this: "In strengthening the foundations for political consensus, the party effort is also functional to the system."[14] Here, we see a shift in emphasis to explaining the *maintenance* of the political system—this is clearly what "functional" means in this context. Using Eldersveld's analysis as a basis, we can succinctly summarize the nature of such an explanation: "A political system S requires for its continued existence, among other things, a certain degree of consensus among its members; political parties contribute to the realization and reinforcement of such consensus; therefore, the maintenance of the system is partially explained."[15] Political party activity is a partial *sufficient* condition, not a necessary one. The most general laws upon which the explanation might be based are: (1) consensus is necessary for a D-type political system; (2) increased party activity tends to strengthen consensus. Thus it can

---

[12]*Ibid.*, pp. 541-42.

[13]*Ibid.*, p. 467.

[14]*Ibid.*, p. 542.

[15]*Ibid.* This is a compact statement of Eldersveld's argument.

be seen why "increased party activity" is a partial (there may be other influencing factors at work at the same time) and sufficient (it is enough, in combination with the other factors to strengthen consensus, yet there may be other elements that could take its place) condition. While it tends to produce consensus, it is possible for other factors to do the job.

Another example of system-maintaining explanation can be found in Donald Matthews' discussion of senatorial folkways, because the maintenance or existence of the Senate is partially accounted for by the existence of the folkways.[16] Thus, "apprenticeship," "courtesy," etc., help keep the Senate a going concern. We see the same pattern here as was manifested in Eldersveld's explanations. To operate, the Senate has to have certain functions performed. The folkways perform them, and so the Senate continues to function. In Matthews' words. "These folkways we have suggested are highly functional to the Senate social system since they provide motivation for the performance of vital duties and essential modes of behavior which, otherwise, would go unrewarded....Without these folkways, the Senate could hardly operate with its present organization and rules."[17] The last clause implies a definition of the political system known as the "Senate." It is maintained with the help of the functions performed by the folkways.

A final example can be cited to indicate just how general this sort of analysis can be. Gabriel Almond has formulated one of the best known and most influential system-maintaining models.[18] It is a general model because he attempts to describe the main political functions of all political systems. He begins by making a list of seven functions that the political system performs for the more inclusive social system.[19] Almond argues that all political systems perform these functions: he calls this phenomena "the

---

[16]Donald Matthews, *U.S. Senators and Their World* (New York: Vintage Books, 1960).

[17]*Ibid.*, p. 116.

[18]Gabriel Almond, "Introduction: A Functional Approach to Comparative Politics," in Gabriel Almond and James S. Coleman, *The Politics of the Developing Areas* (Princeton, N.J.: Princeton University Press, 1960), pp. 3-64.

[19]*Ibid.*, p. 17. Almond distinguishes between input and output functions. The former include "political socialization and recruitment, interest articulation, interest aggregation and political communication." The latter include "rule-application and rule-adjudication."

universality of the political functions."[20] But what is important for us is the fact that different political structures, both within a society and in different societies, can perform the same functions. For instance, in modern political systems, interest groups are the primary performers of the function of "interest articulation." But, "We find in Indonesia that the few and relatively poorly organized trade unions or business associations are not the important interest-articulating structures, that we have to look at the bureaucracy, status groups, kinship and lineage groups and anonic phenomena to discover how interests are articulated."[21] Thus the same pattern appears: the social system requires that certain functions be performed for its continued existence, and political systems perform them *in various ways.* Here, then, is a clear manifestation of the sufficient (partially) and nonnecessary nature of system-maintaining arguments. Interest groups articulate interests in the United States, but not in Indonesia.

We can conclude this section with a favorable comment about system-affecting and system-maintaining approaches. Through their use it is possible to generate hypotheses suggesting that various political institutions can partially explain "a feature of," "the existence of," or "the maintenance of" a political or a social system. It would seem that this is the most important and promising activity among those that are usually classified as functional.

Equilibrium analysis

A special type of system-maintaining explanation is often thought of as a distinct approach to political analysis. This is usually called equilibrium analysis, and it seems to be most widely used in the study of international relations. We will attempt to show that equilibrium analysis is a variation on the system-maintaining approach. The main task of the political scientist would thus seem to be an analysis of how systems retain an equilibrium. Harold D. Lasswell and Abraham Kaplan have defined political equilibrium and at the same time implied its relationship

---

20*ibid.,* pp. 12-17.
21*Ibid.,* p. 13.

to system-maintaining analysis. After speaking of systems and system-maintenance, they make the following observation: "The standpoint of equilibrium analysis directs inquiry to the isolation of such systems and investigation of the conditions of their maintenance: disturbances may lead to a re-establishment of equilibrium or the disruption of the system."[22] We might say that a system is maintained as long as it is in equilibrium.

However, some political scientists have used equilibrium in another way. They assume or attempt to demonstrate that a political system has tendencies toward a steady state. Then, political behavior is explained through the application of the resulting theory. Hans Morgenthau's famous "balance of power" theory can be interpreted as such an undertaking. Morgenthau sees a movement toward equilibrium as one of the main characteristics of all social systems made up of autonomous units.[23] His use of the concept "balance" implies that if there were a grouping of states which did not seek such a balance, they could not be engaged in international politics among themselves.[24] This is acceptable; but one may ask if anything empirical is being said, or is the law really a tautology? Has what is a set of empirical questions: Do nations tend toward an equilibrium of power? If so, to what extent? and, How can this explain international behavior? been transformed into a statement, "A political system is one which seeks an equilibrium," which is true by definition? Quentin Gibson has noted that, "There is of course one infallible way of preserving a higher-level law and that is to make it true by definition."[25] Furthermore "If a procedure of this kind is persisted with, it becomes clear that the alleged empirical law is one which could not be refuted under any conceivable circumstances."[26] This, in a sense, is why Morgenthau can eventually call the present bipolar international system a "new" balance of power

---

[22] Harold Lasswell and Abraham Kaplan, *Power and Society* (New Haven, Conn.: Yale University Press, 1950), p. xiv.

[23] Hans Morgenthau, *Politics Among Nations* (New York: Alfred A. Knopf, 1960), p. 167.

[24] *Ibid.* Morgenthau states "that the balance of power and policies aiming at its preservation are...inevitable...in a society of sovereign states."

[25] Quentin Gibson, *The Logic of Social Enquiry* (London: Routledge & Kegan Paul, 1960), p. 121.

[26] *Ibid.*

even though it diverges greatly from the traditional system upon which his theory is based. The upshot of all this is that while we may better understand what Morgenthau means by "international politics," his "law" can give us no information about the world—it can neither describe nor explain—for it is analytic, not empirical.

Our criticism of Morgenthau's theory implies an important feature of any would-be sound explanation based on an equilibrium theory. If a political system has a tendency toward equilibrium it has ways of maintaining itself. This is why we are discussing equilibrium in this chapter. However, if "equilibrium" is to be employed in a meaningful way, we must be able to state that to a certain degree, the system in question does tend to develop characteristics which perform its necessary functions; in other words that it tends toward an equilibrium. This is what Carl Hempel has called an "hypothesis of self-regulation." It is the basic proposition required to make an equilibrium theory nomological and so potentially useful. Most equilibrium theories do not state such a law, let alone provide it with empirical referents.

However, several political scientists have attempted to give the hypothesis of self-regulation empirical content, in preparation for its use in explanations. For instance, S. Sidney Ulmer has analyzed the voting behavior of Supreme Court judges using the Shapeley-Shubik power index. His objective is the testing of the hypothesis that there is "equilibrium in certain behavior patterns in the Court."[27] Phillips Cutwright has, in a similar vein, searched for an equilibrium law of national political development. The hypothesis he statistically tests is that if a nation is underdeveloped it will tend to improve its position, while an overdeveloped nation will make downward adjustments to bring itself into line.[28] This first calls for the discovery of an equilibrium point at which all types of development are in balance. The difficulty of such an undertaking is obvious; but the *attempt* is what is important for our analysis, because it indicates that some political scientists realize that

[27]S. Sidney Ulmer, "Homeostatic Tendencies in the United States Supreme Court," in S. Sidney Ulmer (ed.), *Introductory Readings in Political Behavior* (Chicago: Rand McNally, 1961), pp. 167-88.

[28]Phillips Cutwright, "National Political Development: Its Measurement and Social Correlates," in Nelson W. Polsby, Robert A. Dentler, and Paul A. Smith (eds.), *Politics and Social Life* (Boston: Houghton Mifflin Co., 1963), pp. 569-82.

equilibrium theory requires an *empirical* law of self-regulation. We have seen the shortcomings of a theory that is not given empirical content.

Functional-teleological analysis

Political scientists sometimes argue that a particular behavior pattern or institution is explained if they can demonstrate that it performs a necessary function for the political system. For instance, the origin and present nature of the interest group would be explained by showing that it performs the functions of interest articulation and integration, functions which, let us assume, have to be performed in every political system. If this kind of analysis helps the researcher sort out structures which might perform important functions, then it is of heuristic value. But as an explanation it is unsound.

Let us examine its methodological weak points. First of all, it is difficult enough to demonstrate that a certain function, interest articulation for instance, is necessary for the maintenance of a system. But it is empirically conceivable. However, it is another thing to demonstrate that a particular political institution or activity is the only one that can perform the function. For it is always possible that another institution might perform the same function. As a matter of fact, we have already pointed out that in assuming that different structures can perform the same function, the functional approach provides a foundation for meaningful comparative analysis. And if it is true that a function is performed by different structures in different political systems, why is it not possible that the function is or could be performed by several *structures* within a political system?

An example might help clarify our argument. We will use Donald Matthews' study of the folkways of the Senate as a *point of departure.* [29] This usage of Matthews' analysis should be emphasized, for we are not claiming that he attempts the unsound kind of functional argument we are criticizing here. We will fit a

---

[29] Matthews, *op. cit.*

part of the discussion of folkways into a schema provided by the philosopher of science Carl Hempel.[30] It is as follows:

1. At time T, S (the Senate) functions adequately in setting of kind C (under certain conditions).
2. S functions adequately in a setting of kind C only if a certain necessary condition N (adequate assignment of work loads) is satisfied.
3. If trait i (apprenticeship) were present in S, then, as an effect, condition N would be satisfied.
4. Therefore, at T, trait i is present in S.

In this way, the folkway of apprenticeship seems to be accounted for. However, it is not in fact explained by showing that it contributes to the maintenance of the Senate. Now, apprenticeship may, as a matter of fact, perform such a function. If such an argument were made, then we would be giving an explanation of the system, using the folkways as causal factors. Thus, the folkways help explain why the Senate continues to function. This, of course, is, in form at least, a sound system-maintenance explanation. However, at this point we need only observe that apprenticeship cannot be explained in the above manner because there might be other ways of assigning work loads. These would be, like apprenticeship, sufficient conditions for carrying out the requisite function. And, there is no way to demonstrate why apprenticeship has a preferred status. It is the possible existence of these "functional equivalents" that deprives the argument of explanatory power. Thus, we see why it is fair to say that the folkways can help explain the maintenance or nature of the Senate, while they themselves cannot be explained on the grounds that they contribute to system-maintenance. Perhaps it is now clear why this functional approach is sometimes labeled *teleological.* The present existence or nature of a political phenomenon is being explained by its end. It exists to perform function X. The influence of biology and physiology can be discerned in such social scientific arguments. In other words, the same approach—the heart is explained on the basis of its blood-circulation function—has long been taken in these fields, and some political scientists have no doubt been impressed.

---

[30]Carl G. Hempel, "The Logic of Functional Analysis," in L. Gross (ed.), *Symposium on Sociological Theory* (Evanston, Ill.: Row & Peterson, 1959), p. 301.

A tempting way out of this methodological bind is to make the folkways part of the definition of the Senate. This can be done if the Senate and its conditions (C) are not clearly described. Then, any functional alternative that is discovered can be dismissed as insignificant since the same system is no longer being referred to. The obvious shortcoming of this tactic is, of course, that analytic statements tell us nothing about the world. Making the statement, "the Senate has the structure apprenticeship," analytic removes it from the class of useful empirical generalizations. These difficulties have led some philosophers to the position articulated by Ernest Nagel: "The cognitive worth of functional explanations modeled on teleological explanations in physiology is therefore and in the main very dubious."[31]

There is another way to interpret some apparent teleological arguments so as to give them a sound logical structure. These are the arguments which refer to human purposes. A behavior pattern is explained by demonstrating that an agent believes that something is functional either for himself or for a valued system, and then employing a law that describes what a person with such a belief and such an intention tends to do. Thus, we know why he performs or seeks it. For instance, referring again to Donald Matthews' study of Senate folkways, we might argue that they are desired by senators. That is, the senators believe that to function efficiently, the Senate cannot allow the public venting of personal animosities. Thus, they have intentionally adopted the folkway, "courtesy." The senators consider the folkways functional for the Senate—they are a means to a desired end. This kind of argument, it would seem, falls within both the functional and intentional approaches. But the important point is that it is not teleological.

---

[31] Nagel, *op. cit.*, p. 534-35.

15 *Communications theory*

It has recently been suggested that an important ingredient of the political process, communications, has been largely ignored in the theoretical literature of political science. Several political scientists have set out to correct this gap by developing models of politics based on this "missing ingredient." Karl Deutsch, the leading proponent of a communications approach to the study of politics, has pointed out that cybernetics, the science of communications and control, "represents a shift in the center of interest from drives to steering...."[1] When applied to politics, this means an emphasis on *decisions, control,* and *communications,* rather than power, which has without a doubt been the primary, and at times exclusive, interest of political scientists.[2]

The communications theorist does not claim that communication is the only topic that should interest political scientists. However, since, quoting Deutsch once again, "It is communication, that is, the ability to transmit messages and to react to them, that makes organizations,"[3] any thorough analysis of political organizations and systems must at least include a consideration of the role of communication.

The ultimate significance of a communications approach does not, however, lie in its concentration on communications but

---

[1]Karl Deutsch, *The Nerves of Government* (New Haven, Conn.: Yale University Press, 1963), p. 76.

[2]Chapter 16 of this book discusses the concept of power.

[3]Deutsch, *op. cit.,* p. 77.

rather the ability to describe and explain the behavior of political systems that follows from such concentration. More specifically, "communications is viewed as vital in implementing man's control of his environment...."[4] This is the key point and the main contribution of the communications approach to the study of politics. Recall the stress in systems theory on inputs and outputs, and in functional analysis on the maintenance of systems. According to the approach now under consideration, it is through communications that inputs are received and acted upon and outputs are generated by a system; in short, the effectiveness of a system, how well it handles the demands of its environment, can be measured in terms of its ability to accurately analyze messages from the environment and effectively transmit messages which express reactions.

Putting it another way, it is through communications that a political system relates to and copes with its environment. A system is constantly bombarded with messages. It must be able to read them and react to them. This is the way a system achieves its goals, including self-maintenance. A quote from the political scientist Robert C. North should clarify the communications theorist's conception of the political process: "Politics could not exist without communication, nor could wars be fought. In these terms a modern nation-state may be viewed essentially as a decision and control system which relies upon the exchange of messages in both its domestic affairs and its foreign relations."[5]

This conception of politics and its emphasis on communications is not surprising when one realizes that its major impetus comes from the already mentioned science of cybernetics. As conceived by its major developer, mathematician Norbert Wiener, cybernetics is the study of communication and control in all types of organizations, from machines to large-scale social organizations.[6] As a matter of fact, the first significant advances were made in the development and study of the former. Cybernetics can be viewed

---

[4]S. Sidney Ulmer, *Introductory Readings In Political Behavior* (Chicago: Rand McNally, 1962), p. 397.

[5]Robert C. North, "The Analytical Prospects of Communications Theory," in James C. Charlesworth (ed.), *Contemporary Political Analysis* (New York: Free Press, 1967), p. 301.

[6]Wiener's basic treatment of cybernetics is *Cybernetics* (2d ed.; New York: John Wiley & Sons, Inc., 1961). A more readable version is *The Human Use of Human Beings* (Boston: Houghton Mifflin Co., 1950).

as the attempt to apply knowledge gained of the workings of such self-monitoring devices as antiaircraft guns, thermostats, and electronic computers to analogous social systems. And communications theory in political science can be viewed as the application of the general approach of cybernetics to political situations.

THE CONCEPTS OF COMMUNICATIONS THEORY

The communications approach to the study of politics assumes that the behavior and survival of political systems can best be analyzed in terms of communication. It attempts to accomplish this task by means of a fairly small set of explicitly defined concepts. Knowledge of the meaning and interrelationships of these concepts provides a basic understanding of the uses and limitations of communications theory.[7]

The first concept is *information,* and the first assumption of a formal theory of communications is that communication transfers information. Information is usually viewed as "a patterned relationship between events."[8] This, then, becomes the basic unit of analysis—information is what flows through the channels of communication, is received, analyzed, and reacted to.

A political system receives information about how its environment is changing relative to the system's goals. In other words, the environment places stress on the system. This is labeled *load.* Communications theory suggests several hypotheses at this point. For instance, "Other things being equal, the greater the load, demands for political equality, let us say, the more difficult it is for the system to adjust and meet the load."

It is at this point that we reach the heart of communications theory, for now the system must cope with the load of its environment. The system receives the information, translates and interprets it, and then decides how to react. The time between the reception of the information (the realization of the load) and the reaction to it is called *lag.* Once again hypotheses are suggested: "The greater the lag, the less efficient a system is—the less able it is to cope with its environment." The fact that a political system

---

7For a thorough discussion of these concepts, see Deutsch, *op. cit.,* Part II.
8*Ibid.,* p. 82.

takes years to process information about basic demands from its environment might be indicative of its inability to maintain itself. Lag has a number of determinants, including the clearness of the meaning of the load and the ability of the system to process load information quickly and accurately.

This suggests another important concept of communications theory, *distortion*. Norbert Wiener notes that "in control and communications we are always fighting nature's tendency to degrade the organized and to destroy the meaningful...." More specifically, the concept of distortion refers to the changes that take place in information between the time it is received and the time it is reacted to. If a system allows or produces much distortion, it is in trouble, for it is not reacting to the actual situation, but a distorted impression of it. One measure of a capable system, then, is the amount of distortion produced in the reception and transmission of information.

The reaction of a system to load is summarized by the concept *gain*. Gain can be defined as the amount of change a system makes as a result of load. If the information is soundly processed, then the gain will be enough to meet the stress or demands of the environment. If the change is insufficient, then the gain has been too small; if the change is more than needed, the gain has been too large. In short, both under-and overreactions are possible.

At this point, the political system will begin to receive information about how successful its reaction has been; in other words, whether the gain was sufficient. This kind of information is called *feedback*. If the system is at all self-monitoring or self-adjusting, it will make adjustments in its behavior when it next reacts to the stress. This is what a thermostat does when it adjusts a furnace to maintain a particular temperature, what an antiaircraft gun does when it corrects its aim in accordance with the speed and flight pattern of its target, and what a President does after he observes the consequences of a particular executive order.

In addition to correcting its reaction to the immediate load, the system will, to a greater or lesser extent, file away information about the success or failure of its reaction; in other words it will *learn*. The information will be stored and used when a similar situation arises. For example, consider what goes on in the mind of a football quarterback who throws a long pass to a new end, only to find that the pass is underthrown because the end is much faster than expected. The quarterback notes that next time he will lead the end more—throw the ball farther ahead of him. So we can say that in any situation in which a political system is responding to its environment, there will be two kinds of relevant information: first, the new information (which might be considered as initial conditions), and second, a storehouse of learned information (which might take the form of generalizations) indicating what the probable outcomes will be if a number of alternative reactions are made. Thus communications theory includes a notion of learning. As a matter of fact, it is this notion that allows us to talk about a political system keeping up with the changes in its environment.

In a simplified environment, a system might be able to react to stress as it occurs, making satisfactory adjustments as it goes, so to speak. Thus, the thermostat on a furnace is able to keep the temperature at the desired level through this simple receive-react pattern of behavior. But a social organization such as a political system faces more complex kinds of stress. If it reacts only to the present load, the environment will probably always be at least one step ahead. It will become increasingly difficult for the system to catch up. This suggests another concept, called *lead* by the communications theorist. It refers to the ability of an organization to predict future states of the environment so as to, in effect, make or anticipate the necessary adjustments in advance. Obviously, a system that can generate this kind of prediction, let us say about potential urban disturbances, is in the long run going to be more effective in realizing goals, including survival, than one that "plays it by ear." Returning to our football example, the most successful passer is one who anticipates his receiver's moves and so throws the ball where the receiver will be, not where he is. This calls for knowledge of the pattern being run and the characteristics of the receiver. Similarly, the decision makers of a political system must attempt to make decisions that take into consideration predicted change of the system and the environment.

THE USES OF COMMUNICATIONS THEORY

Communications theory perceives the political system as an organization (more obviously, a set of organizations) depending upon information about its environment for the making of decisions, and then adjusting its decisions according to the feedback information it receives about the consequences of its decisions. It is not difficult to place this approach within the more general context of systems theory, for, clearly, communication is one aspect of the political system and the political process. As a matter of fact, communications theorists are often less imperialistic than the advocates of other approaches, for they readily admit that their model emphasizes only one aspect of the political system—power, for instance, is still recognized as an important concept in its own right.

But an emphasis on communications is still promising because of the pervasiveness of control and steering in all social organizations and the possibility of describing such behavior in terms of communication. Thus, it comes down to the ability to systematically and meaningfully measure communications. While an analysis of this topic would take us too far afield, let us simply note that political scientists like Deutsch are grappling with the problem of developing units of measure that can catch the significance of information flow in political systems and allow the development of useful hypotheses relating communications variables to variables referring to other aspects of the political system.[9]

---

[9]For an early attempt at empirical application of the approach see Karl W. Deutsch, *Nationalism and Social Communication* (Cambridge-New York: M.I.T. Press-John Wiley & Sons, Inc., 1953). For more recent applications, plus timely analyses of the relationship between communication and political integration and cohesion, see, "Communication Theory and Political Integration" and "Transaction Flows as Indicators of Political Cohesion," both in Philip E. Jacob and James V. Toscano (eds.), *The Integration of Political Communities* (Philadelphia: J. B. Lippincott, 1964), pp. 46-74 and pp. 75-97.

16 *The power approach*

As we saw in the first part of this book, "power" holds a significant place among the concepts of politics. As Harold and Margaret Sprout have put it, "Some concept of power underlies virtually every description of political interaction, domestic as well as international."[1] Many argue that power is especially significant in the field of international politics, where moral and consensual factors seem to be much less important than they are in domestic politics. As a matter of fact, power has assumed such lofty status in international politics that some writers view it as the field's *central* concept.[2] There seems to be a true commonsense core in this position. Be this as it may, we should not allow it to overshadow the importance of power at other levels of politics.

It is difficult to imagine an action between political actors at any level which does not manifest itself in some notion of power. But because there are so many notions, it might be misleading for the political scientist to talk about political power in general. What is clearly needed is a concept of power that is rigorous and at the same time intuitively satisfying. If both conditions are realized, a concept will probably be scientifically useful. Let us recall the requirements of a sound concept: (1) It must have empirical

---

[1]Harold Sprout and Margaret Sprout, *Foundations of International Politics* (Princeton, N.J.: D. Van Nostrand, 1962), p. 136.

[2]See the writings of Hans Morgenthau, for instance, "Power as a Political Concept," in Roland Young (ed.), *Approaches to the Study of Politics* (Evanston, Ill.: Northwestern University Press, 1958), pp. 66-77.

import; that is, it must be directly or indirectly tied to the world of observation. This would mean that, given our definition of power, we could tell if power is present or not in a given situation. (2) A concept ought to have systematic import. If it is to be of immediate use, one must be able to relate it to other concepts in order to formulate generalizations.

This chapter will examine the concept of power and its role as a centralizing and organizing concept in the study of politics. Two general themes will be developed: (1) power is behavioral; (2) the relation between the elements of power and power behavior must be formulated so as to allow for empirical testing if the former are to be of any explanatory and predictive importance.

It is clear that as it is used by many political scientists, "power" is not just one concept among many. It is the common characteristic of all political situations; and so it, better than others, can order and direct the political scientist's research efforts.

THE CONCEPT OF POWER

Power is a relational concept. One nation has power *over* another; Senator Smith controls the Foreign Relations Committee (has power over its other members). However, many students of politics use "power" as if it were something that a nation or a senator might possess without using it. In the words of Harold and Margaret Sprout, "a quantifiable and commensurable mass, something like a pile of bricks or a stone wall perhaps."[3] This point of view is manifested in discussions of the elements of national power, including population, natural resources, and, above all, military strength. In fact, it is not unusual to discover that military strength *is* power in international politics, or that wealth *is* power in domestic politics. Upon further analysis, however, it becomes clear that such discussions usually assume that the elements are significant because they allow a nation or a politician to control or influence others. Danger lies in concentrating upon the elements, for in doing so the need to relate them to power behavior is often obscured. It cannot be overemphasized that if power is to be a

---

[3]Sprout and Sprout, *op. cit.*, p. 136.

useful concept in political research, it must be viewed in relational and behavioral terms. That is, the research focus is on the behavior of one political actor insofar as it influences the behavior of others. If this is so, then it makes no sense to speak of a nation's power if it has not affected the behavior of another nation. The elements are best considered as power bases. Power is not, therefore, military strength; nor is it wealth. The contention that a nation with great military strength is powerful, if true, is true because it has been discovered, through empirical observation, that influence and the ability to control are related to the possession of arms and soldiers.

This analysis seems reasonable enough. However, students of political power have too often overlooked the need to relate power to power-base variables. The most general point of view taken in this chapter is that if the concept of power is to serve as a focal point for models and theories of politics, two tasks have to be undertaken: (1) the development of a sound concept of power; (2) the formulation of hypotheses using this concept which allow political scientists to test assumed relationships between power behaviors, and between behavior and power bases. This ultimately means testing by observing the behavior of political actors.

There are two general reasons for adopting a behavioralistic approach to the study of political power. First, as we have argued, power involves control or influence, and therefore is an activity. The possession of armed forces by a nation A does not necessarily imply that they will be used to control or influence another nation, B. Perhaps there are other features of the situation which prevent such employment, or make it unlikely. For instance, what of the intentions or will of A? It seems clear, then, that a number of factors are necessary if power is to exist. These include the proper bases of power and the ability to use them (the lack of restraint upon them), which together might be labeled *capability*. And secondly, the powerful actor must have the will or desire to control the actions of others, or so it would seem.

But let us consider another situation which might cause us to question the claim that power can only exist if it is exercised. Imagine two geographically adjacent nations, one with a large but inactive army, the other with no army at all. The very existence of nation A's army may influence the behavior of nation B, even though it is never used. This is analogous to the influence that the Presidential veto can have on Congress, even though it is not employed or even mentioned. The solution of this problem is based upon the realization that these are cases of behavioral, and not potential, power. It might be said that the possession of military forces by a nation and the right of veto by an executive are acts of power. Possession in these instances is behavior. This position does not imply that mere possession is always power behavior. For we can distinguish this type of situation from one in which a nation has a substantial military force but demonstrates no desire or will to use it. We might say that its force is not *credible* and so has no influence on the behavior of other nations. In this case, possession does not lead to power.

We can conclude at this point that both capability and will are necessary ingredients of power situations, except in those cases when possession alone leads to influence; and even in the latter case, credibility must be ascertainable.

A second reason for viewing power as a behavioral concept has to do with the basic scientific task of measurement. We will assume that the immediate objective of power theory is to use the concept to measure and compare power. If the "pile of bricks" definition is used, problems begin to arise. The most significant one is that the elements or bases of power provide no *common* unit of measurement. That is, how does one compare a man with a net worth of $10 million and one with a prestigious family background, if the question is which has more power in a particular community? Quincy Wright seems to be referring to the problem in the following statement: "It is difficult to find any common measure by which one of these forms for exerting political and social power can be equated with others as is true of the physical concept of power measured in horsepower or watts."[4] The solution is to use the activity of political actors as the basis of a common measure. Thus, in the example just cited, the behavioral consequences of wealth and prestige could be compared, using, let us say "*X* number of people controlled" as the unit of power. Or, how else would one go about comparing

---

[4]Quincy Wright, *The Study of International Relations* (New York: Appleton-Century-Crofts, 1955), p. 140.

one nation's military forces with another's strategic position? No claim is being made that it is easy to measure or compare power. We will discuss some of the difficulties involved in these activities shortly. The point is that if we are to use power in any scientifically meaningful way, a concept based on behavior will have to be developed.

What, then, is power in behavioralistic terms? The concept surely has a commonsense core, having something to do with control of or dominance over others. But, this doesn't take us far. Robert Dahl attempts a more rigorous definition: "*A* has power over *B* to the extent that he can get *B* to do something that *B* would not otherwise do."[5] A similar definition has been given by Herbert Goldhamer and Edward A. Shils: "A person may be said to have power to the extent that he influences the behavior of others in accordance with his own intentions."[6] Dahl's definition seems to get to the heart of the matter. In form, it harks back to the old argument from moral philosophy that an act cannot be morally good unless it goes against our inclinations or appetites. The point is that if *B* does something that *A* wants it to do, but *B* does not feel the action is in opposition to its interests, then *A* does not have power over *B*. However, it might seem rather difficult to apply this test to political actors. It calls for a knowledge of their intentions and might lead one to overlook manipulation, propaganda, and forms of sublimated aggression as means of influence. A nation may claim that its actions in accordance with the politics of another nation are of its own free will, while, in fact, they may be the result of one of these less overt forms of power. With the complexity of political relations, the ferreting out of such influence is exceedingly difficult.

This is why Goldhamer and Shils' definition might seem more attractive. In using the phrase "in accordance with his own intentions," they make it unnecessary to draw a distinction between acts in accordance with and in opposition to the influenced one's will. But if one ignores this distinction, he is

---

[5]Robert Dahl. "The Concept of Power," *Behavioral Science* Vol. II (July 1957), pp. 201-15. Reprinted in S. Sidney Ulmer (ed.), *Introductory Readings in Political Behavior* (Chicago: Rand McNally, 1962), pp. 344.

[6]Herbert Goldhamer and Edward A. Shils, "Types of Power and Status," *American Journal of Sociology*, Vol. XLV, 1939, pp. 171-82. Reprinted in Ulmer, *op. cit.,* p. 334.

faced with another problem: Does a nation have power every time its wishes are fulfilled?

For example, imagine a small, geographically remote nation which wants to exist in isolation, and because of the play of international forces is not bothered by uninterested nations preoccupied elsewhere. Can we say that this nation is powerful? This is a rough restatement of David Hume's analysis of the problem of causal connections which we discussed in Chapter 6. Recall that we can observe only constant conjunctions, not necessary connections, between events. A broad interpretation of Hume's criticism might allow one to claim that the relationship in the above example is as much a constant conjunction as other power relationships. However, this is the reason for (1) requiring that acts of behavior must be performed by both the influencer and the influenced, and (2) requiring in addition that there be some contact or communication between the parties before they can be said to have a power relationship. unnecessary to draw a distinction between acts in accordance with and in greater the number of interactions and contacts between two parties, the greater the number of opportunities to exercise influence or control of outcomes."[7] This implies that in order for power to be present, there must be some sort of contact between parties. ("Contact" and "communication" must, of course, be defined.) That is, it might be found that there is a direct correlation between the power of a nation and its contact with other nations. In any case, it seems fair to say that any acts of other states in accordance with nation A's interests (as manifested in its words and deeds) which cannot be traced to an act of A cannot be called manifestations of A's power.

A behavioral definition of power refers, then, to behavior in which one political actor influences the behavior of others in accordance with its own intentions. However, in examining the acts of politicians or nations another question arises. It is whether power is a symmetrical or asymmetrical relation. Long ago, Hume argued that all relations must be symmetrical; that is, all actions have reactions and thus there can be no one-way causal

---

[7]Richard Snyder, "Recent Trends in International Relations Theory," in Austin Ranney (ed.), *Essays on the Behavioral Study of Politics* (Urbana: University of Illinois Press, 1962), pp. 114-15.

connections. This is of crucial importance for the study of political power.[8] For it must be recognized that many power actions generate feedback. If nation A influences the behavior of nation B, there is a good chance that B will also influence A. The problem is, how do we measure this type of power relation? One could give up the idea that it is asymmetrical, or that there can be a one-way power flow. This could mean a return to Hume's position. But this would also make it impossible to compare power. As an alternative to this position, an asymmetrical relation operating in the opposite direction to the first may be postulated. Thus we have two relations which, if there is a sufficient time lag, might be individually observed. The amount and direction of the power differential would indicate which party has the most power.

We have given a general definition of power. Influence, as manifested in the acts of political actors, is the key unit of observation and measurement. But a further refinement is needed. There are several types of actions which might be taken by one actor to influence others. These may be classified under three main headings: force, domination, and manipulation.[9] These categories should be fairly easy to distinguish from one another. Force is the only one which involves physical activity, *physical* signifying an employment of visible resources. Domination, perhaps a less well-chosen term, takes place when an actor makes explicit to others what he wants them to do. It can be seen that force and domination will usually occur together, with the former being used to back up the latter. Manipulation is the attempt to influence behavior without making explicit what the desired behavior is. This calls for various sorts of actions which are much less easy to find and observe. Nevertheless, there might be methods of observing such forms of undercover influence. These, then, are the types of actions which might be expected of a nation or politician attempting to gain power over others. They are actions which can be observed and, hopefully, related to other actions and power bases in the form of hypotheses.

But before this can be done, actions must be specified which are

---

[8]The asymmetrical nature of power relations is discussed in Herbert Simon, "Notes on the Observation and Measurement of Political Power," *Journal of Politics,* Vol. XV, 1953, pp. 500-516.

[9]Goldhamer and Shils, *op. cit.,* pp. 334ff.

characteristic of those who are being influenced or controlled. These variables will probably be more difficult to pick out, since they could include a wide range of actions. Nevertheless, certain types of reactions might be discovered which are characteristic of political actors who are acting against their wills. Here we see the reason for making contact or communications between actors a necessary condition for a power relationship. The final step in this strategy would be the empirical linking of the two types of actions to show that those of the first class temporarily precede those of the second. If, after an observable contact between two nations, we observe at least one of each type of act, we may say that this is a power relationship. Suppose that the President has a private talk with a senator who has opposed one of his judicial appointments. When the Senate vote occurs, the senator votes for the appointment. We can conclude that in this case the President exercised power.

Comparing power

Having demonstrated empirically that these two types of action are related, a method still has to be found to compare power. Robert Dahl has pointed out that "the main problem is not to determine the existence of power but to make comparisons." [10] The question, "Who has power?" is in one sense meaningless, for if power is relational, it is relative. Thus, if X has power, it is always power over someone else. This immediately raises several problems. How is one to compare power found in different situations? For instance, suppose (1) nation X has caused nation Y to perform act Z; (2) nation A has caused nation Y to perform act B; (3) nation A has caused nation C to perform act D. Can these situations be compared in order to determine which contains the most power? Can nation X's power in situation (1) be compared with nation A's in situations (2) and (3)? Situations (1) and (2) are alike because nation Y is the influenced nation, while (2) and (3) both have A as the influencer.

It would appear that those sets of situations which have common actors might be compared more profitably than those

---

[10]Dahl, *op. cit.*, p. 349.

which do not. However, has this gained us anything? No common unit has been extracted. Perhaps Dahl has come up with the best test of power.[11] It can be stated by two probability statements: (1) the probability that nation Y will do act A if nation X does act B is N; (2) the probability that nation Y will do act A if nation X does not do act B is N^2. The difference between N and N^2 might be said to be a nation's power—the greater the difference, the more power nation X has. However, the question remains, Can all acts or responses be considered equal? That is, suppose we want to compare the power of India in removing Portugal from Goa and the United States' actions to force the Soviets out of Cuba. Suppose that the $(N - N^2)$ in regard to India is greater than the United States. Can we say that India has more power than the United States? Or are we limited to saying that India has more power in its situation than the United States had in its? The answer clearly is that the situation must be comparable if the relativity of power is to be completely compared. In our example it can be seen that some way must be found of comparing the withdrawal of Portugal from Goa and Russian missiles from Cuba. One possible method is to determine how many nations would be affected by the power relationships. That is, how many nations might have their behavior changed by either the action of the influencer or the reactions of the influenced. In the contemporary international situation, the action of the United States in blockading Cuba affected many nations besides the Soviet Union. But the Indian-Portuguese relationship probably involved only these two nations, or perhaps a few more at most. We can, perhaps, call this the *scope* of power action: How wide are its repercussions in the international sphere?[12]

Measuring power

Even after developing a method of comparing specific events, one still has the feeling that it is not enough. For a statement like, "The United States has more power than England," is not quite clear. Up to now, our comparisons have been of individual

---

[11]*Ibid.,* pp. 347ff.

[12]The notion of the scope of power is discussed in *ibid.*

situations (actions and reactions). But the more general statement seems to go beyond single actions. It encompasses all the acts of a nation of politician. This, then, is a way of determining an actor's total power. That is, the total amount of power of a nation may be measured by the ratio of its successful power acts (those with a certain high difference between N and N^2) to all of its attempted power acts.[13]

Now we might ask, Can one say that the United States is powerful, or must one only say, the United States is more powerful than England? Probably the most meaningful type of proposition is the latter. One can use the methods outlined above and then make comparison by analyzing and totaling the acts of each nation. Thus a nation which is inactive cannot be powerful. But here we can return to the elements of national power which we have discussed and rejected as measures of international power. After going through the steps outlined above for analyzing and comparing the behavior of states, one may notice that certain elements or situational factors are present and evident when certain actions and reactions which we have called power behavior take place. Using the proper empirical methods, one may be able to establish that in a particular type of situation, a given amount of military force will result in a given amount of power (influence over the behavior of other nations). These correlations must be empirically substantiated. No doubt universal laws (those with no exceptions) will not be forthcoming. However, statistical laws (statements of chance) might be obtained. Thus, after making the comparisons, we can empirically determine the conditions that make for influence, that is, the characteristics of nations and of situations that allow us to make predictions about the amount of power a nation will have after it has taken a power-initiating act. It might seem that we have contradicted our previous argument about the shortcomings of using the "pile of bricks" method of equating the elements of national power with behavioral power. This is not the case. Our position has been that (1) there exists the danger of obscuring the behavorial quality of power by emphasizing these elements; (2) if the elements are to have any meaning, they must be empirically related to previously determined power acts.

---

[13]This kind of measure is developed in *ibid.*, pp. 356ff.

As it is often employed by political scientists, the concept of power is deceivingly simple. We can agree with Robert Dahl that "the concepts of influence and power are full of logical traps, and most people — including many people who write about politics— are not accustomed to talking logically about power and influence."[14] We have emphasized one of these traps, the equating of the elements of bases of power with power. It was suggested that approaches using power as a central concept should concentrate on the actions of states, for, methodologically speaking, power does not exist unless it is used. The elements of power would have no significance if politicians and nations did not act. This calls for a behavioral concept of power which meets the requirements of scientific concept formation. It is only after the problems involved in this task are solved that one can undertake the more significant tasks of measuring and comparing power and using power in the explanation of other kinds of political phenomena.

---

[14]*Ibid.*

Index

Index

253

This book has been set in 11 and 10 point Press Roman, leaded 2 points.Part numbers are in 24 point Univers Medium; part titles are in 14 point Univers Medium. Chapter numbers are in 48 point Univers Light Condensed; chapter titles are in 18 point Univers Medium. The size of the type page is 26 by 43-2/3 picas.